ACADEMIC LANGUAGE

LANGUAGE

in Diverse Classrooms

DEFINITIONS AND CONTEXTS

*To our mothers, Anita and Luisa . . . and
strong inspirational women everywhere.*

ACADEMIC LANGUAGE
in Diverse Classrooms

DEFINITIONS AND CONTEXTS

Margo Gottlieb
Gisela Ernst-Slavit

Foreword by Jeff Zwiers

CORWIN
A SAGE Company

CORWIN
A SAGE Company

FOR INFORMATION:

Corwin
A SAGE Company
2455 Teller Road
Thousand Oaks, California 91320
(800) 233-9936
www.corwin.com

SAGE Publications Ltd.
1 Oliver's Yard
55 City Road
London EC1Y 1SP
United Kingdom

SAGE Publications India Pvt. Ltd.
B 1/I 1 Mohan Cooperative Industrial Area
Mathura Road, New Delhi 110 044
India

SAGE Publications Asia-Pacific Pte. Ltd.
3 Church Street
#10-04 Samsung Hub
Singapore 049483

Acquisitions Editor: Dan Alpert
Associate Editor: Kim Greenberg
Editorial Assistant: Cesar Reyes
Production Editor: Cassandra Margaret Seibel
Copy Editor: Cate Huisman
Typesetter: C&M Digitals (P) Ltd.
Proofreader: Susan Schon
Indexer: Jean Casalegno
Cover Designer: Michael Dubowe

Printed in the United States of America.

A catalog record of this book is available from the Library of Congress.

ISBN 978-1-4522-3478-6

This book is printed on acid-free paper.

SFI Certified Sourcing
www.sfiprogram.org
SFI-00453

16 17 18 10 9 8 7 6 5 4 3

Contents

Foreword

Academic language is a tangled web of roots that anchor and nourish most of the learning that students do in school. Yet these roots are deep and difficult to see, especially if we have ingrained habits of focusing on more visible "branches and leaves" of learning, such as discrete facts, grammar rules, right answers in math, and vocabulary definitions. Students need teachers who understand how to fortify learning of content and its language roots at the same time.

I spend a lot of time in classrooms and listen to large amounts of classroom language. In doing this research, several helpful principles for the development of academic language have emerged. First, teachers must be aware of the most important language needed in the lesson and be strategic in developing it both directly and indirectly. Second, students' oral academic language must be developed across content areas. This includes developing their abilities to produce clear and complex output and to engage in authentic interactions in which they build up and fortify ideas in back-and-forth dialogue. Third, academic language grows through authentic and engaged use. When students' brains are involved in a wide range of situations and challenges, they gather more and more language over time and get better at shaping it to understand, communicate, and build ideas (Zwiers, 2008).

Academic Language in Diverse Classrooms: Definitions and Contexts brings these principles into a practical light. It offers educators a concise and insightful guide for understanding the exciting complexities of teaching academic language across disciplines. In Chapter 2, the authors state one of their central themes: "Learning academic language, like learning any other language, requires systematic, deliberate, prolonged, and robust approaches that are rich, contextualized, and meaningful for each and every student." Yet in many settings, approaches for developing academic language, if they exist at all, are not systematic, deliberate, robust, or meaningful—and as a result, student learning suffers—especially learning for students in diverse classrooms.

Academic Language in Diverse Classrooms: Definitions and Contexts shows readers a variety of poignant examples of how teachers across the country are using effective academic language development approaches in different grade levels and content area classrooms. The vignettes allow educators to see the complexity and engagement of the lessons as well as the ways in which the ideas might translate to other classroom contexts.

A wide range of new standards has entered the scene, all of which place high academic language demands on students. The increased emphasis on using more complex texts, for example, means developing our teaching practices to help students learn the language and purposes of challenging texts, so they can construct meaning. Academic language develops when students engage in learning activities that approximate how experts in a discipline think and communicate, encourage the transforming and applying of ideas in new ways, and link concrete and abstract knowledge. Such activities should give students opportunities to engage in meaningful dialogue with one another and become critical consumers of information, as well as foster their abilities to think and talk about how to best think and talk (i.e., to engage in metadiscourse). And this book provides clear examples for designing such activities.

But what should all this look like in a full unit of instruction? Chapter 5 outlines how to weave the necessary elements and practices together to create lessons that are well rooted and well nourished by contextualized academic language instruction. The units also model how to adeptly weave formative assessment across and within lessons, showing how teachers can observe student work and activities to learn where students are and where they need to go with respect to language.

When we dig into the complex questions of teaching academic language across a wide range of grade levels, content areas, and students, we are presented with few simple answers. But over time we can and need to construct our "answers" for our settings, based on insightful research, exemplars from the field, and expert resources. Fortunately, *Academic Language in Diverse Classrooms: Definitions and Contexts* is an expert resource for clarifying the questions and sculpting the answers that you need in your setting.

Jeff Zwiers

Preface

The whispers in the stairwells of laughing children leave much to the imagination. The din of student clatter in the lunchroom is almost deafening. The shouts from team members in the gym almost drown out the coach's directives. Classrooms are abuzz with frenetic activity. Language permeates school!

It is not only the shift to new standards, but also thinking of innovative ways to implement these changes, that is causing teachers, coaches, and school leaders alike to rethink district curriculum around using language for academic purposes. One idea that seems to have gained traction is that professional learning teams, whether pairing content and language teachers or teachers within a department or grade level, have become a more powerful force in designing instructional assessment than individual teachers. Teachers working together can create a synergy for learning, reach mutual decisions with widespread results, and push each other professionally.

We begin our story here with a discussion of the key features of the language of school and how these qualities frame instructional assessment practices. Integral to this conversation is the role of academic language use in today's diverse classrooms as well as in the field of language education. After defining the dimensions of academic language, we illustrate how to purposely integrate language into instructional planning and exemplify how language surrounds and influences every student and teacher.

This foundational book on the value of academic language use for academic success sets the stage for the accompanying six-part series. Accompanying this introduction, individual books of vibrant classrooms reflect three grade-level clusters (K–2, 3–5, and 6–8) and two disciplines (mathematics and English language arts). In today's schools filled with wondrous students, many of whom represent linguistic and cultural diversity, we highlight how teachers infuse the academic language demands of grade-level standards and materials into fascinating units of learning.

CHAPTER OVERVIEW

This foundational book for the series is organized into six chapters:

Chapter 1: What Is Academic Language?

This first chapter defines the focus of the book: the nature of academic language, including an overview of different perspectives for understanding this concept. It explores distinctions and connections between oral and written language and emphasizes the importance of oral language as a vehicle for promoting academic language development. We also include discussions of academic language as a developmental process, the importance of building awareness of academic language use, and students' expression of academic language through multiliteracies. Finally, we describe learning the language of the content areas, with its conciseness, use of high-density information words, and precision of expression in relation to access, equity, and social justice.

Chapter 2: What Are the Dimensions of Academic Language?

This chapter underscores the importance of understanding academic language beyond vocabulary to include discourse- and sentence-level structures. We describe what each of these three levels entails and provide pertinent examples. In addition, we remind readers that academic language learning, like learning a new language, necessitates systematic, deliberate, prolonged, and robust approaches that are rich, contextualized, and meaningful for students. We emphasize the use of strategies that build on students' prior knowledge, including their historical, linguistic, and cultural knowledge, and that engage students in rich and varied language and content experiences to render better academic outcomes.

Chapter 3: How Do Standards Define and Shape Academic Language Use?

This chapter, a crucial reading for educators, school leaders, and administrators, explores the relationship between content and language learning through the lens of standards. It examines academic language within standards and highlights the influence of college and career readiness standards, including the Common Core State Standards and the Next Generation Science Standards, alongside English language proficiency/development standards as the catalyst for designing and aligning curriculum, instruction, and assessment. The chapter concludes with hearty lists of suggestions for redefining teaching and learning around academic language use tailored for multiple stakeholders, including teachers, school leaders, and district administrators.

Chapter 4: How Is Academic Language Used in Content Areas Schoolwide?

This chapter presents brief vignettes that peek into diverse classrooms, where content area teachers and their students are busily using academic language for thinking, knowing, acting, and interacting during subject matter instruction. As readers "visit" music, physical education, arts, mathematics, English language arts, science, and social studies classrooms, they see that academic language is not taught as a list of 10 important words needed for the topic or unit of instruction. Instead, they witness how the full extent of academic language—at the discourse, sentence, and word/phrase levels—is learned as students engage in sophisticated and meaningful disciplinary or interdisciplinary practices.

Chapter 5: How Can Academic Language Be Integrated Into Instruction and Assessment?

This chapter focuses on becoming aware of academic language use in instruction and assessment in classrooms filled with linguistically and culturally diverse students. Following a brief historical overview of language education, we share important aspects of planning instruction and assessment units that revolve around academic language use. Topics related to the design of a curricular unit include selecting a theme and accompanying standards, capitalizing on linguistic and cultural resources to connect home with school, identifying unit targets and differentiated objectives, designing an end-of–unit assessment along with engaging instructional activities and tasks, and understanding the reciprocal relationship between differentiated instruction and classroom assessment.

Chapter 6: How Is Academic Language Situated in Curricular Design and Infused Into Professional Learning?

This last chapter illustrates how a curricular framework can facilitate learning of content and academic language that, in turn, fosters academic success for all students. A brief literature review that traces curriculum from the early 20th century to the present provides the rationale for a Curricular Framework that serves as the basis for the series. Taking an integrated content and language perspective, we describe the usefulness and contribution of each component of the Framework as it relates to academic language use within the mainstay of educational practice. We close by highlighting the importance of professional learning opportunities so that teachers and teacher leaders will have the tools to integrate academic language within curriculum and promote its use.

We realize that in today's busy classrooms, teachers are under tremendous pressure to ensure that their students make ample academic progress. It is our conviction that systematic use of academic language, grounded in both content and language standards, will assist teachers and school leaders alike in reaching their annual goals for student achievement and language development. We hope that incorporating academic language use into school life will yield results that will propel our 21st century students to unforeseen heights.

The K–8 Mathematics Series

Volume	Contributors	Grade Level	Content Topic
1	Catherine Carrison Erika Muir	K	Whole Numbers and Number Sense
	Sylvia Celedón-Pattichis Sandra I. Musanti	1	Base-10 Thinking
	Michael Silverstone Debbie Zacarian	2	Basic Operations– Odd and Even Numbers
2	Judith B. O'Laughlin	3	Time
	Gisela Ernst-Slavit Margo Gottlieb David Slavit	4	Fractions
	Jennifer M. Bay-Williams Rose M. Glasser Tricia A. Bronger	5	Algebraic Thinking— Analyzing Patterns Across Representations
3	Amanda Villagómez Kerri J. Wenger	6	Geometric Solids
	Zandra de Araujo	7	Ratios and Proportions
	Gladis Kersaint	8	Geometry—Similarity and Congruence

The K–8 English Language Arts Series

Volume	Contributors	Grade Level	Content Topic
1	Grabriela Cardenas Barbara Jones Olivia Lozano	K	Reading and Oral Language Development: My Family and Community
	Eugenia Mora-Flores	1	Using Informational Texts and Writing Across the Curriculum
	Sandra Mercuri Alma D. Rodríguez	2	Developing Academic Language Through Ecosystems
2	Terrell A. Young Nancy L. Hadaway	3	Informational and Narrative Texts: Our Changing Environment
	Penny Silvers Mary Shorey Patricia Eliopoulis Heather Akiyoshi	4	Biographies, Civil Rights, and the Southeast Region
	Mary Lou McCloskey Linda New Levine	5	Literature and Ocean Ecology
3	Emily Y. Lam Marylin Low Ruta' Tauiliili-Mahuka	6	Argumentation: Legends and Life
	Darina Walsh Diane Staehr Fenner	7	Research to Build and Present Knowledge
	Liliana Minaya-Rowe	8	A Gothic Story: "The Cask of Amontillado"

Acknowledgments

The two of us have devoted our professional careers to education, being teachers, teacher educators, consultants, and researchers. Throughout the years we have had the privilege of working with many amazing educators and visiting a variety of classrooms and schools in diverse contexts and countries. Our most sincere thanks goes to the students, teachers, and teacher educators who have pushed our thinking about how to conceptualize language for academic purposes and how to maximize its classroom application. As is evident in the pages that follow, we are committed to building on students' strengths to act as linguistic and cultural envoys, integrating language and content instruction, and designing curriculum where all students can achieve academic success.

We would like to applaud Dan Alpert, Program Director, Equity/Diversity and Professional Learning at SAGE, who has been our coach—always available to support us and to answer every question, no matter how trivial, throughout the course of this project. This book builds on conversations about how to elevate the status of diversity by having educators realize the equity issues involved in implementing the new generation of content standards alongside language development standards. Dan has added significantly to the vision and scope of this book and the series as a whole.

Cesar Reyes has been helping us in his capacity as editorial assistant, and Kim Greenberg, as editorial associate editor, has also ensured the quality of our work. We thank them for their commitment and skill in helping to bring this book to publication.

Michael Dubowe, graphic designer, has made this book and the entire series sparkle. He has also provided a common thread that unifies all seven books and yet has made each volume shine on its own.

Our gratitude also goes to Cassandra Seibel, project editor, and our copy editor, Cate Huisman, for their spot on feedback and attention to detail.

Thank you also to Shannon Ray-Cassidy and Jessica de Meurers for using their creative juices and designing skills to enhance our graphics.

Of all the people who have touched our lives during this journey, we are most grateful to five incredible guys—Terry, Graham, Dave, Max, and Arthur; their smiles, encouragement, and understanding have pushed us to excel in this most exciting and rewarding project. Finally, we also would like to give special acknowledgment and thanks to our many colleagues and supporters at World-Class Instructional Design and Assessment, Illinois Resource Center, and Washington State University who have believed in us all these years.

Margo Gottlieb and Gisela Ernst-Slavit

About the Authors

Margo Gottlieb, PhD, lead developer for World-Class Instructional Design and Assessment at the Wisconsin Center for Education Research, University of Wisconsin, Madison, and director, assessment and evaluation, for the Illinois Resource Center, Arlington Heights, crafts language standards, designs multiple forms of assessments, and creates instructional assessment systems for language learners in preK–12 settings. In her capacity as a teacher educator, she has presented in Asia, Central America, Europe, the Middle East, the Pacific, and South America as well as throughout North America.

Dr. Gottlieb has chaired several committees for the TESOL International Association and has served on national expert advisory panels and task forces. In addition, she has published extensively, contributing to or writing over 60 handbooks, chapters, and articles in the field of language education. Her books include *Common Language Assessment for English Learners* (Solution Tree, 2012); *Paper to Practice: Using the TESOL's English Language Proficiency Standards in PreK–12 Classrooms* (with A. Katz & G. Ernst-Slavit, TESOL, 2009); *Assessment and Accountability in Language Education Programs: A Guide for Administrators and Teachers* (with D. Nguyen, Caslon, 2007); and *Assessing English Language Learners: Bridges From Language Proficiency to Academic Achievement* (Corwin, 2006).

Gisela Ernst-Slavit is associate dean and professor in the College of Education at Washington State University Vancouver. She has a PhD in bilingual/multicultural education with an emphasis in cultural anthropology and linguistics from the University of Florida and a master's degree in educational research from Florida State University. Dr. Ernst-Slavit investigates second language development, academic language pedagogy, and language teacher educa-tion using ethnographic and sociolinguistic perspectives. In addition to being the author of many research and practitioner articles, she is coauthor of *Access to Academics: Planning Instruction for K–12 Classrooms with ELLs* (with J. Egbert, Pearson, 2010); *From Paper to Practice: Using the TESOL's English Language Proficiency Standards in PreK–12 Classrooms* (with M. Gottlieb & A. Katz, TESOL, 2009), and *TESOL PreK–12 English Language Proficiency Standards* (TESOL, 2006). Dr. Ernst-Slavit is a native of Peru who grew up speaking Spanish and German at home and English in school. She has given numerous presentations in the United States and North America as well as in Asia, Southeast Asia, the Middle East, South America, and Europe.

In the Beginning . . .

If you talk to a man in a language he understands, that goes to his head.
If you talk to him in his own language, that goes to his heart.

—Nelson Mandela

STUDENTS, TEACHERS, SCHOOLS, AND COMMUNITIES

Schools are experiencing a new student demographic. Each year, more and more teachers look into the faces of linguistically and culturally diverse students. Within this heterogeneous population are English language learners (ELLs), the most rapidly growing student group, whose conceptual understanding, in large part, comes from languages and cultures other than English. As an educational community, our increasing responsibility is to reach out to these students and their families to tap their linguistic capital as a means of promoting their English language development. At the same time, we acknowledge ELLs' cultural backgrounds and integrate their "funds of knowledge" (Moll, Armanti, Neff, & Gonzalez, 1992) into our teaching to ensure that the students can relate to the sociocultural contexts in which learning occurs in school.

English language learners could have begun their lives processing any one of 6,500 living languages (Rieger & McGrail, 2006), but realistically, they have been exposed to one or more of the 400 languages present in the United States. Linguistic and cultural diversity abounds across every one of the 50 states and territories of our nation. This richness of languages and cultures has helped shaped our collective identity. Yet, at the same time, we recognize the force of English as a universal language.

In school, every student is in the process of learning English. For some, English is their one and only language. Other students may use dialectical varieties of English, whether they were born in the United States or in countries, such as India, where British English prevails. For still others, English may be the second or third language of their households or a language newly introduced in school. Learning English should be considered an additive process, where schools work from the premise that students' home languages are valuable worldly possessions (Coltrane, 2003).

The elementary school student population of ELLs in the United States is rapidly growing in size, representation of nationalities, and importance. For decades, California, Texas, Florida, New York, Illinois, and Arizona have enjoyed stability in their significant numbers of linguistically and culturally diverse students. Another dozen states have witnessed hyper-growth of more than 200% in their school-age linguistically diverse populations in the last decade. While there has been an upsurge in numbers in rural and suburban areas throughout all states, large distributions of ELLs and other minorities tend to remain in urban school districts (Payan & Nettles, 2007).

Let's take a peek into a typical elementary or middle school classroom, with its 30+ students, each with a distinct personality, educational history, home background, and life experience. What an eclectic mix! The majority of students have roots in the United States; many have been born within its borders; some are highly transient; others are members of migrant families; still others have remained in the same community for generations. There may be a few newcomers from an assortment of countries, several with strong literacy in their home language, while others have had intermittent time at school. For every student, there is a unique language learning configuration of oral language in relation to literacy development. Look into your classroom, grade, or school to calculate the number of subgroups of students found in Figure 1.

Figure 1 An Inventory of Language Learners in K–8 Classrooms

Student Subgroup	Number in My Classroom, Grade, or School
ELL newcomers to the United States (less than six months in the United States)	
Students with interrupted formal education (SIFE)	
Long-term ELLs (more than seven years of English language support)	
ELLs with learning disabilities	
Other ELLs (in the process of developing English as an additional language)	
Proficient English speakers from linguistically and culturally diverse backgrounds	
Other proficient English speakers	

Why do we begin a book on academic language use in diverse classrooms by introducing the changing school demographic? We believe that students are the center of our universe and that discussion in schoolwide meetings, professional learning communities, and district committees should revolve around how we can provide better educational opportunities for our students. Having a deep understanding of this generation of learners will help us design and differentiate relevant and responsive instruction and assessment that we hope will pave the pathway to their academic success.

PURPOSE OF THE BOOK AND ITS CONNECTION TO THE SERIES

This foundational book examines the theory and research on academic language and its use in varying contexts. In it, we define and illustrate academic language as a construct of schooling and its applicability to the content areas, touching upon language arts, mathematics, science, social studies, music and fine arts, and physical education. Its primary purpose is to provide a rationale for designing and implementing a culturally responsive curriculum schoolwide. In it, we discuss the importance of academic language use and how to incorporate it into instructional routines within and across classrooms. This volume begins to translate abstract theory around language for academic purposes into concrete practice; it is a prologue to a series of six additional books (three on English language arts and three on mathematics) that illustrates standards-driven thematic units of learning for grades kindergarten to 2, 3 to 5, and 6 to 8.

This book stands independently for those readers who wish to dive deeply into the waters of academic language and examine its impact on teaching and learning. It can also be considered a backdrop to use alongside the English language arts books, the mathematics books, or both sets. Together this compendium offers comprehensive insight into the dimensions of academic language use and how it has come to be integrated into the fabric of school.

AUDIENCES AND USES

In the series, our primary focus is on language learners and their teachers in diverse contexts, including mainstream, dual language, and content-based classrooms. In particular, we attend to how teachers delve into investigating academic language in language arts, mathematics, and science materials, sometimes within a single content area, other times from a more multidisciplinary perspective; sometimes in one language, other times in two; sometimes with one teacher, other times in teacher teams. It is our intent to illustrate how these teachers, representing an eclectic array of classrooms across the United States, advocate on behalf of all their students, with particular attention to ELLs.

We would be remiss if we did not acknowledge other educators for whom this book, as well as the series, might be beneficial. Figure 2 identifies those persons along with one or two ways each of them could use the information. The chart is intended to illustrate the broad range of possibilities that, in many instances, can be interchangeable among stakeholder groups.

Figure 2 Potential Audiences and Uses for the Series

Potential Audiences	Ways to Use This Book and the Series
Content and Language Teachers	• Collaborate in planning instruction and assessment • Coconstruct and share content and language targets for units of instruction
Professional Learning Teams or Communities	• Grapple with issues related to curriculum design • Conduct a book study on academic language use
Districtwide Committees	• Offer suggestions and recommendations on standards-referenced themes and units of learning • Reach consensus on ways to collect, interpret, and report classroom data
District Networks	• Plan a classroom database for participating districts • Create a communication plan for exchanging information among schools and districts
School Leaders	• Participate in professional learning teams' study of academic language use in school and the community • Support teams' efforts to be inclusive of all students in planning instruction and assessment
Instructional and Data Coaches	• Serve as liaisons for teachers, school leaders, and administrators in curriculum continuity • Model some of the activities suggested in the case studies in different classrooms
Teacher Educators	• Facilitate teachers' understanding of the dimensions of academic language use • Help teachers differentiate language and content for instructing and assessing heterogeneous groups of students
Preservice Teachers	• Study examples of a variety of units of instruction • Gain insight into the components and purposes of curriculum frameworks

Potential Audiences	Ways to Use This Book and the Series
In-service Teachers	• Apply new instructional and assessment strategies to their classrooms • Team with other teachers to maximize opportunities for student learning
Researchers	• Observe and work with teachers in schools and classrooms • Plan coursework around the process and products of embedding academic language into curriculum design

Every educator has been touched by the increased presence of standards that has become ingrained in school life. With the introduction of the new content standards, in particular the Common Core State Standards (CCSS) and the Next Generation Science Standards (NGSS), the standards movement has reached epic proportion and has gained national momentum.

THE STANDARDS-DRIVEN REFORM MOVEMENT

Standards have been part of the educational landscape for more than two decades. In 1989 the National Council of Teachers of Mathematics (NCTM) published the inaugural content standards for elementary and secondary students in the United States. Other national organizations soon followed NCTM's lead, until an entire suite of standards for the content areas had been produced. In 1997 Teachers of English to Speakers of Other Languages (TESOL) initiated the development of PreK–12 English language proficiency standards that were reconfigured and augmented in 2006 to meet federal requirements.

In fact, federal mandates have fueled the standards movement. The reauthorization of the Elementary and Secondary School Act (ESEA) in 1994, the Improving America's Schools Act, was the first piece of federal legislation to insist that states adopt content standards. The subsequent reauthorization in 2002, also known as the No Child Left Behind Act, required all states to also have English language proficiency or development standards. As a result of this legislative push, the standards originating from national organizations became the prototypes for many states' content standards.

In 2010, we witnessed the collaboration of the Council of Chief State School Officers and the National Governors Association in the creation of the CCSS, a set of content standards in the areas of English language arts and mathematics intended to propel students to college and career readiness.

Adopted by the vast majority of states, the CCSS have come to represent the de facto national content standards initiative. The latest addition to this national conversation was a state-led process managed by Achieve; it resulted in the 2013 NGSS built from the National Research Council's Framework for K–12 Science Education.

The impact of the CCSS and the NGSS has been far reaching, affecting the professional lives of educators from state departments to school boards to classrooms. It has also been influential in spurring the latest round of English language proficiency/development standards designed for the exploding population of ELLs. The common grounding for all of today's standards is grade-level content rigor coupled with rich academic language.

The driving force of the standards movement of this millennium has placed us at a crossroads, poised yet somewhat reticent to accept the new normal and retool curricula to align with the next generation of student assessments. The educational community anxiously seeks exemplars of how to intertwine these different sets of standards into sound instructional practice to ultimately maximize the achievement of all students. To do so, we first need to identify the language of school and seek ways to systematically address its role in our classrooms.

As educators, we seek to provide high-quality educational experiences for all students through language. The new standards, namely, the CCSS and the NGSS, have raised the visibility of language in teaching and learning by immersing language, communication, and collaboration within grade-level content knowledge and skills. In fact, these standards have established a new paradigm around the role of language in teaching across subject area disciplines. (For examples of the language of key concepts within each mathematical domain, according to the CCSS, see Resource A. For specific examples of text types, features, and structures associated with the CCSS for grade levels K–8 and language domains—reading, speaking, listening, and writing—in English language arts, see Resource B). As a result, the saying that "every teacher is a language teacher" has indeed become a reality.

STRATEGIES FOR ACADEMIC LANGUAGE USE: EXAMINING HOME-SCHOOL CONNECTIONS

Academic language helps to define school success for all students. It is the language of textbooks, in classrooms, and on tests. It is different in register, structure, and vocabulary from the casual speech of social interactions, yet that, too, can be academic in nature, especially when introduced in a school environment. *Academic language, the language required by students to understand and communicate in subject area disciplines, forms the heart of grade-level curriculum.*

To equip future generations of students for college and career, schools must be responsive to their ever-growing linguistically and culturally diverse student populations. We need to ensure that classroom instruction and assessment centers on the language of school while remaining congruent with the cultural values of the surrounding communities. Trusted to advance the achievement of students, we must center our attention and reflect on the multicultural frames of reference and range of experiences of our students, as it is through this sociocultural context that we introduce academic language (Gottlieb, 2012a).

One group of strategies that affects academic language development and use revolves around the linguistic and cultural resources of the students, their families, and the communities in which they reside. Building academic language at school is facilitated when it is connected to the students' experiences and backgrounds from home. Figure 3 shows the influences of the students' home and environment on academic language use.

We acknowledge these student resources within the Curricular Framework that highlights academic language (see Resource C or Chapter 1 of each book of the *Academic Language* series), the prototype that guides the design of the units of learning. Through case studies of classrooms, contributors have provided illustrative examples of culturally responsive

Figure 3   Home and Community Influences on the Language of School

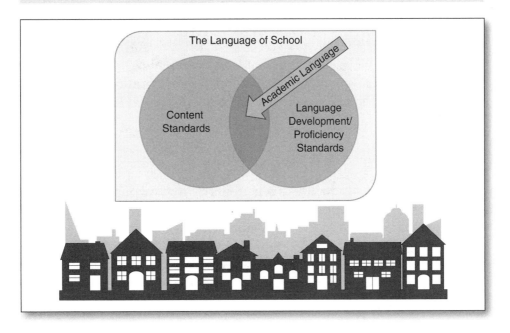

foundations for academic learning in distinct settings. One set of strategies to increase academic language use in classrooms is to examine home–school connections.

A striking example of establishing home–school relations is presented by the kindergarten teacher in the English language arts K–2 volume; she makes home visits to each and every family of her students. This strategy, used throughout the school, helps build grade-level teams and helps teachers gain a collective sense of shared personal and cultural knowledge to better meet the students' individual needs. It also provides teachers with vital background knowledge of each family along with histories and traditions that the students bring to school and the classroom. Equally important, the home visits foster a sense of trust between the families and the school (Cardenas, Jones, & Lozano, 2014).

Another way of highlighting the language of school is by having students extend their academic experiences through field trips. The first grade mathematics classroom showcased in the series, for example, takes the students' base-10 thinking to the local corn tortilla factory. As the entire school population is of Mexican descent, the surrounding community is a reservoir of Latino culture. Upon their return to the classroom, the students are able to better visualize base-10 thinking, apply it to solving problems, and explain their reasoning (Celedón-Pattichis & Musanti, 2013).

Yet one more strategy that utilizes the students' linguistic and cultural resources is seen in a class of fifth grade students studying ocean ecology. To involve the multicultural families in the study of marine organisms and build background for the unit, the teacher prepares an interview for students to give to their family members to identify seafood commonly eaten in their homes. The pride of the students is evident when they bring in their lists and share their cultural information. The teacher herself is surprised to discover that many of her ELLs, including students representing Indian, Burmese, Congolese, and Bosnian cultures, eat a wide range of seafood, providing a most personalized entrée into the unit (McCloskey & New Levine, 2014).

REFLECTION

The complexities of academic language—its definition, purposes, and contexts for use—are foremost in the minds of educators as they attempt to unravel standards in diverse settings and contexts around the country. Interpreting the standards is arduous enough; however, to fully capture the educational potential of ELLs, English language proficiency/development standards must be brought into the fold. In this era of increased content and language expectations, we have to redouble our efforts to ensure accessibility, opportunities, and equity for all students.

Teachers have to take advantage of the rich linguistic and cultural resources of the communities in which their schools are located so that students come to feel that school is an extension of their homes. This fluidity perhaps can lead to more expansive and varied academic language use. With teachers, students, and family members working together toward a unified goal of increased achievement inside and outside of school, a new generation of competent, distinguished, and academically astute individuals will enter college, pursue careers, and contribute to our global society.

1 What Is Academic Language?

Language is the fundamental resource or tool with which teachers and children work together in schools.

—Frances Christie, 2005, p. 2

For the last couple of decades the language education community has been grappling with defining the construct of academic language and situating it within an assets-based model to ensure the academic success of linguistically and culturally diverse students. Along come the Common Core State Standards (CCSS) in 2010, and poof, academic language assumes a front and center position in curriculum design and enactment, impacting every teacher, every day. This chapter summarizes the thinking on academic language use and its application to schooling. It examines the roles of academic language, its dimensions and underlying theories, and the developmental nature of language learning. It concludes with a call for educators to recognize the paradigm shift we are currently witnessing and to seize the opportunity to promote social justice for students everywhere.

THE ROLE OF LANGUAGE IN SCHOOLING AND BEYOND

Language is perhaps the most powerful tool available to teachers, since language is pervasive in every aspect of the teaching and learning process. Whether it is a nod signifying agreement, a command such as "Eyes on me!"

or an explanation such as, "This is one way to simplify an equation," language is always a resource for making and communicating meaning.

Language serves many purposes in schools. In addition to being a place for social networking and for socializing students into ways of "doing school," school is one context for learning. In school, students use language to make sense of the world that surrounds them, and, in the process, they are (1) learning language, (2) learning through language, and (3) learning about language (Halliday, 1993).

One unique characteristic of humans is that we never stop *learning language*. From birth to age 7, children learn an enormous amount of language. Although this amount declines as students reach age 17 or 18, we continue to learn and enhance the language we need as we navigate through new stages and contexts in life.

Language is at the center of the learning process; humans *learn through language*. Language is a way of seeing, understanding, and communicating about the world. Learning in schools and classrooms is largely accomplished through language. In school, "We could virtually say that 'language is the curriculum'" (Derewianka, 1990, p. 3).

Beginning with the early stages of language learning, children formulate—consciously or unconsciously—their own rules about how language works. Later, children add new rules and amend old ones so that their sentences and usages resemble the language used by adults and those that surround them. As children learn the language of the home, they learn several different language styles, which vary according to the setting, the speakers, and the goal of communication. These styles are also called *registers*.

Different Registers

> The concept of register is typically concerned with variations in language conditioned by uses rather than users and involves consideration of the situation or context of use, the purpose, subject-matter and content of the message, and the relationship between the participants. (Romaine, 1994, p. 20)

In the study of language, a register is a variety of a language used for a specific purpose and audience in a particular social setting. Registers are simply a particular kind of language being produced within the context of a social situation. Below are three ways of saying the same thing, depending on the relationship between speakers and the circumstance:

I would be very appreciative if you would make less noise.

Please be quiet.

Shut up!

Throughout the day a person may use several different registers. For example, let's listen in as Nicole, a 37-year-old nurse, uses several registers.

	Message	To Whom	Context
Nicole (nurse, 37 years old)	"That's the optimum, and clinically that's what's advisable."	patient	work
	"What's up, Anne? I haven't seen you in years."	friend	grocery store
	"Way to go, Rudy, you nailed that one."	son	basketball practice
	"let me know where u r when you have a min. thx, luv u"	teenage daughter	text message
	"I never had the opportunity to meet your father, but I know you talked highly of him, and I know your loss is great. Our condolences to you and your family."	neighbor	written message on a card

In school contexts, teachers and students also use a variety of registers. Many researchers and educators have made a distinction between everyday and academic language (Cummins, 1986). Social language is associated with everyday, casual interactions; it's the language we use to order an ice cream, talk with a neighbor, or chat with family members. In schools, this is the language students use in the playground, cafeteria, or in the hallway. However, social language is also very much used in classroom dialog, as illustrated in the following examples:

Consider this . . .

What are some of the ways you typically use language during the day? How might you document differences in academic language use according to the context and with whom you are interacting? What suggestions might you make to increase the rigor of academic language use within classrooms?

"Turn to your elbow partner and figure out the answer." (Grade 2 teacher to students)

"Hold your horses; we are not there yet!" (history teacher to high school students).

"Dunno how to save my work." (Grade 4 student to teacher)

"That's a cool shirt, Dylan. Did you see the game?" (principal to middle school student).

"Dude, you need to get caught up with your group." (Grade 5 teacher to student).

Everyday language is very much a part of classrooms and schools; however, with its colloquial and idiomatic expressions, it can be considered in the academic range for those students who have not previously been exposed to it. At the other end of the academic language spectrum is the more formal, specialized register associated with disciplinary material. With today's emphasis on academic registers, many educators immediately think about vocabulary as the distinguishing feature. Although vocabulary is a very important dimension of academic language, as will become evident in the next sections, it is only one aspect.

THE NATURE OF ACADEMIC LANGUAGE

What's hard about learning in academic content areas is that each area is tied to academic specialist varieties of language (and other special symbol systems) that are complex, technical, and initially alienating to many learners. (Gee, 2004, p. 3)

Although in recent years academic language has been at the center of many educational efforts, educators and researchers have conceptualized academic language in different ways. Several recent studies point to teachers' understandings of academic language as challenging content-area vocabulary, or "hard words" (e.g., Ernst-Slavit & Mason, 2011; Homza, 2011; Lee, 2011; Wong Fillmore, 2011). However, academic language is a complex concept. "The difference in purpose, audience, and context results in clear differences in terms of language use in the selection of words, formality, sentence construction, and discourse patterns" (Gottlieb & Ernst-Slavit, 2013, p. 2).

In this section, we will provide a working definition of academic language, explain its importance in fostering academic thinking, describe the main roles of academic language, and explain three dimensions or components that characterize academic language.

In general terms, academic language refers to the language used in school to acquire new or deeper understanding of the content and communicate that understanding to others (Bailey & Heritage, 2008; Gottlieb & Ernst-Slavit, 2013; Gottlieb, Katz, & Ernst-Slavit, 2009; Schleppegrell, 2004). Because academic language conveys the kind of abstract, technical, and complex ideas and phenomena of the disciplines, it allows users to think and act, for example, as scientists, historians, and mathematicians. Thus, academic language promotes and affords a kind of thinking different from everyday language. As put by William Nagy and Dianna Townsend (2012), "Learning academic language is not learning new words to do the same thing that one could have done with other words; it is learning to do new things with language and acquiring new tools for these purposes" (p. 93).

Viewing academic language not as an end in itself but as a means to foster academic thinking can be very helpful in moving away from a focus on teaching academic language when it is not contextualized in meaningful academic activities. Along these lines, Zwiers (2008) contends that academic language serves three interrelated and broad roles: to describe complexity, higher order thinking, and abstraction. Each purpose is briefly summarized in Figure 1.1.

Throughout this chapter and book series, we discuss academic language as including more than vocabulary or phrases pertinent to the topic at hand. As can be deduced from the above discussion, academic language necessitates more than knowledge of single words to describe complex concepts, thinking processes, and abstract ideas and relationships. The academic language needed for students to access disciplinary content and textbooks and successfully participate in activities and assessments involves knowledge and ability to use specific linguistic features associated with academic disciplines. These features include discourse features,

Figure 1.1 Roles of Academic Language

To Describe Complexity	Academic language enables us to describe complex concepts in clear and concise ways (e.g., explaining the concept of the black hole, the causes of the French Revolution, or the Fibonacci sequence).
To Describe Higher Order Thinking	Academic language enables us to describe complex thinking processes that are used to comprehend, solve problems, and express ideas (e.g., application and problem solving in math, analyzing data in science, constructing an argument in English language arts).
To Describe Abstraction	Academic language enables us to describe ideas or relationships that cannot be easily acted out, pointed to, or illustrated with images (e.g., democracy, altruism, values and beliefs, relationships among objects or numbers, adaptation).

Source: Adapted from Zwiers, 2008, pp. 23–27

grammatical constructions, and vocabulary across different language domains (listening, speaking, reading, writing) and content areas (language arts, mathematics, science, history, among others).

When thinking about academic language use in classrooms, teachers generally start from the bottom level (with words and expressions) and then fold vocabulary into different configurations or syntactic structures that, in turn, combine to create unique genres. However, it might be easier for teachers and students to envision how discourse is the overarching dimension or umbrella that helps shapes the types of applicable sentence structures that, in turn, dictate the most appropriate words and expressions. Figure 1.2 shows the hierarchical nature of the dimensions of academic language along with some examples.

EVOLVING PERSPECTIVES OF ACADEMIC LANGUAGE

The construct of academic language developed from research in the mid 1970s to the 1980s. Since then, academic language—also called *academic English, scientific language, the language of school*—has been defined differently by authors and disciplinary perspectives. This next section provides a brief summary of the different frameworks used in the last decades to approach the construct of academic language. (For reviews of the literature,

Figure 1.2 Dimensions of Academic Language

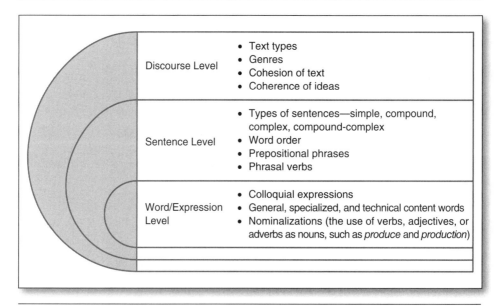

Discourse Level	• Text types • Genres • Cohesion of text • Coherence of ideas
Sentence Level	• Types of sentences—simple, compound, complex, compound-complex • Word order • Prepositional phrases • Phrasal verbs
Word/Expression Level	• Colloquial expressions • General, specialized, and technical content words • Nominalizations (the use of verbs, adjectives, or adverbs as nouns, such as *produce* and *production*)

Source: Adapted from Gottlieb & Ernst-Slavit, 2013

please see Anstrom et al., 2010, and Snow & Uccelli, 2009). To facilitate the discussion, this review is organized around five main orientations:

> **Consider this . . .**
>
> When you think about the dimensions of academic language, do you see them as a cone, from the top down, or as a triangle, from the bottom up? Which visual would be most helpful to explain this concept to your students or other colleagues? Why?

- Academic language versus social language (e.g., Cummins, 1986; Scarcella, 2008)
- Systemic linguistic perspectives (e.g., Gibbons, 2002, 2009; Halliday, 1978; Halliday & Martin, 1993; Schleppegrell, 2004)
- Language skills perspectives (e.g., Bailey & Heritage, 2008; Scarcella, 2008)
- Sociocultural perspectives (e.g., Gee, 2004, 2005; Heath, 1983)
- Language as social action (e.g., García & Leiva, 2013; García & Sylvan, 2011; van Lier, 2007, 2012; van Lier & Walqui, 2012)

Academic Language Versus Social Language Perspectives

In the early 1980s, Jim Cummins, drawing on research with bilingual children, described different kinds of language proficiency, focusing on assessment issues and arguing that assessment of students' language proficiency should involve more than tests of spoken interaction. This pivotal work makes a clear distinction between *basic interpersonal communication skills* (BICS) and *cognitive academic language proficiency* (CALP). In essence, BICS is the casual, everyday language that students use when they are talking to friends and neighbors, during recess, or at the lunchroom (e.g., "Give me that book." "Let's sit by the window." "See ya' later."). BICS, according to Cummins, rely more on contextual cues for transmitting meaning (e.g., body language, facial expressions, gestures, objects). CALP, on the other hand, is more complex and abstract and relies less on contextual cues for meaning. (For example, "Functions are used to solve equations for variables and to show a relationship between the variables." "The process is called photosynthesis." "Meriwether Lewis was born at a time of conflict and just before a major revolution.")

While the BICS and CALP distinction has brought to the forefront the importance of academic language for all students, but particularly for English language learners (ELLs), it has been criticized for its conceptualization of CALP as decontextualized language (see, e.g., Bartolomé, 1998; Gee, 1990) and for promoting deficit thinking by focusing on the low cognitive/academic skills of students (see, e.g., Edelsky, 2006; Edelsky et al., 1983; MacSwan & Rolstad, 2003). This distinction may not suffice to explain the complexities of the language needed to succeed in school, as students are exposed to and interact with multiple literacies (e.g., visual, digital, print) every day. Different kinds of proficiency are needed, including social language. Bailey (2007) has warned us not to believe that "there is something inherent in social language that makes it less sophisticated or less cognitively demanding than language used in an academic context" (p. 9). In fact, social language is much needed to construct meaning in the classroom, but for ELLs who may not be acclimated to school, it's part of the language they must learn!

Systemic Functional Linguistic Perspectives

About four decades ago, Michael Halliday (e.g., 1978) developed an approach to understand how meaning is constructed depending on the different purposes and language choices. Systemic functional linguistics provides a framework to look systematically at the relationships between form and meaning in the language used in various social contexts. More specifically, for scholars espousing a systemic functional linguistic approach, the linguistic system is made up of three strata: meaning (semantics), sound (phonology), and wording or lexicogrammar (syntax, morphology, and lexis).

Researchers have argued that teachers need to be able to conduct linguistic analyses of their curriculum in order to identify potential challenges for students, particularly ELLs (Achugar, Schleppegrell, & Oteíza, 2007; de Oliveira, 2013; Fang & Schleppegrell, 2008; Gibbons, 2009; Schleppegrell, 2001), and functional linguistics provides a framework for conducting such analyses. Language functions are the goals a speaker is trying to accomplish through the use of specific language structures and vocabulary, in other words, the purpose for communicating. In the classroom setting language functions can be equated with the question: What are we asking students to do with language? Examples of the many language functions are describing, listing, and summarizing. (See Chapter 3 for additional examples of language functions found in content and language standards.) Researchers contend that identifying the language functions underlying grade-level content is an important consideration for classroom teachers (Gibbons, 2009; Schleppegrell, 2004). By focusing on the meaning-making role that language plays in content-area learning, this perspective provides "a metalanguage for analyzing language that highlights issues of overall organization and voice and goes beyond structural categories such as noun and verb to show the meanings that follow from different language choices" (Schleppegrell, 2007, p. 123).

The work of Pauline Gibbons (1998, 2003, 2009) is of particular importance for classroom teachers. Influenced by the work of Halliday and Vygotsky (see, for example, Halliday, 1978; Vygotsky, 1978, 1987), Gibbons (2003, 2009) illustrates how language development for learning can be supported, for example, in the context of teaching a science unit on magnetism. Later in this chapter, we point to the different registers used in a science unit, where we observe the different types of language needed to interact in this classroom (see Fig. 1.6). Beginning with language that is more conversational, students eventually move to learn the science concepts and produce the language that is more academic and needed in required oral and written reports.

Language Skills Perspectives

Several approaches focus on the "academic language demands" students must meet to participate in school tasks and activities, specified by educators' grade-level expectations, and required by different standards. The emphasis here is on the language needed to acquire new and deeper understanding of the content areas and communicate that understanding to others (TESOL, 2006; WIDA, 2012). Work in this area has focused on the grammatical and lexical features of written and oral language used in school settings in conjunction with the language functions (e.g., summarizing, explaining) required in most classrooms. For example, important work by Robin Scarcella (2008) discusses the types of cognitive knowledge, skills, and strategies students need to acquire to succeed in the content areas. In her work, mostly with college students, Scarcella highlights the foundational knowledge of English, that is, the basic skills needed to communicate inside and outside of school, such as knowing how to read and write using appropriate verb tenses, as a precursor for academic language. In addition, she emphasizes the importance of learning academic vocabulary (e.g., *argument, empirical*) and language features (e.g., using passive voice, stating a thesis) across content areas as a way of ensuring understanding of and success in content specific classes.

The work of Alison Bailey and Margaret Heritage (2008) provides initial ways of cataloguing the language all students, including ELLs, need to succeed in school. These researchers distinguish *school navigational language* (SNL) and *curriculum content language* (CCL), where SNL is the language used to communicate with teachers and others in the school (e.g., "Get your red pens out." "Do we have to write a summary?"), and CCL is the language used in teaching and learning content (e.g., "The plot revolved around two main characters." "This time we are using an expanded algorithm."). In sum, work in this area describes academic language in terms of its utility in today's standards-driven classrooms.

Sociocultural Perspectives

Sociocultural perspectives view language learning as a social practice, consider students as active participants in the construction of knowledge, and take into account a variety of social and cultural factors involved in the teaching and learning process. From this perspective, there is much more to learning a language than its structural aspects. In classrooms, students need to learn when they can ask a question about a classroom presentation, under what circumstances can they copy information from a text, or when can they speak without raising their hands. Within this stance, language learning is seen as a social practice, where talk and interaction are central to human development and learning.

Sociocultural approaches highlight the role that many factors inside and outside of school play in the acquisition of academic language. In her groundbreaking ethnographic study, Shirley Brice Heath (1983) studied child language and teacher preparation in two working-class communities in North Carolina: Roadville and Trackton. Her findings revealed that the language socialization processes, including home literacy practices, played a pivotal role in students' success at school. In her analysis, Heath explained why some teachers and students had difficulties understanding one another and why typical school questions were not answered. Her work brought forth the fact that certain language socializations were more compatible with school environments than others.

Along these lines, Jim Gee's work (e.g., 1990, 2004, 2005) points to the advantages held by students raised in middle- and upper-class homes, where the language of school might be spoken at home. For these students, a wide range of linguistic, cognitive, and cultural patterns acquired at home support many of the features of school language. Consequently, students from more privileged groups more easily acquire the thinking processes and linguistic conventions necessary to succeed in school. In contrast, for most ELLs who speak another language at home, school might be the only place where they encounter the specialized language of the content areas, via their teachers who model how this kind of English is used (Ernst-Slavit & Mason, 2011). This discussion is elaborated on in the final section of this chapter, Academic Language and Social Justice.

Language as Social Action Perspectives

A relatively recent perspective views language as action. In general terms, action-based learning involves the acquisition of knowledge through activities that involve the concept or skill to be learned. In the field of language learning, this presumes that language must be scaffolded by social activity in terms of actions, interactions, and manipulations (van Lier, 1996). Within this context, the learner's agency and identity need to be located at the center of the teaching and learning process, and learners are seen not only as future competent users of the language to be learned but also as autonomous learners.

In school contexts, an action-based perspective can be understood as somewhat connected to other approaches, such as content-based, project-based, task-based, exploratory, and experiential teaching and learning approaches (van Lier, 2007). A common trait in all these approaches is the emphasis on the learner as an active participant, as someone with agency. Through an action-based perspective, ELLs engage in meaningful activities (e.g., research, projects, presentations) that pique their interest and foster language development through processes that involve perceiving, interacting, planning, researching, discussing, and coconstructing diverse academic products (van Lier & Walqui 2012). In these situations, language development takes place not only because of the meaningful ways in which students are interacting with each other, the teacher, and the materials, but also because activities are carefully planned and language is systematically scaffolded by the teacher.

In sum, an action-based teaching and learning approach places the agency of the learner at the center of the pedagogical process. Language is not seen as a set of rules or list of words but as a type of human action. In addition, language learning is not only a cognitive process but involves the mind, body, emotions, and all the senses. Viewing language learning within an action-based perspective places the forms and functions of language in the backdrop while foregrounding the role that language plays in doing things.

> **Consider this . . .**
>
> Which theoretical orientation(s) of academic language resonates with your thinking? What evidence do you have from teaching to match to your selected theoretical base? Why do you think it is necessary to ground your instruction and assessment in theory?

ACADEMIC LANGUAGE LEARNING AS A DEVELOPMENTAL PROCESS

Academic language is developmental in nature, with increased complexity and sophistication in language use from grade to grade that includes specific linguistic aspects that can be the same or vary across content areas (Anstrom et al., 2010). Lev Vygotsky (1987) saw the fundamental difference between the language a child masters by the age of six, and the many long and hard years of study needed to master academic language and concepts that students face, right up to and beyond the writing of a high school senior project, a grant proposal, a master's thesis, or a doctoral dissertation.

Important to this discussion is the changing nature of academic language throughout the school years. What is considered academic language for children in the early grades becomes part of the everyday language repertoire of high school students. Think about how students in preschool and kindergarten may need explicit instruction to understand the linguistic and conceptual differences among the terms *more, less,* and *same.* Yet, these same terms are used on a regular basis by older students both in and out of school.

Another way to view how linguistic complexity increases throughout the school years is by examining the academic language used in textbooks. A cursory look at a Grade 3 and Grade 10 textbook in any content area will make clear the increase in language demands. With the implementation of the CCSS and the Next Generation Science Standards (NGSS), the level of linguistic complexity in the textbooks is bound to increase, as students are required to read complex texts. In fact, writers of the standards consider that students' ability to comprehend the kinds of texts they will encounter in college and the workplace is perhaps the most critical factor in preparing for postsecondary life. However research discussed in the standards found that, while complexity of texts in entry-level college courses and workplaces held steadily for the most part, the linguistic complexity of texts used in high school declined over recent decades (CCSSI, 2010a, 2010b).

We view academic language as developmental for all students, increasing vertically from grade to grade, year to year. For ELLs, academic language has an additional developmental dimension, that of increasing horizontally from one language proficiency level to the next. Note in Figure 1.3 how grades K through 12 are displayed on the vertical axis, and language proficiency levels 1 to 6 on the horizontal one (Gottlieb & Ernst-Slavit, 2103). Now, let's try to imagine the amount of academic language needed by the four children from an immigrant Honduran family. The two older children came five years ago with their father, while the two younger ones came with the grandma less than a year ago. Gonzalo just started high school and is roughly in Level 4 of English language proficiency (ELP). His sister, Lucia, in fifth grade, is approaching the language proficiency of her English proficient peers and can be considered Level 5. The two younger children are both ELP Level 1, although Humberto in Grade 3 seems to struggle in school more than his little sister, Sandra, in kindergarten. What conclusions can you draw in terms of the academic language in English needed by these four children to be successful in school?

Figure 1.3 The Developmental Nature of Academic Language for ELLs

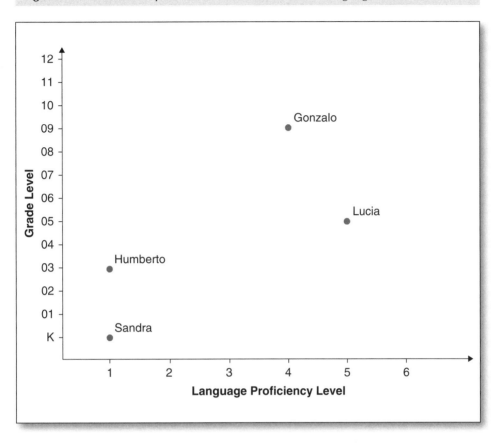

Source: Adapted from Gottlieb & Ernst-Slavit, 2013, p. 4

Considerations for Students With Disabilities

The developmental trajectory for students with disabilities may not be the same as that of their peers; the same principle applies to ELLs with disabilities. However, having a disability does not preclude this group of students from being exposed to age-appropriate academic language and having academic experiences that enable them to perform at their highest level of conceptual and language

Consider this . . .

Think about siblings who speak a language other than English at your school. Are they at the same level of English language proficiency? Who appears to learn English faster? Why might this happen?

expectations. Disabilities also do not necessarily impede this group of students from being able to use language for academic purposes in both their home language and in English. The mere growth of academic language associated with each grade level and language proficiency level for ELLs is not enough to explain its complexity. Also to be taken into account is the building of different types of awareness associated with language within classrooms (Gottlieb & Ernst-Slavit, 2014, p. 9).

ORAL AND WRITTEN LANGUAGES

Most will agree that there are differences between oral and written languages. The language used in a nonfiction book will, in most cases, be vastly different from the language used by two friends chatting in a coffee shop. On some occasions, for example, during a class lecture, a legal consultation, an interaction with a police officer after a collision, or in a text message, there might be some resemblance between oral and written language. Examples of differences between oral and written language occur in texting, tweeting, and other forms of short message services (SMS) normally transmitted through mobile phone connections. However, on most other occasions, when we hear people speaking the way we write or folks writing the way we speak, it may sound strange, funny, unnatural, and even inappropriate. Why? Because generally there are many differences between the ways we speak and the ways we write. For example,

- Spoken language can be more communicative than written language due to extra cues such as body language, tone, volume, and timbre.
- Spoken language often relies on immediate interactions with people.
- Spoken language tends to be full of repetitions, incomplete sentences, corrections, and interruptions, except for formal speeches or scripted presentations.

On the other hand,

- Written language is generally more formal than oral language.
- Written language tends to be more precise than oral language.
- Written language can be more complex and sophisticated than oral language.
- Written language follows certain patterns of organization, explicitness, and logic.
- Written language is usually permanent.
- Written language uses punctuation, headings, layout, colors, and other graphical effects not available in spoken language.

Important to highlight is that neither form of communication is better than the other. The two forms are different and, like different registers, serve different purposes. While some of the above statements do not apply when using text messaging, tweets, or other types of instant communication, the truth is that there are specific suggestions for speakers and writers. Making students aware of the differences between speakers and writers will help them improve both their conversational and writing skills.

What do the differences between written and oral language mean for speakers (during conversations or informal presentations) and writers? Figure 1.4 is a chart that might be useful to students when discussing differences between the language used by speakers and that used by writers.

Figure 1.4 What Speakers and Writers Do

Speakers . . .	Writers . . .
make eye contact with audience.	do not often have readers present.
refer or point to objects in their immediate context.	cannot assume that readers share their immediate context.
can expect encouragement and support from listeners.	have to construct and sustain their own line of thinking.
use all sorts of body language, intonation, stress, and tone to construct meaning.	use punctuation, headings, layout, colors, and other graphical effects to help make their meaning clear.
repeat, restate, and rephrase when they assess that their meaning is not clear.	take time to edit and revise their work to enhance their message.

Source: Adapted from http://englishonline.tki.org.nz/English-Online/Exploring-language/Speaking-and-Writing

Oral Language as a Vehicle for Promoting Academic Language Development

Until recently, students' oral language development in the classroom has largely been neglected due to the prevalence of teacher talk (Rothenberg & Fisher, 2007). The coverage of Listening/Speaking in the Common Core State Standards for English language arts (CCSS for ELA) has helped stimulate student collaboration and

Consider this . . .

Model examples of oral and written language around the same topic for your students. Then pose the questions: "How is oral and written language alike?" "How is oral and written language different?" Have students work in partners or small groups using a graphic organizer, such as a T-chart or Venn diagram, to identify and compare the features of oral and written language.

interaction through conversation. For example, across grades K–2, CCSS for ELA, Speaking and Listening, Comprehension and Collaboration #1 states that students "participate in collaborative conversations with diverse partners about grade [level] topics and texts with peers and adults in small and larger groups" (CCSSI, 2010a, p. 23). By grades 3–8, students are expected to "engage effectively in a range of collaborative discussions (one-on-one, in groups, and teacher-led) with diverse partners" (pp. 24, 49). In high school, the same standard extends to having students "initiate and participate effectively in a range of collaborative discussions (one-on-one, in groups, and teacher-led) with diverse partners on grade [level] topics, texts, and issues" (p. 50).

While the language domains of listening and speaking have always been integral to English language proficiency/development standards and curricula for ELLs, there are now enhanced opportunities for ELLs to have proficient English models (their own peers) with whom to practice their additional language in intentional ways. As a result, dialog and conversation within content area instruction have become venues for elaborating and practicing academic language. To ensure growth in students' oral language development, teachers must plan and orchestrate student–student interaction with clear roles, language targets, and built-in formative assessment strategies to monitor progress on an ongoing basis (Saunders & Goldenberg, 2010).

> **Consider this . . .**
>
> What strategies might you use to ensure that students have time to engage in pointed conversations that involve higher order thinking across all content classes? What is the academic language with which students have to be familiar to meaningfully interact with each other around content topics and issues? How might oral language practice reinforce the students' literacy development?

A language-rich environment that surrounds students with oral and written discourse can be a stimulus for ongoing student exchange and engagement in academic conversations and writing for a variety of purposes (Zwiers, 2008). As learning occurs through social interaction, teachers must organize instruction to facilitate purposeful, academic oral discourse between and among students. As oral language is foundational to literacy development, purposeful talk leads students to develop and deepen their understanding of concepts and ideas that are reinforced through print. Thus, student interaction in authentic contexts should revolve around and be embedded in standards, instructional tasks, and classroom assessment (Fisher, Frey, & Rothenberg, 2008).

Academic conversations are a necessary aspect of schooling. In fact Jeff Zwiers and Marie Crawford (2011) have five distinct categories that justify cultivating and sustaining conversations among students: (1) language and literacy development, (2) cognitive engagement, (3) content learning, (4) social and cultural benefits, and (5) psychological reasons. Figure 1.5 takes the classification scheme of Zwiers and Crawford (2011, pp. 12–25) and places it into a chart.

Figure 1.5   Reasons for Promoting Academic Conversations in School

1. Reinforce Language and Literacy Development	2. Enhance Cognitive Engagement	3. Promote Content Learning	4. Recognize Social and Cultural Benefits	5. Tap Psychological Needs
Conversation: Builds academic language, literacy skills, oral language, and communication skills	Conversation: Builds critical thinking skills Promotes different perspectives and empathy Fosters creativity Fosters skills for negotiating meaning and focusing on a topic	Conversation: Builds content understanding Cultivates connections Helps students coconstruct understandings Helps teachers and students assess learning	Conversation: Builds relationships Builds academic ambience Makes lessons more culturally relevant Fosters equity	Conversation: Develops inner dialog and self-talk Fosters engagement and motivation Builds confidence Fosters choice, ownership, and control over thinking Builds academic identity Fosters self-discovery Builds student voice and empowerment

Oral Language as a Bridge to Literacy

Historically, spoken language has been the precursor of written language. People were speaking for thousands of years before writing was invented; some languages remain only oral. Children use oral language before they learn to read and write. In fact, most folks learn to speak

Consider this . . .

Which of the reasons for promoting conversations between and among students resonates with you? Give a classroom example of the reasons you select. Make an inventory of activities around conversations for building academic language to reinforce students' language and literacy development.

without formal instruction but need assistance when it comes to learning how to read and write.

As discussed in other volumes in this series (Gottlieb & Ernst-Slavit, 2014),[1] oral language is a bridge to literacy, whether in the students' home language or English. According to the Center for Research on Education, Diversity & Excellence (CREDE) and the National Literacy Panel, English oral language proficiency contributes to English literacy development (Goldenberg & Coleman, 2010). In addition, research has substantiated that students who are proficient in both their home language and English tend to outperform their monolingual peers. For Hawaiian students in the Kamehameha Project, oral language development through "talk story" practices, a culturally responsive teaching strategy, improved their literacy when this strategy was integrated into reading instruction (Au, 1998).

What do these findings mean to teachers? It is quite clear that teachers must intentionally build in instructional time for pair and small group work so that students can collaborate, interact with each other, and engage in academic conversations in English and their home languages. This thinking is in concert with the Speaking/Listening standards of the CCSS for ELA; here students are expected to "participate in collaborative conversations with diverse partners about grade-level topics and texts with peers and adults in small and larger groups" (CCSSI, 2010a, p. 23).

Speaking, in particular, in vibrant, topic-focused discussions leads to and strengthens literacy comprehension in ELL classrooms (Snow, Uccelli, & White, 2013).[2] Academic conversations not only fortify oral language and communication skills; these language exchanges tend to build vocabulary, academic language, and literacy, all the while fostering critical thinking and content understanding (Zwiers & Crawford, 2011). As reading expository text tends to be more challenging for ELLs than reading narrative text (Vásquez, Hansen, & Smith, 2010), it is important that students discuss their work with each other to clarify, reinforce, and expand their comprehension of text.

Use of targeted oral language can provide scaffolds for students to enter into academic reading more successfully. Read-alouds, for example, can help build background knowledge about the discourse, spur student interest in the topic, and assist students in acquiring academic language.

Additionally, this strategy helps students (1) develop academic listening comprehension, (2) have multiple exposures to academic words and expressions, (3) cope with complex grammatical constructions within natural contexts, and (4) more readily tackle grade-level text and concepts (Zwiers, 2008). While focused oral language use enhances students' literacy development, there are many areas that challenge language learning, especially when that language is English.

In schools, students need to learn how to use oral language that is more precise, fosters critical thinking, and facilitates understanding of the content areas. What follows is an example from an Australian science classroom where the teacher and her 9- and 10-year-old students are studying magnetism (Gibbons, 2009). One of the teacher's goals for her students, to learn the language of science, becomes apparent when she uses comments such as, "Let's start using our scientific language" and "We are trying to talk like scientists." In this classroom, the teacher interacted with her students in ways that scaffolded their contributions and prepared them for both academic conversations and written texts. Her interchange with them is shown in Figure 1.6.

Figure 1.6 Moving From Oral to Written Language: One Example From a Science Lesson in an Elementary Classroom

Language Mode	Text	Context
Oral	"Look, it's making them move. Those didn't stick."	Students talking in a small group as they were experimenting with a magnet.
	"We found out the pins stuck on the magnet."	Student telling the teacher what she had learned from the experiment.
Written	"Our experiment showed that magnets attract some metals."	Students' written report about the experiment.
	"Magnetic attraction occurs only between ferrous metals."	An entry in a child's encyclopedia about magnets.

Source: Adapted from Gibbons, 2009, p. 49

The example above demonstrates what Gibbons (2003) calls the "mode continuum," which starts from oral language where the speaker and audience share contextual knowledge, and moves to oral language where the audience may not share additional contextual cues (e.g., body language), and goes on to written language. The language needed in these different situations increases in complexity and precision as students move from everyday language to academic language and from oral to written modes as they navigate through the different grade levels.

MULTILITERACIES AND MULTIMODALITIES AS SOURCES OF ACADEMIC LANGUAGE

With the new millennium on the horizon, the New London Group of ten prominent international educators authored a profound article emphasizing the increasing cultural and linguistic diversity around the globe and its impact on the changing social environment facing students and teachers.

With this premise as a backdrop, multiliteracies have emerged as a way to address and make sense of the communicative complexities of the world. Within a relatively short time span, multiliteracies, learning, and teaching have come to be viewed as completely interconnected social processes within the educational milieu. Pedagogically, multiliteracies have taken on a two-pronged approach, recognizing expansion in (1) the number and the integration of different modes of meaning making; that is, where the textual relates to the visual, the audio, the spatial across mass media, multimedia, and electronic hypermedia; and (2) heterogeneity, yet at the same time, the interconnectedness of our global society (New London Group, 1996).

> **Consider this . . .**
>
> What does the term *multiliteracies* mean to you as a teacher, teacher educator, or teacher leader? How has the concept of multiliteracies influenced your thinking about how all students make meaning from the world around them? Is this construct in concert with or different from your personal knowledge base about literacy development?

Len Unsworth (2001) poses a conceptual framework that embraces multiliteracies in school. In it, he suggests three stages: (1) framing perspectives that introduce the changing perspectives of school-based literacy, (2) facilitating knowledge on the role of academic language as a resource for literacy development, and (3) formulating classroom practices where multiliteracies are integrated into content area teaching. The challenge of multiliteracies for teachers is to expand traditional language and print bases of literacy to provide real-life applications for students to express their understanding and learning using multiple modalities.

Today multiliteracies are a means of sense making beyond the printed page, especially for the digital natives sitting in our classrooms who tend to seek information electronically. *Digital literacy* involves the creative use of different forms of technology to support the learning and imagination of students. *Visual literacy* is a way for students to express complex concepts through images without heavy reliance on print. *Oral literacy* has its own genres, encompassing rich storytelling and information sharing. Figure 1.7 lists some of the means students can use to show their conceptual understanding through multiliteracies.

Figure 1.7 Examples of Different Types of Multiliteracies Addressed in School

Print-Based Literacy	Digital Literacy	Visual Literacy	Oral Literacy
• Books • Manuals • Magazines • Newspapers • Brochures • Outlines	• Computer games • Podcasts • Video streaming (e.g., webinars) • Blogs • Social media	• PowerPoints • Photographs • Videos • YouTube clips • Murals • Wordles • Graphics • Sketch noting or visual note taking	• Readers theater • Choral reading • Book reads • Process drama • Read-alouds • Storytelling • Lyrics/songs

Source: Adapted from Gottlieb & Ernst-Slavit, 2014, p. 5

There are new and creative ways of displaying literacy that do not follow the typical horizontal or vertical patterns of print on a page. Think about a typical screen displaying a website for an organization, with its flashing banner and rotating messages. In fact, there may be boxes of varying sizes on this electronic display with illustrated inserts or advertisements. Its contents are generally presented as tabs that serve as a table of contents and open to reveal multiple layers of information. Another form of communication is presented in Figure 1.8, a visual impression of a text that has been made from a Wordle (www.wordle.net), a word cloud from a source text that gives greater prominence to the more frequent words. This word cloud provides an additional medium for students to represent academic language at the word level.

To become effective participants in emerging multiliteracies, students and teachers have to understand the different configurations that result from the interaction among available resources. Put another way, students and teachers alike need to be able to use language in conjunction with images and digital expressions to construct different kinds of meanings. The knowledge of linguistic, visual, and digital meaning-making systems involves metalanguage—language for describing language, images, and meaning-making intermodal interactions (Unsworth, 2001).

Figure 1.8 An Example of Visual Literacy in the Form of a Wordle

Source: nicholaspelafas, 2011

Students have a growing repertoire of literacy sources and a multiplicity of communication channels to access meaning within sociocultural contexts. English language learners, in particular, benefit from having multiple avenues for gaining and demonstrating deep understanding of language and content. Having multiple venues for literacy development allows students to become more motivated and participatory in the process.

RAISING AWARENESS OF ACADEMIC LANGUAGE[3]

Academic language is more involved than terms, conventions, and genres. The teaching and learning of academic language involves more than learning a variety of linguistic components. It encompasses knowledge about "ways of being in the world, ways of acting, thinking, interacting, valuing, believing, speaking, and sometimes writing and reading, connected to particular identities and social roles" (Gee, 1992, p. 73). Put another way, language needs to be understood in relation to the speakers, the purpose of the communication, the audience, and the context for use.

This situated nature of language is integral to content area learning. Moschkovich (2002) proposes a situated-sociocultural view to describe the language ELLs need to successfully navigate instructional activities in the mathematics classroom. That is, language is one of the several resources students need and use to participate in mathematics thinking and learning.

Students also draw on social cues (e.g., gestures) and material resources (e.g., artifacts) as well as the use of their home languages to access and construct meaning as they engage in learning.

Language operates within a sociocultural context, not in isolation. In school, the classroom environment often serves as the sociocultural context for learning academic language. Although the distinct backgrounds, experiences, and views of the students need to be taken into consideration, the classroom becomes the mediator for accruing individual knowledge that leads to shared meaning. Thus, by listening to and coming to understand other perspectives, students become a community of learners with its own cultural practices and social norms. In the examples of content area classrooms described in this volume, we come to see distinct communities of practice with established social and cultural ways of being (Lave & Wenger, 1991).

There is also a growing awareness on the part of teachers and students of the various processes involved in language learning. Besides the sociocultural dimension that permeates the classroom, students are becoming more conscious of how they learn, and teachers are becoming more responsive in how they teach. Figure 1.9 offers teachers ideas of how to tap students' linguistic, cognitive, and sociocultural awareness within the classroom context.

Having established that classrooms are very specialized environments for content and language learning, we now hone in on the relevance of academic language for diverse learners.

Teacher language awareness (TLA) is an area of increasing interest to those involved in preparing teachers to work with linguistically and culturally diverse students. However, over the past several decades, as global migration has made classrooms increasingly heterogeneous, all teachers, regardless of their content area or grade-level expertise, are becoming de facto language teachers. The language awareness movement is rooted in the United Kingdom, where it began in the early 1980s. In its most basic form, "language awareness refers to the development . . . of an enhanced consciousness of and sensitivity to the forms and functions of language" (Carter, 2003, p. 64, as cited in Andrews, 2007). In other words, an understanding of the language used by teachers in the classroom and the ability to analyze it will contribute directly to teaching effectiveness. A general language mindfulness involves at least the following:

A. Awareness of some of the properties of language, its creativity and playfulness, its double meanings.

B. Awareness of the embedding of language within culture. Learning to read the language is learning about the cultural properties of the language. Idioms and metaphors, in particular, reveal a lot about the culture.

Figure 1.9 Building Awareness of Academic Language in the Classroom

Type of Awareness	Classroom Examples
Metalinguistic Awareness	• Recognizing and identifying cognates in multiple languages • Comparing the similarities and differences of forms and structures • Transferring information and literacy across languages
Sociocultural Awareness	• Using language and culture as resources • Considering and incorporating the students' cultural norms and traditions • Being aware of the situation or context for language learning
Metacognitive Awareness	• Reflecting on how students learn language • Talking and writing about language learning • Discussing with learners about how they do things in the classroom, such as their comprehension strategies

Source: Gottlieb & Ernst-Slavit, 2013, p. 5

C. Awareness of the forms of the language we use. We need to recognize that the relations between the forms and meanings of a language are sometimes arbitrary, but that language is a system with patterns and exceptions.

D. Awareness of the close relationship between language and ideology. It involves "seeing through language," in other words. (Carter, 1994, as cited in Andrews, 2007)

Consider this . . .

For additional information, see *Teacher Language Awareness* (2007) by Stephen Andrews or the *Language Awareness* journal. Several variations have evolved under the language awareness umbrella: *teacher language awareness* (TLA), *critical language awareness* (CLA; for a partial review, see Svalberg, 2007); and *critical language study* (CLS).

ACADEMIC LANGUAGE AND SOCIAL JUSTICE

In a study focusing on the classroom talk used by elementary teachers working in mainstream classrooms, Ernst-Slavit and Mason (2011) found that ELLs had limited opportunities to hear and use different academic discourses. In fact, teacher talk during content area instruction heavily relied on everyday language and was filled with contractions, colloquialisms, indefinite referents, homophones, heteronyms, and idiomatic expressions, all of which have the potential to cloud understanding.

Learning the language of the content areas—with its conciseness, use of high-density information words, and precision of expression—is difficult for all students. Schools might be the only setting where they hear that "metamorphic rocks that have their grains arranged in parallel bands or layers are classified as foliated," or that "Melville's crew in the Pequod predicted America's demographic diversity federated along one keel." For many students, their teachers might be the most significant single source of oral academic discourse (Bartolomé, 1998; Ernst-Slavit & Mason, 2011).

Academic language has become increasingly important in K–12 settings; this increase has been fueled, in part, by the implementation of college and career readiness standards, in particular, the CCSS and NGSS. If schools are going to require students to use certain linguistic repertoires to demonstrate conceptual understanding, educators will have to systematically model the kind of academic registers needed to achieve academic success. "Those academic and professional uses of language require conformity to elaborate, explicit, and often quite mysterious sets of rules" (Gottlieb & Ernst-Slavit, 2014, p. 8). Not teaching those rules to our students is equivalent to what Macedo (1994) calls a "pedagogy of entrapment," when schools require students to use the different academic registers that they do not teach. Simply put, all educators must be aware of the importance of teaching academic discourses to all students, but particularly to those students for whom English is a second, third, or fourth language and for students from underrepresented backgrounds who may not be surrounded by the types of thought and academic registers valued in schools.

Implementation of the new generation of content (college and career readiness) standards and language development standards can be seen as an opportunity for advancement for all students and a renewal of equity in the classroom. Belief in academic success for all students, coupled with appropriate, scaffolded, and stimulating instruction and assessment, will lead to the creation of a generation of students prepared for exciting and challenging postsecondary experiences.

FOR FURTHER THINKING . . .

During the last three decades, the construct of academic language has been central in the work of researchers and practitioners searching to advance educational opportunities for students for whom English is an additional language. Only recently, due in part to the introduction of new content standards including the CCSS and the NGSS, has the focus on language learning become central to the educational success of all students. As a result, all teachers have become language teachers, regardless of their content area.

With an emphasis on developing verbal and analytical skills, the new standards are propelling educators to acknowledge the importance of preparing all students to use language in sophisticated and academic ways as they participate in meaningful academic practices. This emphasis on language learning places proficient English speakers and ELLs on equal footing, as all students will need to learn academic language as they become ready for college and careers.

The following questions are intended to spark discussion among teachers and teacher leaders as they deal with academic language use on a daily basis.

1. Make a list of all the activities you do in your classroom that involve the use of academic language. What proportion of your list involves written texts? What proportion is devoted to oral language?

2. What strategies do you use in your classroom or school to foster academic language learning for all your students? What additional steps can you take to keep enhancing the acquisition of academic language for students?

3. Do you remember learning a second language in high school? What were some practices used by your teachers that helped you learn or that hindered your learning of the new language? For example, was there an overemphasis on teaching vocabulary and grammatical structures in isolation?

4. Look at a couple of pages in your grade-level content area textbook. Aside from new or difficult academic vocabulary, what are the grammatical structures that might be challenging for students to understand or produce?

NOTES

1. Text in this paragraph and the following one was previously published in Gottlieb & Ernst-Slavit, 2014, pp. 12–13.

2. Text in this paragraph and the following one was previous published in Gottlieb & Ernst-Slavit, 2014, p. 14.

3. The next five paragraphs and Figure 1.9 were previously published in Gottlieb & Ernst-Slavit, 2013.

2 What Are the Dimensions of Academic Language?

High thoughts must have high language.

—Aristophanes (405 BCE)

IDENTIFYING ACADEMIC LANGUAGE WITHIN AND ACROSS CONTENT AREAS

The teaching and learning of academic language requires *more* than linguistic knowledge—it also involves cultural knowledge about ways of being in the world, ways of acting, thinking, interacting, valuing, believing, speaking, and sometimes writing and reading, connected to particular identities and social roles (Gee, 1992, p. 73). Ultimately, one important goal for learning academic language, as discussed in Chapter 1, is to afford and promote thinking and communicating about issues in more abstract, technical, and deeper ways. As shown in Figure 2.1, having teachers and school leaders recognize and incorporate the linguistic and cultural influences of home and community into school enables students to unite their experiential and academic worlds to build their academic language use.

For some years we have known that many students may encode and decode words as they read and write and yet still not understand the texts. With the current emphasis on academic language of text in college and career readiness standards, namely, the Common Core State Standards

Figure 2.1 The Larger Context of Academic Language Use

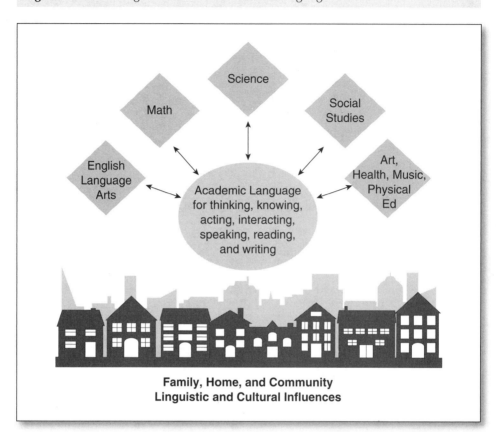

(CCSS) and the Next Generation Science Standards (NGSS), there is the impetus to prepare our students for success after secondary school. What are schools doing to ensure that students are prepared to meet the challenges of our changing society? How can educators prepare students to readily access linguistically demanding texts and to wrestle with real-life problems? If students are to become creative problem solvers, they will need to learn the academic language of diverse texts and acquire the skills, habits, and knowledge needed to succeed in the 21st century.

While most agree that the teaching of academic language is an imperative, unfortunately many efforts focus only on increasing academic vocabulary. Thus many important aspects of the language of the disciplines—such as reducing long sentences into shorter phrases, using connectors to link technical vocabulary, focusing on details, excluding ambiguous interpretations, assuming an impersonal authoritative voice, and, most important, using academic language for thinking and knowing—are often visibly absent.

In the following sections, we describe selected dimensions of academic language, taking into account that learning academic language, like learning any other language, requires systematic, deliberate, prolonged, and robust approaches that are rich, contextualized, and meaningful for each and every student. In addition, the teaching and learning of the academic register needs to consider the individual needs of students as well as their linguistic and cultural resources. Only with this kind of additive mindset can instruction be effective.

ANALYZING ACADEMIC LANGUAGE WITHIN DISCOURSE

In this book and series, *discourse* refers to the larger bodies of language—their organization, coherence, and cohesiveness. It involves oral and written language use in varying social contexts beyond the sentence level. Within discourse are *genres* (and *text types*); that is, specific ways in which discourse communities are constructed, interpreted, and used (Bhatia, 2005). Examples of different genres prevalent in school include lab reports in science, timelines in history, word problems in mathematics, digital story telling in English language arts, and sheet music in music.

While there are many similarities in terms of how academic discourse is constructed across disciplines—conciseness, high density of information-bearing words, and formal tone—there are also many differences in terms of formats and expectations. Figure 2.2 presents examples of different texts students encounter in their various content areas that represent unique discourses.

Discourse alludes to the different ways in which text can be organized in relation to voice/perspective, coherence of ideas, and transition of thought. For example, young elementary students can learn about bats by reading *Bats!* (Iorio, 2005), a publication from *Time* magazine filled with colorful photographs and facts about bats. Children can also learn about bats by reading *Stellaluna* (Cannon, 1993), a fictional narrative about the adventures of a young female fruit bat. While both books are written for

> **Consider this . . .**
>
> The term *discourse*, like so many other words in the English language, has several meanings. On the one hand, there is a traditional definition of discourse—dialog or conversation between two parties, but on the other hand, there is what Gee (2011) refers to as "Discourse with a big 'D'" (p. 34). His definition of Discourse with a big "D" is socially acceptable ways of using language—"of thinking, valuing, acting, and interjecting, in the 'right' places and at the 'right' times with the 'right' objects" (p. 34). Being a competent user of academic language means knowing what to say, when to say it, and how and when to say it within the different oral and written disciplinary contexts.

Figure 2.2 Examples of Discourse Across Content Areas

Content Areas	Examples of Discourse
Mathematics	Proofs, story problems, graphs
English language arts	Editorials, autobiographies, plays, blogs
Science	Articles in science journals, lab directions, science reports
Social studies	Historical diaries, speeches, folktales
Other content areas	Art encyclopedias, health compendia, performance evaluations (music)

children, their purposes and organization are different. *Bats!* is an informational book with paragraphs, challenging vocabulary, detailed diagrams, captions, fact boxes, and interviews with experts. *Stellaluna,* on the other hand, is an uplifting fictional story with short sentences and paragraphs and realistic illustrations that describes the trials and tribulations of one baby bat which, after being separated from her mother, lives with a family of birds. Both books help students learn much about bats; however, their purpose, voice, and organization of text are different. In addition, the two books pose different kinds of academic language demands for students. The difference between *Bats!* and *Stellaluna* speaks to one of the important instructional shifts in the CCSS, that is, the call for an increased focus on informational texts.

Balance Between Informational and Literary Texts

In an attempt to make stronger connections between school and societal needs, the CCSS call for a more balanced distribution between informational and literary texts. The expectation is that by fourth grade, half of what students read should be informational text, and this should increase to 70% by 12th grade. The CCSS authors based their recommendations partly on a chart prepared by the National Assessment of Educational Progress (NAEP) Reading Framework regarding the distribution of texts by grade level, shown in Figure 2.3.

While there is some debate about whether the prescribed proportion of literary/fiction and informational texts might be healthy—or lethal—doses for students, school districts and educators are making the necessary curricular adjustments to satisfy these guidelines. Pertinent to this discussion is the distinction between fiction and informational texts. A common misconception is that fiction consists of narrative text structures

Figure 2.3 Distribution of Literary and Informational Passages by Grade in the 2009 NAEP Reading Framework

Grade	Amount of Literary Text	Amount of Informational Text
4	50%	50%
8	45%	55%
12	30%	70%

Source: National Assessment Governing Board, 2008

(i.e., writing that tells a story), while informational text uses expository text structures (i.e., writing that explains). This distinction is too simplistic, as fiction and nonfiction both use narrative and expository writing, as well as text structures (Short, 2013). The main difference between these two types of texts is that informational texts are about facts and principles related to the real world, while anything can be made up in fiction writing.

Nonetheless, students can learn important content and lessons from fictional materials. Starting in the early years, educators can help children enjoy both kinds of text while, at the same time, teaching young learners how to tease apart fictional from nonfictional elements. Fictional texts can also be powerful learning tools in diverse content areas, as the above discussion of *Stellaluna* suggests. Another example of a powerful fictional book to aid students' understanding of big numbers is the children's book *How Much is a Million?* (Schwartz, 2004). This book, while fictional with its whimsical artwork, a mathematical magician, and a unicorn, is filled with illustrations and concepts that are simple enough for children to conceptualize astronomical numbers like a million or a trillion. (For example, seven pages of the book are filled with tiny stars that represent approximately the number 10,000).

> **Consider this . . .**
>
> What kinds of adjustments have you made as a teacher, teacher leader, or teacher educator to represent or use grade-level informational and fictional texts in your educational context? Which examples of these text types have you found that best illustrate students in linguistically and culturally responsive classrooms?

In some cases, valuable historical and scientific information comes packaged as a narrative. Consider, for example, *The Immortal Life of Henrietta Lacks* (Skloot, 2010). In this narrative about the life of a poor African

American woman whose cells (which were later to become one of the most important tools in medicine) were taken from her without her permission, the author discusses issues about DNA, biology, chromosomes, and bioethics. This *New York Times* bestseller has provided many readers with a refresher course in biology, ethics, and social justice, all within the context of a riveting narrative about the life of Mrs. Henrietta Lacks.

The value of informational texts cannot be underestimated. In today's information age, students "are bombarded with informational text; they see billboards, newspapers, brochures, pamphlets, text messages, web pages, advertisements, and use electronic devices such as smartphones and mobile computers" (Mora-Flores, 2014, p. 83). Each type of text serves a distinct purpose. The ability to access and produce diverse texts partly determines students' success in school and beyond. Thus, students need to work with informational texts beyond the traditional school essay to include more diverse and authentic forms found in the real world. Regardless of whether students are writing a traditional school essay or a more authentic experiential recount, students still need to select a topic, take into account the audience, become familiar with the selected genre of the written text, draft, revise, edit, and publish their work (Mora-Flores, 2014).

Differences Between Nonfiction and Informational Texts

Earlier in this chapter we discussed misconceptions about the difference between fiction and informational texts. Equally important is the need to clarify the differences—and similarities—between nonfiction narrative and informational texts. While the terms *informational text* and *nonfiction* are often used interchangeably, they are not the same. As illustrated in Figure 2.4, there are marked differences between these text types in terms of their focus, purpose, authenticity, voice, and other kinds of features.

Figure 2.4 Characteristics of Nonfiction Narratives and Informational Texts

Characteristics	Nonfiction Narratives	Informational Texts
Focus	Center on a single individual or group in specific points in time (e.g., Anne Frank's biography)	Center on whole classes of things in a timeless way (e.g., group—"Llamas, originally from South America, are members of the camelid family.")
Purpose	To entertain readers	To provide readers essential fact-based information about a topic

Characteristics	Nonfiction Narratives	Informational Texts
Authenticity and Research	Emphasize the emotional or moral truth of a story	Make use of research, paying attention to sources and providing a list of references
Features	Use detail to create setting, character, and theme Aim to bring events to life for readers	Include comparative and classificatory structures, technical vocabulary, navigational aids, such as indexes and headings, descriptions of attributes and characteristic events, and various graphical devices such as diagrams, tables, and charts
Voice	Give readers a sense of author's style via the use of storytelling elements	Use a common voice that is accessible to audiences
Examples	Personal essays Biographies Resumés Blogs Memoirs	Handouts Textbooks Websites Brochures

The experiences and strategies needed for students to be better prepared for future college and career experiences, as defined by the CCSS and NGSS, exceed those needed in reading and writing nonfiction texts. Informational texts span all disciplines, build connections among content areas, and provide opportunities for students to deepen their knowledge and understanding of the world that surrounds them.

However, not all informational texts are written using academic language features such as long sentences, abstraction, precision of expression, conciseness achieved by avoiding redundancy, and avoidance of personal opinions and relations. The two excerpts shown in Figure 2.5, from an article in *Science* by Catherine Snow (2010), point to the wide range of informational texts.

Consider this . . .

1. While in both science texts in Figure 2.5 (see pages 34 and 35) the authors are writing to inform, what specific differences can you find in terms of the nature of the text (e.g., voice, organization, coherence of ideas, cohesion)?

2. What other differences can you identify in relation to vocabulary and sentence level structure?

3. What inferences can you make about the language demands that each of these texts places on readers?

4. What inferences can you make about the language demands that each of these texts poses for students who are learning English as a second or third language?

Figure 2.5 Examples of Nonacademic and Academic Informational Texts

From http://www.lowrider.com/forums/10-Under-the-Hood/topics/183-HP-vs-torque/ posts (spelling as in the original posting)

Often times guys get caught up in the hype of having a big HP motor In their lolo. I frequently get asked whats the best way to get big numbers out of their small block. The answer is not HP, but torque, "You sell HP, you feel torque" as the old saying goes. Most of us are running 155/80/13 tires on our lolo's. Even if you had big HP numbers, you will *never* get that power to the ground, at least off the line. I have a 64 Impala SS 409, that i built the motor in. While it is a completely restored original (I drive it rolling on 14" 72 spoke cross laced Zeniths), the motor internals are not. It now displaces 420 CI, with forged pistons and blalanced rotating assembly. The intake, carb and exhaust had to remain OEM for originality's sake, and that greatly reduces the motors potential. Anyway, even with the original 2 speed powerglide, it spins those tires with alarming ease, up to 50 miles per hour!

In my 62, I built a nice 383 out of an 86 Corvette, i built it for good bottom end pull, since it is a lowrider with 8 batteries. And since it rides on the obligatory 13's, torque is what that car needs. it pulls like an ox right from idle, all the way up to Its modest 5500 redline. But I never take it that high, as all the best power is from 1100 to 2700 RPM.

So when considering an engine upgrade, look for modifications that improve torque. That is what your lolo needs!

Posted by Jason Dave, Sept 2009

Jason you are right on bro. I have always found an increase in torque placement has not only provided better top end performance but also Improved gas mileage in this expensive gas times.

Posted by Gabriel Salazar, Nov 2009

From http://www.tutorvista.com/content/physics-iii/rigid-body/torque.php

Torque is the product of the magnitude of the force and the lever arm of the force.
What is the significance of this concept in our everyday life?

Dependence of torque on lever arm
To increase the turning effect of force, it is not necessary to increase the magnitude of the force itself. We may increase the turning effect of the force by changing the point of application of force and by changing the direction of force.

Let us take the case of a heavy door. If a force is applied at a point, which is close to the hinges of the door, we may find it quite difficult to open or close the door. However, if the same force is applied at a point, which is at the maximum distance from hinges, we can easily close or open the door. The task is made easier if the force is applied at right angles to the plane of the door.

When we apply the force the door turns on its hinges. Thus a turning effect is produced when we try to open the door. Have you ever tried to do so by applying the force near the hinge? In the first case, we are able to open the door with ease. In the second case, we have to apply much more force to cause the same turning effect. What is the reason?

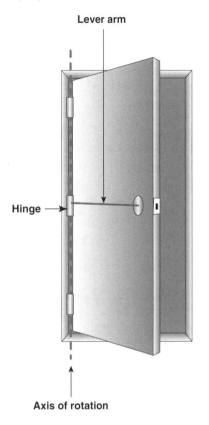

Lever arm

Hinge →

Axis of rotation

The turning effect produced by a force on a rigid body about a point, pivot or fulcrum is called the moment of a force or torque. It is measured by the product of the force and the perpendicular distance of the pivot from the line of action of the force.

Moment of a force = Force × Perpendicular distance of the pivot from the force.

The unit of moment of force is newton metre (N m).
In the above example, in the first case the perpendicular distance of the line of action of the force from the hinge is much more than that in the second case. Hence, in the second case to open the door, we have to apply greater force.

Source: Snow, 2010

Both examples above, available on the web, discuss the concept of torque, a topic covered by many state science standards that can be embedded under the topics of force and motion within the NGSS. As the analysis by Snow suggests (2010), there are differences between the two excerpts in terms of voice. For example, the first excerpt, written using everyday language, has a greater number of expressive, interpersonal markers, such as "guys get caught up," "most of us," and "Jason you are right on bro."

The second example maintains an authoritative stance by using a reduction of personal pronouns. Maintaining the impersonal authoritative stance creates a distanced tone that is often puzzling to adolescent readers and is extremely difficult to emulate in writing (Snow, 2010). Just like many texts written by scientists, the discourse in the second excerpt is filled with technical terms and features needed to describe the natural and physical world. In addition, there are no stories or personal accounts, although, like many science texts, the second excerpt has a diagram with text that aids understanding of abstract concepts. There are additional differences that can be identified between these two excerpts. Our analysis will continue as we discuss additional features of academic language at the sentence and word/phrase levels in the next sections.

EXAMINING SENTENCE-LEVEL STRUCTURES

At the sentence level academic language is characterized by grammatical structures, language forms, and conventions that are encountered primarily in textbooks, assessments, and school-based tasks. For all students, including English language learners (ELLs), learning and understanding grammatical structures facilitates English language development (Fisher, Rothenberg, & Frey, 2007) and content-area learning. However, many features of academic English are not intuitively obvious. In fact, some basic structures of the English language are illogical or dissimilar to structures of other languages making them difficult to understand, even when taught in context. Think about the following examples:

Why do students *play at a recital* and *recite in a play?*

To *overlook something* and to *oversee something* are very different.

Yet, *quite a lot* and *quite a few* can be the same.

Even everyday English can be confusing! We encounter additional irregularities in academic English. In addition to the use of irregular count nouns, prepositions, and interrogatives, academic language includes more complex sentence-level structures (e.g., parallel clauses, passive voice, and complex noun sentences). While there are numerous grammatical structures that cross content areas and disciplines, some are used more often in some disciplines than in others. Figure 2.6 provides selected examples of grammatical structures within sentences found mostly in English language arts classrooms.

Figure 2.6 Examples of Selected Complex Sentence Structures

Sentence Structures	Definitions	Examples
Complex Noun Phrases	Phrases made by the addition of multiple modifiers	Overhead Overhead projector Overhead projector light Overhead projector light bulb
Complex Sentences	Sentences with one independent clause and at least one dependent clause	While all of his writings are enthralling, Miguel de Cervantes's *Don Quixote,* full of idealism and madness, is his magnum opus.
Conditional Forms	Clauses that include an action reliant on something else, also called *if-clauses*	**If** I had seen the movie I would have better understood the plot. Their teacher will be sad **if** they do not pass their test.
Nominalizations	Verbs or adjectives are turned into nouns	Election, abortion, taxation, stewardship
Parallel Clauses	The use of the same pattern of clauses within a sentence	The students expected **that they would present** their report on Tuesday, that **there would be** enough time for them to use their PowerPoint, and **that other students would ask** questions.
Passive Voice	Sentences where the subject is acted upon, receiving the action expressed by the verb	The final exam was failed by over three fourths of the eighth graders.
Syntactic Ambiguity	Words, phrases, or sentences that may be reasonably interpreted in more than one way	She saw the president with binoculars. They were milking cows. Bruno shot a soldier with a gun.

Source: Adapted from Gottlieb & Ernst-Slavit, 2014, pp. 6–7

The academic language used to express concepts and ideas in the content areas necessitates the use of grammatical devices that allow speakers and writers to pack a lot of information into coherent and logical sequences. Determining how much information to pack into one sentence or sequence requires a balance between including enough information so the audience can understand the meaning but not so much as to cause confusion.

Continuing the analysis of the two science excerpts about torque discussed earlier (see pages 34–35), we find some of the grammatical structures listed in Figure 2.5. For example, in this sentence from the second excerpt: "We may increase the turning effect of the force by changing the point of application of force and by changing the direction of force," the words *application* and *direction* are nominalizations representing entire propositions. *Application* is short for "where we apply," and *direction* is short for "how we direct." Nominalizations are very common in academic writing, partly because they contribute to making texts concise and abstract. Syntactic structures, like the ones listed above, can be difficult for students to process without explicit instruction about their formation and structure.

Language Functions as Expressions of Sentence-Level Meaning

Language functions can be considered either discourse-level or sentence-level features that are part of the way we define academic language use. Academic language functions refer to the purpose of language use or, put more simply, why we use language to communicate—how we might wish to describe, explain, identify, or clarify (among others) concepts and ideas.

Language functions often trigger specific grammatical structures within sentences. Figure 2.7 depicts a set of language functions and their

Figure 2.7 Selected Academic Language Functions, Their Purposes, and Key Words of Associated Grammatical Structures

Academic Language Function	Purpose	Key Words and Phrases Within a Sentence
Cause and Effect	To show the reason behind an outcome or to show the consequence of an event	*as a result* *consequently* *due to* *for this reason* *is caused by* *therefore* *thus* *when . . . then*

Academic Language Function	Purpose	Key Words and Phrases Within a Sentence
		since because so
Compare/Contrast	To show similarities and differences between two things, people, places, ideas, concepts, actions	although similarly on the other hand unlike however instead of even though for this reason
Define Concepts	To state the meaning of a concept using appropriate supporting details	refers to that is characterized by in other words for instance usually stated differently
Sequence	To explain a chronology of events	first finally immediately later first, second, third starting today not long after
Describe	To help the reader/listener form images or visualize processes	above across along the side of as in behind beside between down the road from in front of looks like over to the left/right of under

(Continued)

Figure 2.7 (Continued)

Academic Language Function	Purpose	Key Words and Phrases Within a Sentence
Generalize	To organize information into overall statements with supporting details	always in fact overall in most cases for the most part one can generalize that generally speaking
Problem Solve	To identify problems/issues and pose solutions	*conclude that* *research shows* *the evidence points to* *a solution to* *the problem* *the question*

Consider this . . .

Cause and Effect is a prominent and naturally occurring academic language function in content areas like science and social studies. Recognizing cause-and-effect relationships in texts help students understand why events happened and remember what they are reading. Explaining that an action (cause) has consequent reactions (events) leading to an outcome (effect) can be helpful. Sometimes students ask why they have to use different words (e.g., *therefore, consequently, as a result*) to show cause and effect, when they could simply use *so* or *because*. Part of the explanation can include that language patterns have evolved over the years to a point where certain words fit certain patterns. Consider, for example, this sentence: "He is a wonderful role model; *consequently,*

purposes, and it gives examples of key words and phrases within their grammatical structures. Systematic modeling combined with practice of these language functions is recommended as students learn grammatical structures of sentences within academic language use.

The CCSS for English language arts and mathematics as well as the NGSS are filled with language functions. In Chapter 3, Figure 3.4 exhibits a sampling of academic language functions that are explicitly stated in these content standards. Language functions also exemplify how to represent language development standards. For instance, the CCSS for mathematics, Grade 2 Measurement and Data, state that students are to "solve word problems involving dollar bills, quarters, dimes, nickels, and pennies, using $ and ¢ symbols appropriately"; this standard is more procedural than language dependent. However, students still need to have the academic language of mathematics, in particular for the topic of "money" to access and successfully manipulate the denominations. In order to do so, it is helpful to plan what students are expected to do with language. Examples of such expectations (or model performance indicators) include "sequencing sentences to decide how to solve word problems involving money" and "categorizing word problems involving money according to their operation (i.e., addition or subtraction)" (WIDA, 2012, p. 60). These examples underscore the benefit of content and language teachers collaborating in planning and enacting of units for learning.

> many teachers want him as a guest speaker." As is evident, not all the terms listed for cause and effect in Figure 2.7 can be used to replace *consequently* in this sentence.
>
> Since we know that students need to learn to use English academically, can you think about specific ways of teaching cause and effect within your grade-level content?

IDENTIFYING VOCABULARY—WORDS, PHRASES, AND EXPRESSIONS

Almost everyone recognizes the importance of teaching vocabulary to enhance students' understanding of academic and complex texts. When discussing academic language at the word or phrase level, we refer to both written and spoken forms. Average five-year-old proficient English speakers enter kindergarten knowing at least 5,000 words, and they acquire approximately 3,000 new words every school year (Nagy & Anderson, 1984). With this statistic, it becomes evident that ELLs have to learn many more terms in English than their fluent English peers and, in addition, continue to learn new words as they progress through their schooling. Thus, it is vital that educators enhance ongoing efforts to help all students, especially those who may have to accelerate their growth in English language vocabulary.

There are two points we want to underscore. First, vocabulary is only one aspect of academic language instruction. An individual can know many words in a language and yet not be able to read a newspaper article or an academic text or put words together in sentences or longer chunks of texts that convey meaning. Second, teaching words in isolation, as definitions that may occur sporadically during a unit, is not helpful. Only strategies that engage students in rich and varied language experiences in meaningful contexts and that include systematic word instruction and word awareness will translate into successful academic vocabulary learning.

It is important to recognize here that individual words are parts of larger linguistic systems. The ability to use individual words requires understanding of how word meanings are part of a network of concepts. The example in the next paragraph exemplifies how it is not the vocabulary that is clouding students' understanding of a word problem in mathematics, but the students' inability to make sense of how the terms relate to each other.

In her analysis, Lily Wong Fillmore (2004) discusses the following item from the National Assessment of Educational Progress (NAEP) test:

> The rectangle is twice as long as it is wide. What is the ratio of the width of the rectangle to its perimeter?

Although it may not seem like a difficult question, only 11% of US eighth graders answered it correctly. The test item doesn't include numbers to compute, and the technical terms do not seem that difficult. For example, although there are technical terms like *perimeter, rectangle, long, wide,* and *ratio,* it appears that the terms alone are not the problem, as most eighth graders understand their meaning. What might trouble students is making sense of what is being asked by looking at the relationships among those terms. For example, students need to interpret the descriptor *perimeter* as meaning twice length and width from the dimensional terms *long* and *wide.* Next, comes the tricky part, recognizing what the question asks for; this is what 89% of US students failed to address. In conclusion, learning mathematics is not just learning the technical terms or procedural fluency; it's about conceptual understanding, reasoning, and sense making. The goal is to focus on mathematical practices, not vocabulary, single words, or a list of definitions (Moschkovich, 2013).

> **Consider this . . .**
>
> Continue with the analysis of the two science excerpts in Figure 2.5 (p. 34) by comparing the vocabulary used. You should notice, for example, that in the first excerpt, a nonacademic informational text, the less familiar words are *torque, lolo, lowrider, upgrade, carb, HP, exhaust,* and *spin.* The second excerpt, however, contains many content-specific terms, such as *magnitude, force, lever arm, hinges, pivot, fulcrum, significance, moment of a force, perpendicular distance,* and *axis of rotation.* The amount of content-specific and technical terms used in the second excerpt is typical of science texts packed with precise information.

Development of Academic Vocabulary

There is considerable research that links students' word knowledge to their academic success. More specifically, many studies demonstrate that readers' knowledge of the words on printed materials improves text comprehension. Michael Graves (2007) emphasized the crucial role that vocabulary plays in schooling for all students, emphasizing the knowledge of words specific to each domain or content area. Unfortunately, the school success of ELLs is often predicated on their English vocabulary even though they may have large vocabularies in their home language (Garcia, 1991).

The process of learning words varies. William Nagy and Judith Scott (2000) demonstrated that most words are learned in stages. Some words are learned faster than others, some words have multiple meanings, and yet others sound alike. Throughout their schooling, students have to learn a wide range of words with varying levels of complexity. The number of new terms or academic words in textbooks increases drastically in the middle and high school years. Research has shown that, in one case, students were required to learn at least 3,500 new vocabulary words just to comprehend their science book (Bravo & Cervetti, 2008).

While there is a realization that there are different kinds of words within the K–12 curriculum, there is not agreement on how words should be organized. In fact, there are different ways of classifying the words that students need to learn to be successful academically. Isabelle Beck and collaborators (Beck, McKeown, & Kucan, 2008) provided a three-category system for classifying English words. Tier 1 consists of the most basic words. These words rarely require instruction for proficient English speakers, although the words may be unfamiliar for ELLs or contain multiple meanings (e.g., *table, pencil, happy, box*). Tier 2 consists of high-frequency words that appear in various contexts and play an important role across several content areas (e.g., *predict, maintain, summary, justification*). Finally, Tier 3 represents low-frequency words, domain-specific or technical words that appear in specific fields or topics (e.g., *mitosis, egregious, quadratic equation, vagrant*). What is not considered in this scheme is that while Tier 1 words may be challenging for ELLs, Tier 3 words often are cognates that may be familiar to ELLs and support their vocabulary learning across languages.

Similarly, the preK–12 English language proficiency standards from Teachers of English to Speakers of Other Languages (TESOL, 2006) classify academic words into three categories where ELLs, rather than proficient English students, are the primary audience: (1) general academic vocabulary encountered across content areas, (2) specialized academic vocabulary that is specific to a content area, and (3) technical academic vocabulary necessary for discussing specific topics within a content area. Figure 2.8 displays examples of vocabulary types categorized by content area.

There are also lists of academic vocabulary that include words or word families recurrent in academic texts. The academic word list compiled by Averil Coxhead (2000) consists of 570 word families that are not among the 2,000 most common words in English but that occur frequently across a wide

Figure 2.8 Vocabulary Type by Content Area

Academic Vocabulary	General	Specialized	Technical
English Language Arts	appropriate articulate assess assumption	semantic metaphor voice limerick	soliloquy romanticism gothic burlesque
Mathematics	conclusion context decline demonstrate denotes	angle ordered pair percent random	coefficient statistical variability right prism x-axis
Social Studies	distribute generic inference itemize opposition	revolutionary constitutional policy supply	chauvinism Magna Carta prime meridian signatory powers
Science	prompt restate reveal solution	asteroid range inquiry variable	atmospheric biotic convection prototype
Other Content Areas (e.g., Art, Music, Health, Physical Education)	structure summary superfluous though trait wonder	aesthetic consonance offside Renaissance period	blues progression body mass index vivace law of specificity

range of academic and scientific texts. These 570 words are grouped into ten sublists that reflect frequency and range. For example, the term *establish* is located in Sublist 1, which contains the most frequent words, while the word *albeit* is located in Sublist 10, which includes the least frequent words. Coxhead developed this list with college students in mind; however, because of the extensive nature of the list and the fact that it is not restricted to a specific field, it can be helpful for middle and high school students. Several other word lists, developed in the last 10 years, can be found in publications and on websites from school districts, learning centers, and textbook companies.

One important aspect to recognize about vocabulary teaching and learning is the large number of infrequent words compared to the very small number of frequent words. According to Elfrieda Hiebert (2005), the 100 most frequently used words account for 50% of the words in a typical text; the 1,000 most frequently used words account for about 70%; and the 5,000 most frequently used words for about 80%. One important implication can be gleaned from this research: If students don't know these frequently used words, they will consistently stumble over them in a variety of texts. Hence, via systematic and effective vocabulary teaching, educators should strive to teach 2,000 to 4,000 of the most frequently used words in a variety of word families (Graves, August, & Mancilla-Martinez, 2013).

> **Consider this . . .**
>
> Many educators recommend that students use the dictionary.
>
> How effective do you think it is to ask students to refer to a dictionary when they encounter a new word?
>
> How effective do you think it is for ELLs to have a bilingual dictionary at all times?
>
> If you have encouraged your students to use a dictionary often, has it helped them improve their vocabulary? Why or why not?

The next section offers a robust plan for teaching vocabulary based on current literature along with a selection of strategies to teach academic vocabulary within a larger context.

Teaching Academic Vocabulary in Authentic Contexts Through Meaningful Interactions

Explicit vocabulary instruction—not in isolation, but within meaningful and relevant content area instruction—has a positive effect on reading and content area learning (Gottlieb, Katz, & Ernst-Slavit, 2009). In fact, work by Janet Allen (1999) and Paul Nation (2001), among others, indicates that purposeful vocabulary instruction in the content areas

a. increases reading comprehension,

b. develops knowledge of new concepts,

c. improves range and specificity in writing,

d. helps students communicate more effectively, and

e. develops deeper understanding of words and concepts.

In recent years, research has identified a number of methods to develop students' academic vocabulary. A common theme in these studies indicates that vocabulary instruction must occur in authentic contexts, where learners have ample opportunities to learn how target words interact with, garner meaning from, and support meanings of other words (Nagy & Townsend,

2012). Michael Graves, Diane August, and Jeannette Mancilla-Martinez (2013) propose a four-pronged program for vocabulary instruction for ELLs. The program builds upon decades of work in this area (e.g., Blachowicz, Fisher, Ogle, and Watts-Taffe, 2006; Graves, 2006, 2009; Nagy & Townsend, 2012; Stahl & Nagy, 2006) and has four main components, as illustrated in Figure 2.9.

Figure 2.9 A Four-Part Vocabulary Program

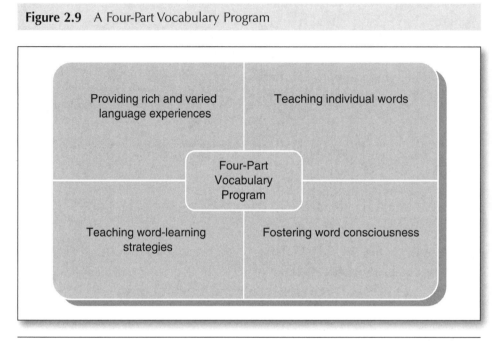

Source: Graves, August, & Mancilla-Martinez, 2013

Providing Rich and Varied Language Experiences

If students are to learn and accrue new words, terms, and expressions, they need to be immersed in a rich array of meaningful language experiences that include using the four language domains—listening, speaking, reading, and writing. As Michael Graves (2006) so eloquently stated,

> The probability of learning a word from context increases substantially with additional occurrences of the word. That is how we typically learn from context. We learn a little from the first encounter with a word and then more and more about a word's meaning as we meet it in new and different contexts. (p. 25)

Overall, research indicates that teaching students to use context clues is critical in learning vocabulary. All students, including ELLs, learn word meanings from context and benefit from participating in authentic interactions in which they have opportunities to thoughtfully discuss topics and engage in reading and writing in a variety of genres, including prose and poetry, in narrative and informational texts.

Teaching Individual Words

One well-known way of building students' vocabularies is by teaching individual words of an excerpt, a concept, or a lesson. However, simply giving students a set of words relevant to a topic and asking them to look up their meaning is just one step in learning basic meanings of the word. "Vocabulary instruction is most effective when learners are given both definitional and contextual information, when learners actively process the new word meanings, and when they experience multiple encounters with words" (Graves, August, & Mancilla-Martinez, 2013, p. 4). Vocabulary instruction that involves activating prior knowledge, comparing and contrasting word meanings, planning for repeated thoughtful encounters with the words, and using semantic mapping can improve word learning, as illustrated in the graphic organizer in Figure 2.10 (Graves, 2006).

Figure 2.10 Example of Generating Categorical Relationships Among Words Using a Semantic Map

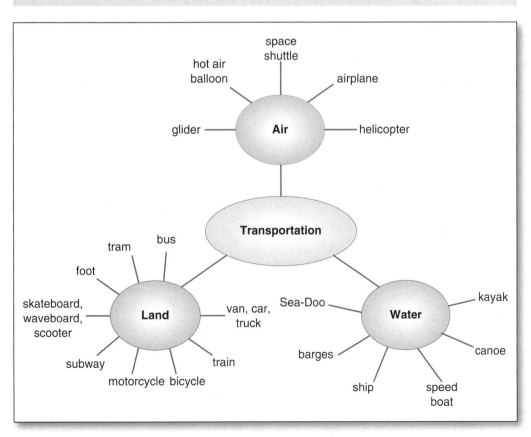

Consider this . . .

Morphology, the study of word structure, including roots, bases, and affixes, can be extremely useful in building academic vocabulary proficiency. Good readers have the ability to figure out a word by using diverse strategies such as finding its roots, suffixes, and prefixes (Blachowicz et al., 2006). When students encounter an unknown word, they might realize that they know parts of the word already. For example, students might not know what *ferromagnetic* means, but they do know the meaning of *magnetic.* Once they figure out the meaning of the prefix *ferro-*, they can have a sense of the meaning of *ferromagnetic.* In this case, a Spanish-speaking student will most likely be able to decipher the meaning of *ferromagnetic* because the Spanish word *fierro* refers to *ferro* (pertaining to iron and nickel), and the Spanish cognate for *magnetic* is *magnético.*

Teaching Word-Learning Strategies

Another way to increase students' vocabulary is to teach a variety of word-learning strategies. An example is using word parts, such as using prefixes, suffixes, and roots, to recognize and understand word families and decipher the meanings of unknown words (e.g., *analysis, analytical, analyzing*). Figure 2.11 presents a list of words using the prefix *photo-* created in a sixth grade classroom. Once students understand the meaning of the prefix *photo-*, meaning "light," they are able to realize the meaning of many technical words like the ones included in their word web.

Fostering Word Consciousness

The term *word consciousness* is used to refer to an awareness of and interest in words and their meanings. In essence, this process includes a twofold stance for developing a long-lasting

---

Figure 2.11   Example of a Word Web Created by Sixth Graders Using the Prefix *Photo-*

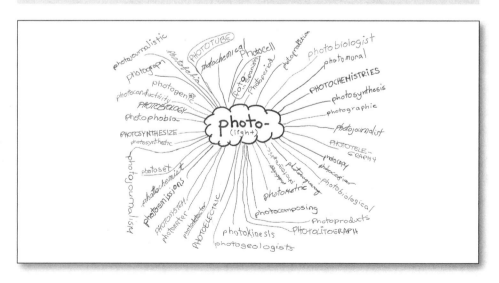

interest in learning and using new words that is both cognitive and affective. William Nagy and Judith Scott (2004) believe that word consciousness also involves knowledge and beliefs about word learning. For teachers and students to be word conscious, they should know that

- Word knowledge is complex and involves more than knowing a definition.
- Word learning is incremental and involves many small steps.
- Words are heterogeneous and require different learning strategies.
- Definitions, context, and words parts can be helpful in deciphering the meaning of a word, but they have their limitations. (Nagy & Scott, 2004, p. 204)

> **Consider this . . .**
>
> What strategies do you use to help your students learn the meanings of new or unfamiliar words?

Vocabulary Instruction for English Language Learners (ELLs)

While the vast majority of studies on vocabulary development have been conducted with proficient English speakers, in the last few years there has been an increase in the number of studies that focus on ELLs. When deciding on an instructional plan that addresses the needs of ELLs, educators need to consider the following:

- The students' English language proficiency
- The students' proficiency in other languages
- Home, community, and school factors
- The instructional context

First, ELLs come to school with **differing levels of English language proficiency** in each language domain and with different sets of strengths and needs; they move along a continuum of English language development at different rates, depending on their age, schooling, and their entry level of English language proficiency.

Second, as mentioned above, **ELLs' proficiency in their home language** influences their learning additional languages. Thus, students who have high levels of literacy in their home language, given the right context and instructional approaches, will most likely achieve high levels of literacy in English. The purposeful use of cognates (words in different languages that are similar both orthographically and semantically) can render excellent results, particularly when there are a large number of cognates between English and a student's home language. For example, in an eighth grade unit on Poe's *The Cask of Amontillado,* Liliana Minaya-Rowe

(2014, in this series) discusses how the teacher uses English–Spanish cognates throughout the unit to enhance the linguistic, cognitive, and academic opportunities of his Spanish-speaking students.

Gisela Ernst-Slavit and Michelle Mason (2011) discuss other types of "opaque" language that can hinder students' understanding, such as the use of slang (terms and expressions that are not considered standard) and "Americana" terms (words and phrases used to refer to artifacts of the history, folklore, and culture of the United States). In their study of upper elementary classrooms, they found many examples of teachers using terms and phrases that may be challenging for ELLs, such as *stars and stripes, touchdown, left field, sad as Eeyore, we're gunna work together, I wanna use the picture, don't forget to include all that stuff in your paper, dude,* and *we gotta finish.*

Equally important is helping students learn idiomatic expressions, colloquialisms, and words with multiple meanings (Ernst-Slavit & Mason, 2011). According to the *Dictionary of American Idioms* (Makkai, Boatner, & Gates, 2004), there are about 8,000 idioms in the English language. Educators might be surprised at how often idioms are used in K–12 classrooms. In a study of fourth and fifth grade mainstream classrooms with at least five ELLs by Ernst-Slavit and Mason (2011), referenced above, there were many idioms heard during content area instruction, including these:

Barking up the wrong tree

Bend over backwards

Couch potato

Cry wolf

Down to the wire

Hit the books

Hit the nail on the head

Hold your horses

Icing on the cake

Off on the wrong foot

Play it by ear

Pulling my leg

Rule of thumb

Walk me through it

Words that hold us up

Since idiomatic expressions are pervasive in school, educators can help students become aware of and learn popular idioms. This will not only help students comprehend different kinds of texts but also allow them to give their oral and written language a more authentic feel.

> **Consider this . . .**
>
> Have fun with idiomatic expressions by keeping a tally of the different ones that you encounter in books, hear, or say throughout the day. Challenge your students to also keep a journal page or an interactive wall showing idiomatic expressions and what they might mean. Invite students to deepen their understanding by refining the definitions over time, like articles in Wikipedia.

Home, community, and schooling factors affecting student achievement cannot be underestimated. As the opening figure in this chapter suggests, students' languages and cultures are firmly anchored in the linguistic and cultural traditions of their families, friends, and communities. For example, it is widely known that the education levels of parents, coupled with socioeconomic status, are strong predictors of academic success for students. In the case of ELLs who may have had interrupted schooling experiences, schools can bridge that gap via high-quality instruction, increased home–school connections, and tapping into the linguistic and cultural resources of families and communities. One specific example that has been successful in enhancing vocabulary learning for diverse students includes shared book reading, in which adults read aloud to children, periodically stopping to highlight and discuss individual words and other aspects of what they are reading (Graves August, Mancilla-Martinez, 2013).

Finally, a comment needs to be made regarding **the role of instructional context** in language learning. In a study cited by Graves, August, and Mancilla-Martinez (2013) about vocabulary instruction in fourth through eighth grades in Canada, Judith Scott, Dianne Jamieson-Noel, and Marlene Asselin (2003) found that about 12% of language arts instructional time was dedicated to vocabulary instruction. However, only 1.4% of the time was spent on vocabulary instruction in other content areas.

Given the emphasis on academic language use across content areas placed by the college and career readiness standards, we need to shift the way language and content are taught. Figure 2.12 presents a variety of helpful strategies for teaching academic language to all students.

Figure 2.12 Strategies for Teaching Academic Language With Attention to ELLs

Strategy	Explanation	Examples
Encourage **oral language use.**	Give reasons for students to speak to each other in class. Structure academic conversations around texts and topics of interest that enhance language learning.	Teachers/students ask questions that require more than yes or no answers. Teachers design authentic interactive activities.
Promote a **wide range of reading and writing.**	Incidental learning of language increases when students have many opportunities to read diverse texts and write about them.	Fiction Nonfiction Informational texts
Focus on **cognates.**	About 40% of all English words have cognates in Spanish. Teachers and Spanish-speaking students, among others, can use cognates to enhance understanding and communication.	Students search for cognates on the web. Students identify cognates as they read or as the teacher reads aloud.
Highlight **critical academic words in context.**	Special attention needs to be given to words that appear across multiple grade levels and content areas.	Students discuss the use of words such as *summarize, resolution, appropriate,* and *recall* in multiple contexts.
Foster a **love of words and language** in your classroom.	If students are aware of the language around them and actively pursue trying out new words, they will take ownership of their language learning.	Interactive word/phrase walls Displays of original student work Sentence frames with discourse
Make use of **visuals** when appropriate.	These are especially helpful for concepts that are difficult to explain verbally but that are suited to nonverbal explanations.	Pictures/illustrations Symbols Multimedia (e.g., videos) Diagrams
Model, model, model.	Students need to hear how academic language is used orally and in writing from their teachers.	Use expressions in context. Use morphology to unpack complex words (e.g., "that's another word that ends in -*ology*").
Provide opportunities **to act out the meaning** of words or expressions.	Younger children can learn language by acting out actions, for example, and by role-playing.	Students follow commands such as "jump high to the sky," "squat down," and "stretch your legs" as they move along a path.

Strategy	Explanation	Examples
Review **common academic words.**	Review and reinforce common academic words that might be unfamiliar for beginning or intermediate ELLs.	Think about words important to the big ideas of the lesson as in *product, setting, graphic organizer, visual*
Teach **word- and sentence-learning strategies.**	Help students learn how to use word and sentence parts in context.	Prefix maps Word/expression webs Common families of root words
Use multiple resources such as **audio books, computers, and videos.**	By hearing and seeing the language used in context, ELLs can learn their meaning, gain skills in understanding prosody and syntax, and increase their oral fluency.	Original student work Listening centers Computer work
Use **student-friendly, yet grade-level, definitions** of words, expressions, and concepts.	Provide student-friendly definitions, or have students restate, in their words, what they think a word, expression, or passage means.	Frayer graphic organizers Four-corners vocabulary Match-up cards

FOR FURTHER THINKING . . .

In this chapter we have reviewed the dimensions of academic language use and how different discourse patterns require students to understand and use the structure of texts. Understanding academic language at the sentence level is also crucial for all students, especially since academic language often reduces large ideas into fewer words and phrases that are linked with specific connectors that denote certain kind of relationships. In schools, students will not only have to access academic texts but also produce them both orally and in writing. Last but not least, we cannot forget that vocabulary, consisting of words, phrases, and expressions, forms the building blocks for expression through sentences that relate to one another through discourse.

The academic register of school may not be the language students use at home or in their communities. However, important connections may be available for some students whose languages have cognates with English or use many of the Greek and Latin roots pervasive in scientific texts.

Finally, we need to understand that academic language development is not an end in itself but an ongoing process. Academic language is a tool to help students broaden their thinking and understanding of complex problems, scientific matters, and local as well as global issues. Ultimately, what we want is for students to be able to think, talk, act, and use language like scientists, mathematicians, historians, psychologists, reporters, musicians, archaeologists, and physicians, among many other possibilities. Here are some questions that invite you to apply the contents of this chapter to your setting.

1. Think about your own use of academic language at home and in the community. What ideas might you have to increase your students' use of academic language outside the boundaries of school?

2. Discourse is composed of multiple sentences, and sentences, in turn, consist of words. How might you help your colleagues as well as students understand the relationship among these dimensions of academic language?

3. What is one new strategy for vocabulary development that resonates with you? How might you apply it to your classroom or professional learning?

4. What is a particular teaching strategy to enhance academic language use for ELLs that you might adopt? Which ones have you already tried successfully?

3

How Do Standards Define and Shape Academic Language Use?

Language is the blood of the soul into which thoughts run and out of which they grow.

—Oliver Wendell Holmes

In today's classrooms with their heterogeneous mix of learners, what does the use of language for academic purposes mean? How can it become central to instruction and assessment, so students can advance cognitively and linguistically? Keeping in mind the prominence and importance of academic language to schooling, this chapter examines the relationship between content and language learning through the lens of standards. It underscores the influence of college and career readiness standards, including the Common Core State Standards (CCSS) and Next Generation Science Standards (NGSS), alongside English language proficiency/development standards as the springboard for designing and aligning curriculum, instruction, and assessment.

Academic language encompasses a broad range of language competencies necessary for students to fully participate in classroom activities and function as accepted and valued members of content-centered communities (Gottlieb, Katz, & Ernst-Slavit, 2009). Its role is elaborated for linguistically and culturally diverse students who have the added resource of other languages and cultures to draw from and attach to their learning experiences at school. For these students, both content and language standards assist teachers in supporting student learning. With standards as a reference, educators can gain a deep understanding of academic language use in curriculum, instruction, and assessment.

THE IMPACT OF THE NEW STANDARDS ON SHAPING ACADEMIC LANGUAGE

The arrival of the college and career readiness standards, in particular, the CCSS in English language arts and mathematics in 2010, followed by the NGSS in 2013, precipitated a scientific revolution (Kuhn, 1962) within US educational circles. That is to say, the momentum for educational change reached a critical mass that evoked a paradigm shift in educators' thinking about schooling and enacting curriculum. While many states are still in the midst of planning for full implementation of these new content standards, school leaders and teachers are beginning to understand their potential for elevating the status of our country on the world stage. Academic language, the register of school, is central to this discussion as a necessary 21st century competence for communicating meaningfully within classrooms and across international borders, whether person to person or in cyberspace, at a high level of sophistication. Figure 3.1 describes some of the primary differences in the views and roles of academic language use before and after the introduction of college and career readiness standards.

In the context of the CCSS and the NGSS, almost all students can be considered academic language learners (Sanders, 2013). If this statement holds true, in today's standards-driven classroom all educators have a shared responsibility for producing a generation of learners who excel in their chosen fields and endeavors. Given that enormous challenge, educators must do their best to make each student's educational experiences from class to class and from day to day as seamless and as meaningful as possible.

> **Consider this . . .**
>
> Rigorous content standards are one of the hallmarks associated with the renewal of the US education system (National Education Goals Panel, 1993). According to their report, "Without high standards, we will not be able to rebuild America's education system—they are absolutely pivotal if we are to thrive and prosper" (p. 10). It is now two decades later. Do you think the United States has made any strides in that direction with the new wave of content standards? What evidence might you cite?

Figure 3.1 Perceptions of Academic Language Before and After the Introduction of the College and Career Readiness Standards or the Common Core State Standards (CCSS)

Before CCSS	After CCSS
Academic language is implicit in standards.	Academic language is more explicit in standards.
Academic language is considered secondary to key concepts and skills of content standards.	Academic language is embedded in and a focus of standards.
Academic language demands of content standards are variable from state to state.	Academic language demands of standards are uniform within consortia of states.
Academic language is primarily associated with English language proficiency/development standards.	Academic language is shared between English language proficiency/development and content standards.
Academic language is largely perceived as vocabulary.	Academic language is extended to include the dimensions of sentence and discourse features.
Academic language is generally confined to English language arts.	Academic language is extended across every school discipline.
Academic language is often taught in isolation or frontloaded prior to a lesson.	Academic language is taught in context within a lesson.
Academic language is the purview of language teachers.	Academic language is the responsibility of all teachers.

It is in this spirit that we underscore language for academic purposes as an educational opportunity for the youth of this generation.

The new content standards have been the impetus for a shift in thinking in regard to the rigor and relevance of language and literacy across the curriculum. Figure 3.2 illustrates four major changes in educational practice evoked by the CCSS for English language arts, namely, (1) stronger content area knowledge (and its accompanying academic language), (2) increased sophistication of texts (along with their greater linguistic complexity), (3) a balance of informational and literature-based texts (and their varied discourses and genres), and (4) evidence and justification for writing from text (through explanation or argumentation). These shifts place academic language front and center in the discussion on effective teaching in today's classrooms.

The new content standards dictate increased grade-level expectations. To be responsive to this new paradigm, students are required to analyze

Figure 3.2 Common Core Influences on Academic Language Use

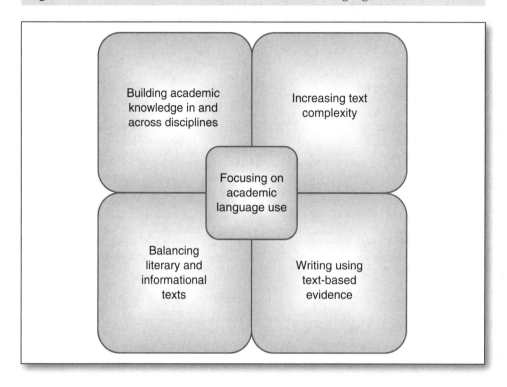

complex text. To enable their students to do so effectively, teachers have to have an awareness of the

1. features of academic language, from the discourse or text type to individual words and expressions;

2. challenges students will encounter along the way, especially English language learners (ELLs), such as understanding the use of idiomatic expressions, unfamiliar grammatical structures, and words with multiple meanings; and

3. compatibility of the backgrounds and experiences of the students with the texts with which they are expected to interact.

In redefining teaching and learning, academic language is the vehicle by which teachers translate the new standards into viable instructional assessment practices. Academic language is the means to empower language learners in their quest for success. As illustrated in Figure 3.3, content and language standards, assessment, and instruction are an outgrowth of academic language.

Where is the academic language situated within state standards? Sometimes it's quite visible; at other times, academic language is rather

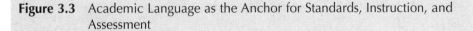

Figure 3.3 Academic Language as the Anchor for Standards, Instruction, and Assessment

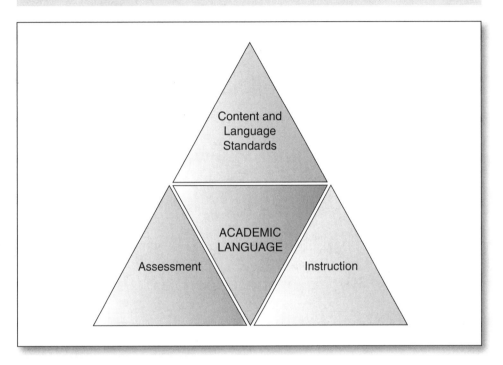

hidden. Academic language, shared among the standards, serves as the crosswalk between each set. The academic language encapsulated in content standards needs to be totally compatible with, if not duplicative of, the academic language embedded in language proficiency/development standards. A direct correspondence between content and language standards enables teachers to collaborate in the design of curriculum from both sets.

Content standards, specifically the CCSS and the NGSS, have had undeniable influence on language proficiency/development standards. The question at hand, though, is, how can the simultaneous use of multiple standards make sense to teachers and school leaders? In content standards, academic language is intertwined and at times undecipherable from grade-level knowledge and skills of the discipline. Language proficiency/development standards, in contrast, identify academic language in the service of content; the differentiation of language expectations by language proficiency levels gives ELLs access to the content expressed in companion content standards. Figure 3.4 shows the centrality of academic language across standards.

Let's look back to Chapter 2 at the dimensions of academic language. What would it mean if we superimposed the major features of academic language onto language proficiency/development standards? The message it would give is that when examining each language standard and

Figure 3.4 Academic Language Shared Among Content and Language Standards

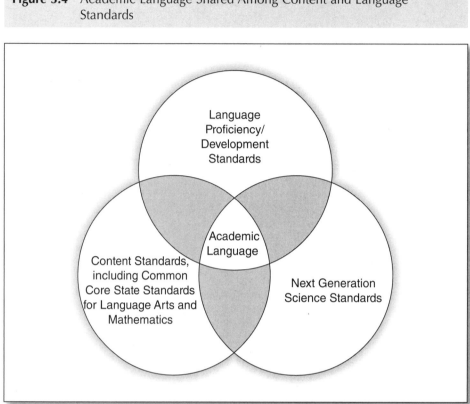

Consider this . . .

Which standards do you, your school, or your district use? If you have students in dual language settings, do you reference additional standards, such as those for Spanish language development or for students in early childhood? (See www.wida.us, for example.) Discuss why all teachers of language learners must be familiar with and use multiple sets of standards.

its accompanying materials, educators should think about its associated discourses, sentence structures, and words/phrases and expressions. In a standards-referenced curricular framework that centers on academic language (see Chapters 5 and 6), these three dimensions help drive the shape of the curriculum and how it is enacted in classrooms. Figure 3.5 illustrates how the dimensions of academic language are represented in WIDA's/TESOL's English language development/proficiency standards.

Given that both the new content and the language standards play an important role in advancing the academic achievement of students, imagine the potentially powerful force of their combined contribution to education.

Figure 3.5 Three Dimensions of Academic Language Superimposed Onto Language Development/Proficiency Standards

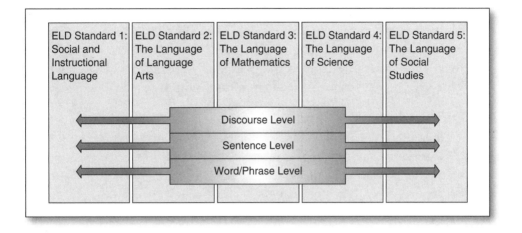

BRINGING STANDARDS TOGETHER: CONTENT LEARNING THROUGH LANGUAGE AND LANGUAGE LEARNING THROUGH CONTENT

Historically there has been a divide between content teachers, who have envisioned their primary responsibility as improving the academic achievement of their students, and language teachers, who have focused on the growth of students' language proficiency. Since the publication of Bernard Mohan's seminal book *Language and Content* (1986), where the two constructs are seen as an integrated whole, the language education field has slowly been moving in that direction. On the one hand, some language educators have used content as the driver, such as in content-based instruction and sheltered instruction, where teachers deliver grade-level content in ways that are accessible and comprehensible to all learners. On the other hand,

Consider this . . .

To delve more deeply into the dimensions of academic language, professional learning teams could select a universal theme applicable across all the standards, such as "foods around the world." Then its members could divide up and each select one English language proficiency/ development standard and a grade or grade-level cluster. What would be the discourse, types of sentences or grammatical structures, and vocabulary that would typify the standard for the theme? In this jigsaw, members would come back together to discuss similarities and differences in the use of academic language across the standards.

others have been more language centered, either keeping to English as a Second Language methodologies isolated from content, or using content as the context or backdrop for language learning. Figure 3.6 outlines these subtle distinctions.

While content and language learning have slowly started to be viewed as a totality, it is academic language that has served as the gatekeeper for the two. Academic language as the principal register of school has been recognized as central to learning, as it helps students

- Successfully navigate school.
- Develop oral language and literacies.
- Deepen their conceptual understanding.
- Engage in scientific and mathematical practices.
- Prepare for college and careers.

Figure 3.6 Differences Between Content and Language Learning

Content Learning Through Language	Language Learning Through Content
The focus is on attainment of skills and conceptual understandings.	The focus is on communication centering on the four language domains.
Language is the medium of instruction for content area disciplines.	Content area disciplines provide the contexts for language learning.
Students' demonstrate mastery of skills and concepts.	Students' demonstrate processing and production of language.
Students' accuracy and precision in showing their knowledge and skills are paramount.	Students' consistency of language use is most important.
Achievement is measured in relation to content standards, including college and career readiness.	Language proficiency is measured in relation to language development/ proficiency standards.

Consider this . . .

Understanding that the goal of schooling is to mesh content and language within students' learning experiences, how might the subtle differences between the two constructs be useful to you? What do you see as the relationship between content and language in teaching and learning?

Academic language is extended, reasoned discourse that is logically connected through grammatical devices and precise word use (Wong Fillmore, 2004). It spans content and language learning within sociocultural contexts. In this conceptualization, concepts are reinforced through language, and language is the medium for accessing content, while the sociocultural context frames each learning situation.

Academic language use, by straddling content and language learning, can be viewed as an equalizer in helping students remove the "dis" from "disadvantaged." In this vision, "There are many different school languages, different styles of language used in different academic practices. . . . None of these styles of language are decontextualized. They are all—just like 'everyday' face-to-face language—contextualized" (Gee as cited by Faltis, 2013, p. 4). Figure 3.7 illustrates how academic language use binds content and language learning.

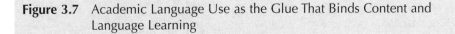

Figure 3.7   Academic Language Use as the Glue That Binds Content and Language Learning

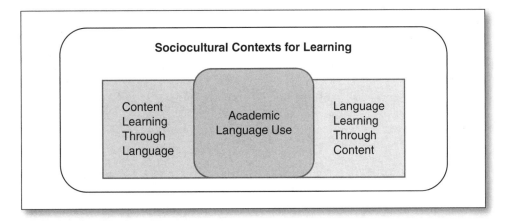

Content and Language Learning for English Language Learners

All students acquire, use, and demonstrate their conceptual understanding of content through language, no matter which and how many tongues are involved. However, simultaneously, all ELLs must also learn English as an academic register within school. Put another way, language can no longer be dichotomized as demanding or not, as "all language is demanding. . . . It is important to stress that social language is just as cognitively challenging in some cases as it is in academic settings" (Lillie, 2013, p. 226).

Consider this . . .

Sociocultural context is the backdrop for content and language learning. How would you describe the sociocultural context of your classroom and school? How can the sociocultural context cast a positive light on how to envision schooling for different groups of students? How are students' linguistic and cultural diversity part of the sociocultural context? What insights does sociocultural context bring to teaching and learning?

To reinforce this notion of the complexity of language learning, Deborah Short and Shannon Fitzsimmons (2007) aptly claim that adolescent ELLs, like all ELLs, are subject to "double the work" of their English-proficient peers. This group of students is subject to accountability for grade-level content mastery while still in the process of developing academic English. To that end, the authors pose the following attributes to define academic literacy, the heart of school success, for ELLs. Academic literacy

- Includes reading, writing, and oral discourse for school;
- Varies from subject to subject;
- Requires knowledge of multiple genres of text, purposes for text use, and text media;
- Is influenced by students' literacy in contexts outside of school;
- Is influenced by students' personal, social, and cultural experiences. (Short & Fitzsimmons, 2007, p. 2)

What is often not taken into account, however, is that ELLs are spread across a continuum of English language development. At one end are newcomers, that is, students who have been enrolled in the US school system for under two years, whose conceptual understanding most likely is in a language other than English. On the other end of the spectrum are ELLs who have reached a threshold of English language proficiency and are approaching linguistic parity with their English-proficient peers. With such a heterogeneous mix of students, language learning through content must be carefully scaffolded according to the students' levels of language proficiency to maximize linguistic access to and support of their content learning experiences.

As previously discussed in Chapter 1, language learning is a developmental process; one of the variables to consider in instructional planning is the students' grade or grand band, as that is a proxy for age and cognitive development. Another factor is the context or situation in which learning occurs, such as a classroom activity. For ELLs, yet another consideration is their levels of language proficiency, in the students' home language and English. Examining the students' cognitive development or grade in relation to their levels of language proficiency enables teachers to begin to project the expectations of academic language use (see Gottlieb & Ernst-Slavit, 2013).

The next sections peek into how academic language is represented in content and language standards. It provides resources for teachers and examples that can be applied to diverse classrooms.

THE IMPACT OF STANDARDS IN SHAPING GRADE-LEVEL LANGUAGE FOR ACADEMIC PURPOSES

Academic language use is gaining prominence in school, starting with standards. Both content and language standards contribute to our understanding of how we use language for multiple purposes in a variety of contexts, grade by grade.

Academic Language Within Content Standards

Academic language is pervasive in the CCSS for English language arts and for mathematics as well as the NGSS. Students are required to use academic language functions, or in other words, show what they can do with language to demonstrate their content understandings and skills. Topics encountered in the CCSS for mathematics with examples of academic language use along with examples of text types/genres, text features, text structures, and language structures from the CCSS for English language arts are reproduced in Resources A and B. These charts provide some insight into the magnitude of academic language coverage in the core content areas, grades K–8. In addition, Figure 3.8 offers examples of specific academic language functions within the CCSS for English language arts and mathematics, as well as those for science.

In addition, a prominent Speaking and Listening standard in the CCSS for English language arts under Comprehension and Collaboration encourages students to "engage in a range of collaborative discussions (one-on-one, in groups, and teacher-led) with diverse partners starting in kindergarten" (www.corestandards .org/ELA-Literacy/SL/K). This standard works alongside the College and Career Readiness Anchor Standard that states students "prepare for and participate effectively in a range of conversations and collaborations with diverse partners, building on others' ideas and expressing their own clearly and persuasively" (http://www.corestandards.org/ELA-Literacy/CCRA/SL). Together, these standards prompt strong motivation for teachers to provide students with ample opportunities to interact

Consider this . . .

How might you use the academic language functions in Figure 3.8 for instruction and assessment? How might these functions point to the necessary language for accessing grade-level content? How might you complement these functions with those found in language proficiency/development standards (see Figure 3.12) to obtain a full repertoire of what students are expected to do with language?

Figure 3.8 A Sampling of Academic Language Functions Explicit in the CCSS and the NGSS

Academic Language Functions in English Language Arts	Academic Language Functions in Mathematics	Academic Language Functions in Science
• ask and answer questions • recount information; recall information from experiences • tell stories • describe characters, settings and major events, the structure of stories, relationships • compare and contrast themes, two versions of the same story, texts in the same and different genres, important points and details, structure of two texts • explain processes, how authors use reason and evidence • identify words and phrases in stories, main topics • explain differences between books • summarize points of a speaker • interpret information from diverse media • draw evidence from literary or informational texts • present claims and findings	• interpret equations, multiplication as scaling • compare two-digit numbers, two decimals, properties of two functions • describe the relationship between two quantities • explain why addition and subtraction strategies work, patterns, a proof • relate volume to operations • summarize numerical data sets	• compare the effects of different strengths or different directions, life in different habitats, multiple solutions • describe patterns, different kinds of materials • construct an argument with evidence • ask questions to obtain information • determine cause and effect relationships • define design problems

with one another, to exchange information and ideas, to share findings, and to justify their views.

For ELLs, oral language is an important component of literacy; findings from the *Report of the National Literacy Panel on Language-Minority Children and Youth* (August & Shanahan, 2006) substantiated by more current research confirm that for ELLs, oral language is a necessary requisite for enhancing literacy development. Practice using oral language to communicate in authentic situations for defined purposes produces more confident and proficient learners (Zwiers & Crawford, 2011).

In conjunction with academic language use, the new content standards require students to engage in higher order thinking throughout their school careers. Such cognitive demands include all those in Bloom's revised taxonomy (except the lowest level, remembering): understanding, applying, analyzing, evaluating, and creating (Anderson et al., 2001). For example by eighth grade, the CCSS for English language arts, Reading Informational Text, expect students to *"analyze* how a text makes connections among and distinctions between individuals, ideas, or events; *analyze* in detail the structure of a specific paragraph; and *analyze* a case in which two or more texts provide conflicting information on the same topic" (CCSSI, 2010a, p. 39, emphasis added). The coupling of high cognitive engagement with academic language increases the rigor of content standards for all students.

The NGSS are based on the National Research Council's framework of "language-intensive science and engineering practices, requiring students to engage in classroom science discourse" (Lee, Quinn, & Valdes, 2013, p. 224). Furthermore, "Engagement in any of the science and engineering practices involves both scientific sense-making and language use. These practices offer rich opportunities and demands for language learning at the same time they produce science learning" (Lee et al., 2013, p. 225). It is quite apparent from this statement that the NGSS are forging a partnership between content and language teaching.

With teachers becoming more acclimated to college and career readiness standards, the opaqueness of language in content standards has now become more visible (Boals, 2013). Content teachers must come to see the critical role academic language plays across the curriculum, while language teachers need to have an understanding of the conceptual base onto which language is overlaid. Content and language teachers have to work together as partners to maximize the opportunities for success of their students. In essence, this new generation of content standards has been the stimulus for redefining teaching and learning around academic language use.

Resources for ELLs for the New Content Standards

More and more digital resources are becoming available that leverage the new content standards for ELLs. The group of researchers that form the Understanding Language initiative at Stanford University has been a think tank for analyzing the CCSS and the NGSS in light of their linguistic influences on ELLs. A compendium of academic papers and videos devoted to "analyzing the shifts, challenges, and opportunities in the Common Core State Standards and Next Generation Science Standards and open-source teaching resources that support language development and learning in

Consider this . . .

What other digital and print resources on academic language in content standards, including the CCSS and the NGSS, might you add to the ones mentioned here? How might you share these resources with colleagues?

the content areas" can be found on the initiative's website, http://ell.stanford.edu/.

As an extension of the work put into the CCSS and the NGSS, the Council of Chief State School Officers (CCSSO) has published the *Framework for English Language Proficiency Development Standards Corresponding to the Common Core State Standards and the Next Generation Science Standards* (2012) for states. This document articulates a process for determining the match between state content and language standards to maximize support for ELLs as the students are simultaneously learning grade-level content and language. It identifies language practices extracted from the CCSS for English language arts and mathematics as well as for science that students need in order to perform analytic tasks using specified language functions.

A practical, teacher-friendly interpretation of the CCSS for ELLs can be found on the Colorín Colorado website at www.colorincolorado.org/. An extensive array of resources, including classroom video modules, educator interviews, bilingual parent tip sheets in multiple languages, a blog, and news from the field are available at the tap of a keypad or a click of a mouse.

Examples of Academic Language in Content Standards

Content standards are a source of academic language, as students' knowledge, skills, and conceptual understandings are largely expressed through oral and written language. In this section and the next, we review some of the content and language standards used in the thematic units of learning throughout the mathematics and English language arts series on academic language. There are many different ways to identify academic language, and it is strengthened when content standards are coupled with language standards; here are two exemplars.

Exemplar 1

Common Core State Standards, Fourth Grade Mathematics
The first exemplar that utilizes content standards in conjunction with language standards in a unit on fractions is taken from the CCSS for mathematics (see Ernst-Slavit, Gottlieb, & Slavit, 2013).

| 4.NF.1 | Explain why a fraction *a/b* is equivalent to a fraction *(nxa)/(nxb)* by using visual fraction models, with attention to how the number and size of the parts differ even though the two fractions themselves are the same size. Use this principle to recognize and generate equivalent fractions. |
| 4.NF.2 | Compare two fractions with different numerators and different denominators, e.g., by creating common denominators or numerators, or by comparing to a benchmark fraction such as ½. Recognize that comparisons are valid only when the two fractions refer to the same whole. Record the results of comparisons with symbols >, =, or <, and justify the conclusions, e.g., by using a visual fraction model. |

Source: CCSSI, 2010b, p. 30

In order to demonstrate their mathematical reasoning and know-how of these two mathematics standards, students are expected to be skillful in the academic language functions of "define equivalent fractions," "explain equivalency," and "compare fractions with unlike numerators and denominators." Figure 3.9 provides a couple examples of the language students might be processing and producing for particular tasks or mathematics problems generated by these standards.

Figure 3.9 Examples of Academic Language Associated with Fourth Grade Fractions in the CCSS for Mathematics

CCSS for Mathematics Topic	*Examples of Academic Language Use*
4. NF.1 Fraction Building	Three and two-thirds *means that....*
	Another way of saying four and two fifths is
4. NF.2 Fraction Equivalence and Ordering	One-half *is the same as* three-sixths or 1/2 = 3/6.
	One-half *is greater than* three-eighths or 1/2 > 3/8.

Source: Gottlieb & Ernst-Slavit, 2013, p. 37

The second exemplar, based on the Virginia Standards of Learning, along with the CCSS for English language arts, is foundational for a middle school unit on research (see Walsh & Staehr Fenner, 2014).

Exemplar 2

This case study revolves around using technology as a vehicle for delving into research. Teachers select the following state content standards for the unit:
   Virginia Standards of Learning (SOLs) Seventh Grade English Language Arts
   7.9 The student will apply knowledge of appropriate reference materials to produce a research product.

(Continued)

(Continued)

(a) Collect and organize information from multiple sources including online, print, and media.

(b) Evaluate the validity and authenticity of sources.

(c) Use technology as a tool to research, organize, evaluate, and communicate information.

(d) Cite primary and secondary sources.

(e) Define the meaning and consequences of plagiarism (Board of Education, Commonwealth of Virginia, 2010, p. 3).

The seventh grade collaborative learning team chooses to deconstruct the content standards by extracting the applicable language functions and then pairing them with language arts content for the research project. Figure 3.10 shows how the team analyzes the standards to produce a graphic organizer that helps guide instructional and assessment activities.

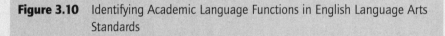

Figure 3.10   Identifying Academic Language Functions in English Language Arts Standards

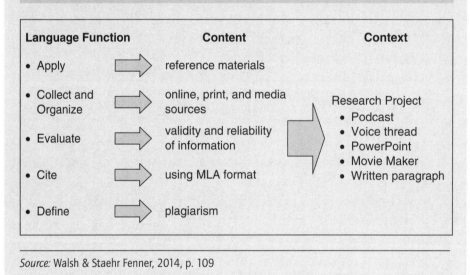

Source: Walsh & Staehr Fenner, 2014, p. 109

Academic language is equally present within language proficiency/ development standards. The question that teachers have to ask when approaching these standards is, "What is the academic language (i.e., discourses, sentences, and words/phrases) that students need to access grade-level content knowledge, skills, and understandings?"

ACADEMIC LANGUAGE IN ENGLISH LANGUAGE DEVELOPMENT/PROFICIENCY STANDARDS

Content standards must partner with English language development/proficiency standards to have a meaningful impact on teaching practices and achievement of diverse students. That is, there must be reciprocity and correspondence between the two sets of standards so that students can learn content through language and language through content. Academic language permeates both sets of standards. In Figure 3.11, the content standards of English language arts, mathematics, and science are connected to their corresponding English language development (ELD) standards through academic language, as exemplified in three of the five ELD standards from World-Class Instructional Design and Assessment (WIDA). In sum, academic language permeates both content and language standards.

Consider this . . .

Start with identifying a content standard from one grade level to extract its academic language. Then search for the corresponding representation of academic language in English language development/proficiency standards. What conclusion can you draw from your cursory analysis? Why is it important to view academic language use from both a content and a language perspective?

Figure 3.11 Academic Language as the Crosswalk Between Content and Language Standards

College and Career Readiness Standards		
The Common Core State Standards for English Language Arts	The Common Core State Standards for Mathematics	The Next Generation Science Standards
Academic Language Use Across Content and Language Standards		
WIDA's ELD Standard 2: The language of Language Arts	WIDA's ELD Standard 3: The language of Mathematics	WIDA's ELD Standard 4: The language of Science
English Language Development Standards		

In 2006, the TESOL International Association, which originally published preK–12 ESL standards in 1997, produced an augmentation of WIDA's English language proficiency (ELP) standards and subsequently published a guidebook for classroom implementation (Gottlieb, Katz, & Ernst-Slavit, 2009). These documents have contributed to the conversation on academic language and its role in schooling language learners.

At present, there are two multistate consortia that are using ELD/ELP standards to develop the next generation of English language proficiency assessments. WIDA, with 37 states having adopted its ELD standards, has an extensive website (www.wida.us) that extends into professional development for teaching and learning, academic language and literacy initiatives, and research. Additionally, the Council of Chief State School Officers (CCSSO), on behalf of the English Language Proficiency Assessment for the 21st Century (ELPA21) Consortium, has produced a set of ELP standards that map onto the CCSS. Several states with the country's largest ELL populations, including California, Texas, and New York, have also designed their own language standards.

Academic Language Use in Language Standards

Academic language functions, in part, represent language proficiency/development standards; that is, they are descriptive of what students are expected to "do" with language. A variety of language functions may be used to scaffold language across levels of language proficiency when the cognitive demand is held constant. Academic language functions always work in tandem with a specific context for language use. Figure 3.12 (parallel to Figure 3.8 for the CCSS and the NGSS) offers some examples of academic language functions within model performance indicators for three English language development standards (WIDA, 2012).

Content standards, in particular the CCSS and the NGSS, working in tandem with language proficiency/development standards, are a powerful force to harness in planning and implementing an integrated curriculum. Referring back to the first exemplar on fractions in this chapter (4.NF.1 and 4.NF.2, see pages 69–70), it becomes readily apparent that the scaffolded language representing ELD Standard 3, the language of mathematics, can assist language learners in better understanding the concepts and skills of the CCSS for mathematics, in this case, for the academic language function *explain.* Figure 3.13 shows one way that the language of fractions can be expressed along a developmental continuum.

Other exemplars illustrate academic language found in English language proficiency/development standards. In this first case study, an eighth grade class is studying similarity and congruence of polygons. The

Figure 3.12 A Sampling of Academic Language Functions Representing Three English Language Development Standards

Academic Language Functions for the Language of English Language Arts	Academic Language Functions for the Language of Mathematics	Academic Language Functions for the Language of Science
Describe parts of stories Retell stories Identify language that indicates narrative points of view Compare and contrast narrative points of view Explain editing of peers' writing Discuss themes related to the main idea Predict the evolution of literary characters, themes, and plots	Sequence sentences to solve word problems Define types of lines and angles Ask and answer simple wh- questions related to coordinate planes Explain choices based on rate calculations Identify key language patterns to solve real-life mathematical problems Describe scenarios for right triangle word problems	Describe in detail the stages of life cycles Explain outcomes of experiments Order paragraphs associated with Earth's rotation Identify functions of organisms within ecosystems Summarize scientific questions and conclusions Discuss how energy transfers

Figure 3.13 The Language Function "Explain" Scaffolded Across Levels of English Language Proficiency (ELP)

ELP Level 1	ELP Level 2	ELP Level 3	ELP Level 4	ELP Level 5
Explain by labeling fractional parts using diagrams or realia in conjunction with number word/phrase banks	Explain what the fractional parts mean using diagrams or realia in conjunction with phrases or short sentences	Explain step-by-step process for solving problems involving fractions using diagrams in conjunction with a series of related sentences	Explain strategies for solving problems involving fractions using diagrams in conjunction with paragraphs	Explain differences in solving problems involving fractions for different real-world scenarios or situations

Source: Adapted from WIDA, 2007, p. 34

teacher decides to integrate the four language domains to create a thematic unit of instruction, as shown in Figure 3.14.

Figure 3.14 Representation of the Language of Mathematics in an Integrated Thematic Unit

English Language Development Standard 3
English language learners **communicate** information, ideas, and concepts necessary for academic success in the area of MATHEMATICS

	Level 1 Entering	Level 2 Emerging	Level 3 Developing	Level 4 Expanding	Level 5 Bridging
Listening	Point to the figures that share the described features (e.g., congruent, similar) with a partner based on oral statements	Classify polygons and properties of figures and transformation with a partner based on oral descriptions	Classify and compare similar polygons from those that are not based on oral directions with a partner	Classify and compare polygons and properties of figures based on classroom discussions	Classify and compare polygons and properties of figures based on information from complex oral discourse
Speaking	State or repeat processes shared in class using manipulatives or other visual supports in small groups	Use mathematics vocabulary and simple phrases to communicate observations (e.g., "These two are similar.") in small groups	Use sentences to describe methods for determining the relationship between two figures or steps for solving problems in small groups	Outline approaches to determine the relationship among the figures in small groups	Discuss and explain the relationship between two figures (e.g., similar, congruent) and describe the mapping that takes one to the other
Reading	Match words to the concepts being explored from illustrated text with a partner	Recognize key terms and phrases that provide information to solve the problem from illustrated text with a partner	Sequence phrases and sentences to decide how to solve problems involving congruence and similarity from illustrated text with a partner	Locate key information to solve problems involving congruence and similarity from simplified text with a partner	Identify key implicit information to solve problems involving congruence and similarities from grade-level text
Writing	Make visual representations from models	Describe the properties of figures using vocabulary, phrases, and visual representations	Illustrate the relationship between polygons using vocabulary, sentences, symbols, and visual images	Provide justifications for conclusions about properties of similar and congruent figures and transformations using visual representations and related sentences	Summarize outcomes of investigations that explain the relationship between figures in paragraph form

Source: Kersaint, 2013, p. 119

From this standards matrix, the teacher dissects the academic language the students will be using in the unit. In Figure 3.15, the academic language associated with the mathematics topic of similarity and congruence is displayed at the word/expression, sentence, and discourse levels.

In this second classroom, a pair of second grade dual language teachers uses the Texas English language proficiency standards (ELPS) in the design of a unit on ecosystems. They realize that the Texas ELPS are a helpful complement to the Texas Essential Knowledge and Skills (TEKS) standards.

Figure 3.15 Range of Academic Language Used in a Unit on Similarity and Congruence

Word/ Expression Level	*Prerequisite mathematics vocabulary:* congruent, polygons, triangles, round to the nearest. . . . , *Words encountered most often in mathematics classes:* measurement, polygon, congruent/congruence, transformation, rotation, translation, scale factor, ratio, proportions/proportional, hypotenuse, right angles, coordinate plane, square (x^2), segment *Everyday words with specific meanings in mathematics:* dilation, reflection, legs, sides, scale, drawing, formula, compositions
Symbols	$=, \sim, \cong$, AB, $\overline{AB}$, $\angle ABC$, 30°, $\pm$, $\sqrt{2}$
Sentence Level	A *transformation* that takes triangle ABC to triangle DEF **is called a** _____. *Syntax and Semantics:* If two triangles are similar, the ratio of their areas **is equal to** the *square* of their scale factor. **Suppose** $\angle A$ measured 15°. What **would be** the height of the tree? *Directions:* Determine whether each pair of polygons is similar. Explain. Find each missing side measure. Find the height of . . . if . . . Draw a diagram. Explain your reasoning.
Discourse Level	Description of a theorem or definition of terms/phrases within story problems such as: similar polygons, transformations, translation, reflection, rotation, dilation

Source: Kersaint, 2013, pp. 121–122

The teachers catalog the different ways that the students could demonstrate their learning strategies and academic language for each language domain; the list is reproduced in Figure 3.16.

Figure 3.16 Looking at Academic Language Across Language Domains and Learning Strategies

Listening	Speaking	Reading	Writing	Learning Strategies
Follow directions. Retell or summarize. Relay spoken messages. Respond to questions and requests. Collaborate with peers. Take notes.	Use grade-level content area vocabulary in context. Share information in cooperative learning groups.	Engage in shared reading. Retell or summarize material. Respond to questions. Take notes. Summarize text, and distinguish main ideas from details. Make connections between ideas.	Produce different sentence lengths and patterns. Connect words to combine phrases, clauses, and sentences.	Concept mapping Drawing Comparing Contrasting

Source: Mercuri & Rodríguez, 2014, p. 124

What often is forgotten in a discussion of student standards are the students in our classrooms and what they bring to the learning situation. For linguistically and culturally diverse students, and, most important, ELLs, teachers should have a sense of the students' literacy in their home language to better predict the students' pace of achievement in English.

THE IMPACT OF HOME LANGUAGE ON ACADEMIC LANGUAGE DEVELOPMENT

Home languages and cultures are powerful forces in shaping the social, emotional, and linguistic disposition of students. As students enter school, they bring their identity along with a set of concepts and skills that has been crafted from their home language and cultural experiences (Miramontes, Nadeau, & Commins, 2011). Research provides irrefutable evidence that the home language of linguistically and culturally diverse students positively impacts their English language development (Coleman & Goldenberg, 2012; Genesee, Lindholm-Leary, Saunders, & Christian, 2006; among others). As there is a strong relationship among language, culture, identity, and cognition, students' accumulated knowledge in their home languages will ultimately enhance their abilities to learn in English (Egbert & Ernst-Slavit, 2010).

Similarly, many literacy practices have widespread applicability across languages. Research is clear that strong literacy in students' home languages accelerates literacy development in English (Collier & Thomas, 2009; August & Shanahan, 2006). Students who are literate in their home languages bring concepts, skills, and attitudes about reading and writing that readily transfer to other languages, thus easing their transition to literacy development in English (Peregoy & Boyle, 2013). Ultimately, when schools promote bilingualism and create additive learning environments, students reach higher levels of academic achievement (Wagner & King, 2012).

The acceptance of students' pursuit of multiliteracies has expanded the scope of their expression of understanding that is demonstrated in nontraditional venues, such as through the visual arts and other multimedia. Multiliteracies also encompass and embrace expression in multiple languages and cultures. Sensitive to their cultural roots, linguistically and culturally diverse students can voice their perspectives or worldviews by displaying or incorporating their home language alongside English in authentic and meaningful ways, such as in digital formats. The acknowledgment of home languages and cultures within the school environment can thus lead to rich and creative ways of translanguaging among emergent bilinguals, where students interact in two or more languages in naturally occurring situations to bolster their language development.

Many of today's instructional practices that capitalize on students' home languages as linguistic assets and contributors to learning in English emanate from the theories of Roger Shuy (1981) and Jim Cummins (1981).

> **Consider this . . .**
>
> To what extent have you considered or are you currently incorporating multiliteracies into curriculum, instruction, and assessment? What are some examples you can share with other teachers? Why are multiliteracies an important aspect of building students' 21st century skills, especially for linguistically and culturally diverse students?

These theorists both posed an iceberg metaphor to illustrate how academic language, closely tied to literacy and universal aspects of literacy, lies beneath the surface of each individual language. Furthermore, Cummins' interdependent hypothesis points to the effectiveness of using the student's home language to promote proficiency in another language and attributes transfer between languages to both exposure and motivation. In recent years that notion of using two languages to promote literacy development has been refined. Today, it is the strategic and intentional use of the students' home language in school that helps ELLs, even those with learning disabilities, make explicit connections between languages, learn grade-level content while acquiring English, and reinforce the bond between home and school (Beeman & Urow, 2013; Klingner, Hoover, & Baca, 2008).

SUGGESTIONS FOR REDEFINING TEACHING AND LEARNING AROUND ACADEMIC LANGUAGE USE

Changing the culture of school to be inclusive of all students, in particular, making language learning integral to every discipline and classroom, is going to require a tremendous amount of effort on the part of educators. School leaders and district administrators have to be sensitive to the changing student demographic, infuse academic language into policy and practice, and support teachers in sustained professional learning. Teachers, in turn, have to believe in their students—their values, identities, languages, and cultures, and embrace the communities in which they live.

We believe that having academic language at the center of the design and implementation of standards-referenced curriculum, instruction, and assessment will foster student growth and achievement. Therefore, we offer the following set of suggestions to facilitate the process of transforming schools so they highlight a strengths-based approach to teaching and learning.

Teachers should encourage students to

1. Use their linguistic and cultural prowess to make sense of the world of school.

2. Engage in performance-based activities, tasks, and projects that emphasize academic language use.

3. Interact with other students in academic conversations and form partnerships for learning.

4. Access technology to learn through multiple modalities and show their learning.

5. Become familiar with standards-referenced criteria for success and participate in self and peer assessment.

6. Use their metalinguistic, metacultural, and metacognitive awareness to enhance learning.

7. Apply pointed, descriptive feedback from peers and teachers to improve their performance.

School leaders should encourage teachers to

1. Integrate content and academic language learning throughout the school day.

2. Participate in department or grade-level teams or professional learning communities in designing standards-referenced content and language targets for units of learning for all students.

3. Think about and discuss with colleagues how academic language at the discourse, sentence, and word/phrase levels is organized for each subject area.

4. To the extent feasible, organize curriculum around grade-level themes that relate to the students' experiences and identify text types/genres that exemplify those themes.

5. Form professional learning teams around promoting instructional and assessment strategies that enhance academic language use.

6. Honor the linguistic and cultural resources that the students bring to school, and place them at the forefront of instruction.

7. Engage in the discussion and use of academic language, from standards to assessment.

District administrators should encourage school leaders to

1. Support teachers and give them power to make decisions around academic language use in instruction and classroom assessment.

2. Contribute to grade-level, department, or professional learning teams in their exploration of academic language within and across standards and content areas.

3. Review curriculum in light of the presence of and emphasis on academic language.

4. Schedule protected joint planning time for grade-level content and language teachers in every school across the district.

5. Enable coaches and mentors to participate in and provide sustained professional learning to teachers and teacher teams around the language of school.

6. Analyze students' achievement data in relation to their language proficiency data as a requisite for decision making.

Academic language, as a register of school, strings together the components of an educational system. Starting with standards, academic language is shared between the concepts and skills of content and the language required to access that content. Subsequently, academic language is central to assessment of both academic achievement and language proficiency. And, in an aligned system, standards-referenced assessment informs the curriculum and related instruction within educational programs.

Academic language is also an expression of the sociocultural contexts in which it operates. Within these contexts, students' home languages, cultures, and understandings facilitate the making of connections between their home backgrounds and school. If students are to be viable participants in 21st century life, it is critical that schools reflect their multicultural frames of reference and range of experiences (Ladson-Billings, 1995). One of the most powerful responses that schools can make to this call for culturally responsive teaching and learning is to ensure the congruence of instruction and assessment with the cultural values of the surrounding communities (Osher & Fleischman, 2005).

Figure 3.17 depicts academic language as the unifying thread that binds standards, assessments, and educational programs. It serves as the mediator at school, in the communities in which our students reside, and ultimately in the society at large. In order for students to succeed academically and in other facets of their lives, there has to be coherence between academic language use inside and outside of school. Therefore, it is the responsibility of teachers, school leaders, and administrators to redefine teaching and learning around the tenets of academic language so that there is meaning to school and a seamless transition for students to the world around them.

State content standards, including the CCSS and the NGSS, have pushed the educational community to reexamine grade-level expectations that mark student success in elementary and secondary school as students prepare for college and careers. Corresponding English language

Figure 3.17 Academic Language Use Within Sociocultural Contexts for Learning

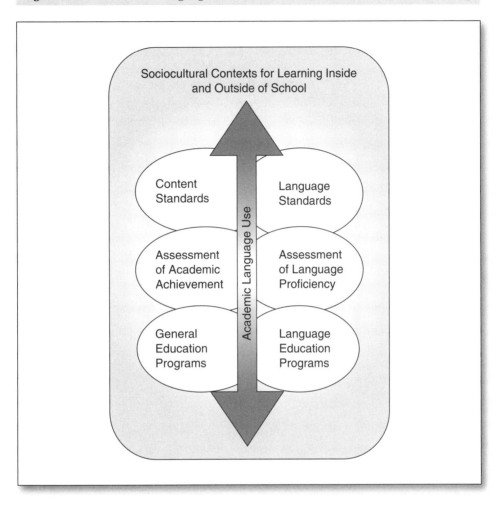

development standards have provided representative ways in which to scaffold academic language across students' levels of language proficiency without diminishing the cognitive demands of learning. Students of the 21st century can reach these outcomes only through the collective revisioning and redefining of teaching and learning.

FOR FURTHER THINKING . . .

Academic language has come to be situated smack dab in the middle of the standards movement and is the focal point for curriculum design and delivery. In this chapter, we have viewed how academic language use has facilitated the fusion of content and language standards as well as its integration in teaching and learning. You are welcome to extend your thinking about academic language use by pondering the following questions:

1. What is a metaphor you or your professional learning team might use to describe the role of academic language use in teaching and learning?

2. How have college and career readiness standards impacted your teaching? Give some examples of how the standards have made a difference in other aspects of schooling.

3. In what ways do you and your colleagues collaborate in the use of content and language development standards? If you do not, what strategies do you have to ensure that you identify the language within the standards for academic purposes?

4. What are some suggestions you might share with other educators on how to integrate content and language standards when planning a unit of learning?

4 How Is Academic Language Used in Content Areas Schoolwide?

A language, which we do not know, is a fortress sealed.

—Marcel Proust, *Within a Budding Grove*

In the last five years there have been increased research efforts examining the nature of academic language and an explosion of publications for practitioners discussing the teaching of academic language in elementary, secondary, community college, and university settings. While not everyone agrees as to how to define the notion of academic language (see Chapter 1 for a historical overview of this construct), there is consensus regarding the centrality of academic language in fostering student academic success in school. Students cannot engage in complex academic practices and accumulate deep content area knowledge if they do not have the linguistic tools for thinking, processing, participating, and, ultimately, learning during content area instruction. The pivotal role of academic language in today's educational arena has been further accentuated with the introduction of college and career standards, namely, the Common Core State Standards (CCSS) and the Next Generation Science Standards (NGSS). While many publications provide ways of teaching academic vocabulary or may offer suggestions for teaching selected features of academic language, many educators still wonder, who should be teaching academic language? How can I teach academic language if I teach mathematics? Where can I find academic language in school?

SEEING ACADEMIC LANGUAGE THROUGHOUT THE SCHOOL DAY

The following brief vignettes offer opportunities to peek into diverse classrooms where content area teachers and their students are busily using academic language for thinking, knowing, acting, interacting, speaking, reading, and writing during subject matter instruction. In these classrooms academic language is not taught as a list of ten "critical" words related to a topic, but as part of deep, technical, and meaningful interactions during a variety of disciplinary or interdisciplinary practices and activities. The classrooms depicted are populated by diverse students and by teachers with diverse backgrounds and life experiences. While the vignettes present real classroom experiences, they depict only a momentary slice of time in the life of an instructional unit. This consideration is important, since, as we know, student understanding of academic content and its associated language builds over time with many topics and ideas requiring extended revisiting throughout the year. Finally, most of the vignettes presented here are part of the chapters from our six-book series Academic Language in Diverse Classrooms: Promoting Content and Language Learning. Each chapter in the Mathematics or English Language Arts series presents detailed descriptions of a unit of learning—aligned with state content standards in combination with English language proficiency/development standards—that is filled with rich descriptions of the students, the unit theme, and the different components involved in planning, designing, implementing, and reflecting on the unit.

LISTENING IN THE MUSIC CLASSROOM

The first thing we see when we enter Mr. Nikolai's music classroom is a bulletin board divided in two by a line of multicolor musical note silhouettes. On one side there are pictures of classical composers framed by the question: Who are they? Students have posted notes and identified the likes of Beethoven, Vivaldi, and Mozart but there are still many others without names. On the other half, there is a big sign "The Music Literacy Challenge: Do you know?" Below this sign there are about a dozen different paper squares, each with a different challenge:

- Do you know . . . how many lines and spaces are on the staff? Can you locate space three? Can you locate line two?
- Do you know . . . how to sing the scale on solfege syllables: do, re, mi, fa, so, la, ti, do? Can you sing them going up the scale?

- Do you know ... the style of music that your heritage country is known for?

Many would say that music is an international language because it can be universally appreciated, interpreted, and internalized. In fact, you do not have to understand German to be uplifted by listening to a choir singing the *Ode to Joy* or speak Italian to be moved by Puccini's heartfelt notes in *O Mio Babbino Caro.* However, as the three questions above illustrate, you *do* need to know the language of music to know what the three challenges above entail. Music, like other arts and disciplines, has also its own language, with written and spoken parts, theory and syntax, an alphabet, symbols, punctuation, and a vast vocabulary.

Consider this . . .

When describing and communicating the concepts of music, some common everyday words will have specific musical meanings. These multiple meanings can indeed be challenging for English language learners in a music appreciation class.

Term	Meaning in Everyday Language	Meaning in Music
beat	To hit something repeatedly, to beat by stirring	A rhythmic stress, or the rhythmic effect of these stresses
fifth	Number five in a series	The interval between two notes. Three whole tones and one semitone make up the distance between the two notes.
key	A usually metal instrument to turn the bolt of a lock	System of notes or tones based on and named after the key note
major	Large in number amount or extent	One of the two modes of the tonal system. Music written in major keys has a positive affirming character.
meter	The base unit of length, about 39.37 inches	The basic recurrent rhythmical pattern of note values
note	To notice or observe with care	Symbol or sign used to indicate both duration and pitch
pitch	To throw a baseball to a batter	Position of a single sound in the complete range of sound
staff	A long stick carried in the hand for support in walking	The horizontal lines with their spaces on which music is written—called also *stave*

Mr. Nikolai's students are learning the language of music as they sing, play music, explore a variety of written texts, and talk about music. For example, during rehearsals, Mr. Nikolai guides his students' performances by using Italian terminology used for rehearsals: *Fortissimo* (very loud), *allegro* (fast), *poco meno mosso* (less speed/movement), and *tutti* (all). It is also in this context where students can hear Mr. Nikolai speak to portions of the music they are playing using both a language students can connect to and an academic register when he is presenting didactic analysis of the music, providing a historical background, or speaking about the music in more abstract, transcendental levels.

In developing academic language in the music classroom, Mr. Nikolai has to consider the breadth of the language that students need to learn to succeed in his class. Most of his students come to his music room needing to essentially learn a new language; this places English language learners (ELLs) on the same footing as their English-proficient peers.

Students in Mr. Nikolai's class also read about music to become familiar with the concepts and the historical and technical aspects of music. Through reading informational text, the students can learn about the discourse features and the specialized vocabulary of the language of music. For example, in addition to reading sheet music and understanding that the black dots on the lines convey meaning, students have to read about those classical composers displayed on the bulletin board as they learn about different musical and historical periods. Listening skills are particularly important in learning and using the language of music. When studying minor tonalities, students listen to a variety of music as they discuss pertinent music terminology—*mode, tonality, minor*—and feelings inspired by the music—ecstatic, sad, melancholic.

In sum, in Mr. Nikolai's class there is always something to listen to. You can hear students singing or playing instruments, you can hear music on the teacher's iPod—from Vivaldi's *Four Seasons* to the Monkees' version of *I'm a Believer*. In addition, between musical pieces, you can hear the teacher and students use a particular register to talk about music.

Throughout the different classrooms and spaces in the school, we can hear and view the academic register in action. For example, in physical education (PE), in addition to performing the physical skills, it is essential for students to express their understanding of the skills, concepts, and rules of playing specific sports or discussing health issues verbally and in writing. Students can practice the language of PE when they exercise and practice movements, watch videos or demonstrations, engage in constructing word walls and posters, or when they interact, read, or write about those activities.

In physical education, particularly at the high school level, students are expected to access and produce a variety of different texts and genres.

These texts are dependent upon the situational context (e.g., the newspaper article about the Friday night football game, a description of personal exercise training, or the weekly test) and specific to the activity or the players (e.g., lacrosse rules for parents and students, ground routines for swimmers, agility training). In PE, students also use a variety of language functions in order to participate in learning, practice, and assessment tasks, such as

- Discussing ideas and asking questions.
- Describing thought processes.
- Following and giving instructions.
- Acting out a minilesson.
- Listing steps and procedures.
- Providing evidence supporting an opinion.
- Summarizing instructional and disciplinary texts.
- Explaining strategies that apply knowledge of the rules of games on tests.

At the sentence level, since many of the topics studied in physical education are related to science, texts and instructional materials may include complex grammatical structures and conventions. Some of these features (e.g., complex noun phrases, cause and effect, time order, compare and contrast) may present challenges to students, especially when their expectation for PE content is to exercise and practice sports, rather than do reading and writing tasks.

Similarly, there are many academic terms and concepts frequently used in PE and health education classes. These can be grouped in four categories: (1) general academic vocabulary (e.g., *pressure, power, resistance, flexibility*), (2) specialized academic vocabulary (e.g., *muscular strength, body composition, backstroke*), and (3) technical vocabulary (e.g., *cardiovascular endurance, anaerobic, isokinetic exercise*) along with the myriad of (4) acronyms typical of this field (e.g., FITT, BMI, CPR).

MOVING FROM A PHYSICAL EDUCATION CLASS TO THE ARTS

Moving along our tour of a school, we encounter academic language in the art studio. The arts are integral to a well-rounded education and can provide many opportunities for students' artistic and cognitive development while enhancing their literacy and language development. In fact, the arts provide a variety of avenues for students to develop their visual awareness, take pride in their heritage, express themselves, and develop their own identity. In art there are also different types of discourses, that is, particular ways of talking about a piece of art, an era, or an artist. As an example, let's enter into Ms. Hodnett's visual arts studio to examine a newspaper article brought in by students as part of their assignment to read art reviews before they wrote their own. The excerpt below, by Mary Abbe (2013), is from a review of Claes Oldenburg's 1960s work at the Walker Art Center published in the *Minneapolis Star Tribune*.

> Oldenburg was among the fresh faces. Born in Sweden, he grew up mostly in Chicago, where his father was a diplomat. After studying at Yale and the Art Institute of Chicago, he settled in New York in 1956 and has lived and worked there ever since. . . . The Walker's three-gallery show opens with crude drawings and rough card-board cutouts from "The Street," a 1960 installation of graffiti-like figures and bruised body parts whose edgy chaos conveyed a sense of urban decay. Snapshots from the artist's notebooks of the time footnote Manhattan's shabby industrial underbelly.

Exploring the linguistic complexity of these five sentences reveals several aspects that can impede understanding. In addition to discipline-specific terms (e.g., *three-gallery show, drawings, cutouts*), the writer uses metaphors (e.g., *fresh faces, footnote, underbelly*), and nominalizations (e.g., *installation*) to communicate specific and nuanced feelings. Complex sentences are characteristic of academic language as exemplified by the fourth one—a long statement filled with many adjectives (e.g., *crude, rough, graffiti-like, edgy, urban*). Also in this short excerpt is an abundance of locations (e.g., Sweden, Chicago, New York, Yale) aside from the mention of the gallery where the exhibit takes place.

Academic language in any content area serves to describe abstraction, complexity, and higher order thinking (Zwiers, 2008). An abstract concept is an idea or relationship that we cannot easily represent by drawing, pointing, or acting out. For example, in the newspaper excerpt above, *fresh faces* does not refer to the artist's youth or physical health (in fact, he is 84 years old), but it is used in relation to the previous paragraph in the newspaper article describing the artist's role in "somber-minded Abstract Expressionism" five decades ago. Thus, the metaphor *fresh face* is an abstraction, shorthand for the information conveyed earlier. This kind of abstraction is a necessary part of academic discourse. In the arts, abstraction refers to an art form or method of working that focuses on certain aspects of an image or object to the exclusion of others. As a way of illustrating abstraction, let's look at the painting reproduced in Figure 4.1. Just as in language, abstraction refers to

Figure 4.1 "Enigma" by Heinz Ernst

Used with permission.

ignoring or hiding details to capture some kind of commonality between different instances; in the painting in Figure 4.1 we observe aspects of a person's face removed, while others are emphasized. It would be difficult to decipher who this person is or to identify the gender without talking to the artist or knowing more about the context of this painting.

Content area disciplinary language reflects the subject matter and nature of a discipline. This language compounds that of learning other academic registers. All educators, regardless of their subject matter or where they teach—in a studio, gym, music room, video room, film studio, lab, or classroom—need to be aware of the linguistic demands of their content area and provide opportunities for students to learn the necessary register.

LOOKING INTO MATHEMATICS CLASSROOMS

Learning to communicate mathematically encompasses a variety of skills and processes to access information, to think and problem solve, and to communicate mathematical knowledge to different audiences using multiple representations. Academic language in mathematics includes a variety of representational forms beyond oral and written language, such as mathematical symbol systems and visual displays. Figure 4.2 is a semantic web that offers a visual representation of the complexity of academic language in mathematics, consisting of layers of everyday language, technical terms and symbols, grammatical conventions unique to mathematical discourse, and oral or written language tailored for different purposes and audiences.

Students are no longer simply asked to articulate definitions and steps to solving problems. An important aspect of the CCSS for mathematics is explicit student expectations related to communicating reasoning. Students are expected to (a) communicate their reasoning through multiple representations (including, e.g., pictures, words, symbols, tables, graphs, pictures), (b) engage in productive oral, written, and symbolic group work with peers and teachers, (c) explain and demonstrate knowledge using emerging language, and (d) extract meaning from written mathematical texts (Moschkovich, 2013). This shift in mathematical practice indicates the need to have students actively participate in mathematical discourse practices around language functions (e.g., justifying, explaining) that move them beyond the "correct usage" of vocabulary or the learning of a set of formulas.

In the classroom, mathematics instruction needs to recognize the complexity of the language of mathematics and provide all students, especially ELLs, with the necessary scaffolds and differentiation to support their learning of both the language of mathematics and the related mathematical content. In essence, and as stated by Moschkovich (2013), mathematics instruction for ELLs should

1. Support ELLs' participation in mathematical discussions as they learn English.

2. Draw on multiple resources available in classrooms (objects, drawings, graphs, and gestures) as well as home languages and experiences outside of school.

3. Focus on students' mathematical reasoning, not on their accuracy in using language.

4. Emphasize mathematical practices, not "language" as vocabulary, single words, grammar, or a list of definitions.

5. Treat everyday language as resource, not as obstacle. (Moschkovich, 2013)

Figure 4.2 Complexity of Academic Language in Mathematics

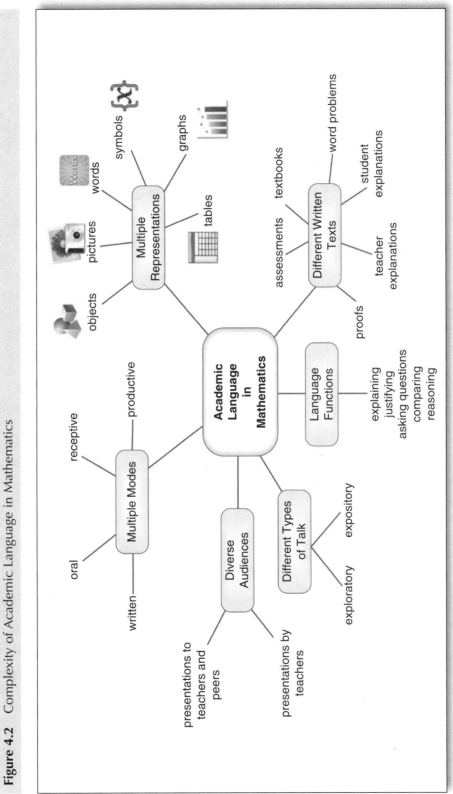

Consider this . . .

Three important aspects are emphasized in the CCSS for mathematics: *Coherence* (thinking across grades and linking to major topics), *rigor* (pursuing conceptual understanding, procedural skill and fluency, and application), and *focus* (narrowing the scope of content and deepening understanding). In addition to the content standards, there are standards for mathematical practice, which describe ways students come to interact with content as they grow in mathematical maturity and expertise throughout their schooling (CCSSI, 2010b). The eight Mathematical Practices work in tandem with the mathematics content standards and describe essential mathematical habits of mind and action that can guide K–12 curriculum, pedagogy, and assessment:

1. Make sense of problems, and persevere in solving them.

2. Reason abstractly and quantitatively.

3. Construct viable arguments, and critique the reasoning of others.

4. Model with mathematics.

5. Use appropriate tools strategically.

6. Attend to precision.

7. Look for and make use of structure.

8. Look for and express regularity in repeated reasoning. (CCSSI, 2010b)

It is obvious that communication and meaningful use of the language of mathematics play a pivotal role in the implementation of each of the recommended mathematical practices.

As we look into two classrooms— Grade 8 and Grade 1—we find examples of how instruction can create opportunities for mathematical reasoning and support students as they learn to manipulate the language needed to explain their reasoning and understanding to others.

The first vignette is set in an eighth grade classroom located in an ethnically diverse middle school in the southeast United States. Ms. Jackson, a veteran middle school mathematics teacher endorsed in teaching English to Speakers of Other Languages, carefully tailors instruction that builds on student strengths and addresses the needs of her 10 ELLs at various stages of language development (Kersaint, 2013). Based on her prior experiences teaching this unit on similarity and congruence, Ms. Jackson knows that most students find it difficult to understand those concepts and their associated academic language. Her perspective on viewing all her students as mathematics language learners has transformed her teaching into instructional activities where language is used to deepen students' understandings of mathematical concepts.

At the beginning of the unit, Ms. Jackson decides to spend time helping students comprehend the key features of similar and congruent figures. She realizes that this foundational knowledge will not only help students as they navigate throughout the unit, but also lay the foundation for conversations that make use of important mathematical language. As expected, with this background knowledge, the class quickly moves through the sections on *finding missing measures* and *solving problems involving similar triangles*. Throughout the unit, she reinforces students' use of mathematics language as they discuss problems, share results, and explain their thinking to the class.

A major section of the unit focuses on the use of the Pythagorean theorem. Ms. Jackson knows that her students have varying familiarity with right triangles, but she wants to make connections to students' prior knowledge. For that purpose, and as illustrated in the next segment, Ms. Jackson engages students, including Elidor, an ELL at the beginning level of English language proficiency, in a conversation to find out what they know about right triangles.

Ms. Jackson: [pointing to an image of a right triangle displayed on the board] We have already been working with *right triangles*. Let's go over what we know. What do we know about right triangles? Elidor?

Elidor: 90 degrees.

Ms. Jackson: What about 90 degrees? Please remember to use a complete sentence.

Elidor: [Looks at his notes] The angle is 90 degrees?

Ms. Jackson: Yes. It has *one angle* that measures 90 degrees. How do we show that we have a 90 degree angle?

John: With a square.

Ms. Jackson: We use a square to show the *right* or the *90 degree* angle. [She used her clicker to add a square to indicate the right angle.] What do we call the side opposite the 90 degree angle? [She used her clicker to add an arrow that pointed toward the side opposite the right angle.]

George: The longest side is the hypotenuse and the other two sides are legs. [As the student said this, Ms. Jackson uses her clicker to add the words hypotenuse and legs to the slide to indicate the names of the other parts.]

Ms. Jackson: We will use this information as we learn about the Pythagorean Theorem [the words are displayed]. Let me hear you say Py-tha-go-re-an [said slowly] Theorem.

Choral Response: Pythagorean theorem. (Kersaint, 2013, pp. 134–135)

Ms. Jackson observes that nearly all students had familiarity with the main mathematical concepts of this part of the unit, but not all students appeared to say the words. She realizes that she will need to provide opportunities for individuals to practice. The teacher and students also accessed the Internet and applets to provide visual proofs of the theorem.

Later in the unit, Ms. Jackson again used visuals to begin the section on transformations. Because she wanted students to gain an informal understanding of the motions involved in reflection, translation, and rotation, she used a suite of tools, shown in Figure 4.3, that allowed students to observe and apply the various motions.

Figure 4.3 Suite of Tools to Explore Congruence and Similarity

Understanding Congruence, Similarity, and Symmetry Using Transformations and Interactive Figures

Rotations; translations, or slides; and reflections, or flips, are geometric transformations that change an object's position or orientation but not its shape or size. The interactive figures in this four-part example allow a user to manipulate a shape and observe its behavior under a particular transformation or composition of transformations.

Activities like these allow students to deepen their understanding of congruence, similarity, and reflection, and they also contribute to the study of transformations, as described in the Geometry Standard.

	Visualizing Transformations (6.4.1) Choose a transformation and apply it to a shape to observe the resulting image.
	Identifying Unknown Transformations (6.4.2) The user is challenged to identify the transformation that has been used.
	Composing Reflections (6.4.3) Examine the result of reflecting a shape successively through two different lines.
	Composing Transformations (6.4.4) Users are challenged to compose equivalent transformations in two different ways.

Engaging conversations, animated group work, carefully planned tasks, and meaningful assessments contributed to the success of this unit. While Ms. Jackson used the textbook as the main source for her teaching, over the years she has increased the use of technology and manipulatives to actively engage students, foster understanding, and scaffold language learning (Kersaint, 2013).

If you were to walk down a virtual hall, you would see a whole classroom of first grade students of Mexican descent. Ms. López and her students are part of a Title I bilingual elementary school. While many of the subjects are taught in two languages, mathematics is taught mostly in English. Ms. López, a native Spanish speaker, works to create a mathematics discourse community, where students are learning to be successful problem solvers surrounded by a mathematics environment with unique ways of thinking, acting, and speaking (Celedón-Pattichis & Musanti, 2013). During this base-10 unit, Ms. López helps develop mathematical discourse with her students by encouraging them to retell the story embedded in the problem, share their mathematical thinking, rephrase questions and answers, and, for beginning ELLs, use sentence frames to communicate their mathematical thinking in English.

In reviewing the different texts that students use throughout the unit, Ms. López identified several aspects of academic language. For example, in terms of discourse, she realized that story problems present many challenges for all students (Gottlieb & Ernst-Slavit, 2013); however, the issue becomes accentuated for ELLs who are not familiar with the context of the story problem (e.g., ping pong balls, spinners) (Bay-Williams, Glasser, & Bronger, 2013; Ernst-Slavit & Slavit, 2013; Turner, Celedón-Pattichis, Marshall, & Tennison, 2009). Consequently, Ms. López planned tasks related to base-10 thinking by connecting to familiar items, such as crayons, and familiar places, such as the corn tortilla factory (close to the school), *el mercado* (supermarket), and *la pulga* (the flea market) in the community. It was easy for Ms. López to make home–school links, since she lived in the same neighborhood as her students (Celedón-Pattichis & Musanti, 2013).

To observe student performance on base-10 thinking, Ms. López asked students to represent their solutions using illustrations, symbols, and words (orally and in writing) on a single worksheet (see Figure 4.4). To support all her students, she brought bags of corn tortillas. For her students in the early stages of English language proficiency, she prepared a base-10 assessment in Spanish (Figure 4.5). In addition to the written assessment, Ms. López also assessed her students orally by asking them to respond to the story using the bags of tortillas as realia.

Figure 4.4 Base 10-Thinking Problems Using Corn Tortillas

Problem	Draw the bags and the extra tortillas.	Write a number sentence.	Write your solution using words to explain your thinking.
Example: You have 3 bags of tortillas and 4 extra tortillas.	$\boxed{10}$ $\boxed{10}$ $\boxed{10}$ | | | |	10 + 10 + 10 + 4 = 34	*I have 3 bags of tortillas. That is the same as 30. I also have 4 extra tortillas. 30 plus 4 is the same as 34.*
1. Anali has 5 bags of tortillas and 0 extra tortillas.	Draw the bags and the extra tortillas.	Write a number sentence.	Write your solution using words to explain your thinking.
2. Pedrito has 8 bags of tortillas and 6 extra tortillas.	Draw the bags and the extra tortillas.	Write a number sentence.	Write your solution using words to explain your thinking.
3. Citlali has 7 bags of tortillas and 19 extra tortillas.	Draw the bags and the extra tortillas.	Write a number sentence.	Write your solution using words to explain your thinking.
4. Consider the tortillas that Pedrito and Citlali have. Who has more? How many more?	Draw the bags and the extra tortillas that belong to Pedrito and to Citlali.	How did you know? Write your solution using words or number sentences.	

Source: Celedón-Pattichis & Musanti, 2013, pp. 120–121

Overall this was a successful unit, as students in Ms. López's classroom were able to solve story problems using larger numbers than what is expected for first graders. In addition, the use of all four language domains enhanced students' abilities to connect mathematical notations and representations, describe their understanding of story problems, challenge the thinking of others, and present solutions. For additional examples of mathematics units of instruction taught in mainstream classrooms with ELLs, see Carrison and Muir (2013), de Araujo (2013), O'Loughlin (2013), Silverstone and Zacarian (2013), and Villagómez and Wenger (2013).

Figure 4.5 Assessment in Spanish

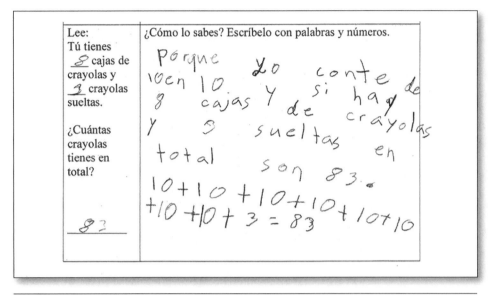

Source: Celedón-Pattichis & Musanti, 2013, p. 121

ENTERING AN ENGLISH LANGUAGE ARTS CLASS

Of course we teach academic language! That's what we do in language arts; we teach language and literacy; we teach English all day.

—Seventh grade teacher

English language arts teachers play an essential role in teaching academic language to all students, as conclusively affirmed by the seventh grade teacher quoted above. However, with the changes in demographics and the implementation of college and career readiness standards, many teachers are left wondering how can they meet the needs of all their students. Some of the questions we have heard language arts teachers ask include, "How can teachers assist students who are at the early stages of learning English as an additional language or ELLs with learning disabilities to learn academic language?" "How can ELA teachers help students understand that the American romantic movement is not about red roses, beating hearts, or awkward declarations of adoration?" "How can teachers help students understand allegory and symbolism in Poe's work?"

To address these questions, at least in part, we will "enter" one English language arts (ELA) classroom to explore how teachers assist students in the learning and production of academic language. The classroom we visit

Consider this . . .

For additional examples of how to design, implement, and reflect on standards-referenced language arts units in elementary and middle school diverse classrooms, see Cardenas, Jones, and Lozano (2014), Lam, Low, and Tauiliili-Mahuka (2014), McCloskey and New Levine (2014), Mercuri and Rodríguez (2014), Mora-Flores, Silvers, Shorey, Eliopoulis, and Akiyoshi (2014), Walsh and Staehr Fenner (2014), and Young and Hadaway (2014).

is based on Chapter 4 of *Academic Language in Diverse Classrooms: English Language Arts, Grades 6–8: Promoting Content and Language Learning,* written by Liliana Minaya-Rowe (2014), where Alberto and his eighth grade students are engaged in a unit on gothic literature in a New England classroom.

In planning for this unit, Alberto considers using an adapted version of Poe's "The Cask of Amontillado." Several questions guide Alberto's thinking, including

> What is the academic language that students will encounter in these two texts (the original and the adapted version)?

What are the words and grammatical structures that might prevent ELLs and their proficient English peers from comprehending the selected short story?

To answer these questions, Alberto searches for the different dimensions of academic language in the two texts. Figure 4.6 illustrates the academic language in the introductory paragraph of the adapted versions of "The Cask of Amontillado." The bottom part of the figure depicts the kind of academic language students need to successfully participate in two of the activities planned for this gothic literature unit.

In this ethnically diverse classroom, two thirds of the students speak Spanish at home and are at various levels of English language proficiency. Within this context, Alberto decides to point out and contrast English and Spanish prefixes and suffixes. Alberto and his colleagues know that this kind of word-learning strategy helps students increase their metalinguistic awareness and improve their spelling. Figure 4.7 illustrates the kind of suffix patterns in English and Spanish that bring a wealth of awareness and learning of linguistic patterns across languages.

However, the comparisons between English and Spanish do not stop at the vocabulary level. There are many instances in this unit where the teacher builds on the students' linguistic repertoires and connects to students' interests. One specific example of connecting between the students' languages and cultures and the focus of the unit is the comparison Alberto and his students construct between a written gothic story

Figure 4.6 Academic Language in the "The Cask of Amontillado"

Text Type	Discourse Level	Sentence Level	Word/Expression Level	
Literature short story	Narrative	Complex sentences: Deep in my _____ I _____ him, but I never said or did anything that _____ him how I _____ felt. But I couldn't find you and I was ____ he would sell the cask of _____ to someone else. The _____ _____ is just beyond these _____ where the ____ of my family are _____. I smiled to _____ and stopped working so that I could ____ _____ listening to the noise.	• punish • deep in my heart • weak spot • insults • powerful wine • cellar • costly • judge • twisting stairway • stored • stone blocks no longer wrapped around buried tombs • play a good joke • dead • barrel • damp underneath • loud screams	• solid • deeper and deeper • the thought of carnival season • look like • stepped into • really • moaning • suddenly • pretended • cask of amontillado • half a century • fear • shallow • shovel • intriguing
Gothic literature	Interactive dialog– discussion Essay writing	Elaborate responses to complex questions: e.g., How does Poe create a sense of fear in "The Cask of Amontillado"? Is Montresor's revenge justified?	• unity of effect • bizarre world • intense emotion • foreshadowing • setting • symbolism • grotesque • fantasy and reality • allegory • paraphrasing • restating • summarizing • tone • theme	• devices • horrific • allegory • metaphor • intriguing • malice aforethought • motive • emotional effect • hostile environment • human condition

Source: Minaya-Rowe, 2014, p. 147

Figure 4.7 Suffix Patterns in English and Spanish

Nouns	Adjectives	Verbs	Adverbs
-tion = -ción	**-ous = -oso/a**	**-ate = -ar**	**-ly = mente**
retribution/retribución	furious/furioso/a	decorate/decorar	really/realmente
attention/atención	spacious/espacioso	celebrate/celebrar	immediately/inmediatamente
satisfaction/satisfacción	curious/curioso	illustrate/ilustrar	seriously/seriamente

Source: Minaya-Rowe, 2014, p. 150

("The Cask of Amontillado") and an oral gothic story from Latin America ("El Chupacabra," or "The Goat Sucker") known by many of the students. The comparison centers on the devices used in each story that contribute to unity of effect, such as setting, symbols, foreshadowing, mood, and tone.

While Alberto teaches English all day in classes that include many ELLs, he uses many resources to assist students navigate his five-week unit. For example, Alberto works with a team of teachers in his middle school to plan, collaborate, and reflect about everyday teaching. In addition, Alberto regularly and systematically uses English language proficiency standards to differentiate language, plans for ways of making strong home–school connections, provides continuing scaffolds, differentiates instruction, and makes deliberate efforts to systematically teach the different dimensions of academic language. As a result, by the end of the unit, while his students may not be able to fully understand the romantic period, they will have acquired important content and language knowledge. Students are able to articulate features and characteristics of gothic stories, including those from other languages and cultures, and to make connections between Edgar Allan Poe's tales of mystery and the macabre with contemporary novels and movies. Alberto is pleased that his class can articulate the meaning of allegory and symbolism in both written and oral gothic stories using grade-level academic language.

VISITING A SCIENCE CLASS

In a fifth grade classroom in the southeastern United States, Maria and her 24 students embarked on an interdisciplinary unit on ocean ecology with strong ties to literature (McCloskey & New Levine, 2014). In this section, we present highlights of the unit and focus on selected practices that encourage academic language use, both orally and in writing.

Like other teachers in her school, Maria has a linguistically and culturally diverse group of students, including seven ELLs, two of whom were recently reclassified as English proficient, and five who are proficient English speakers from diverse language backgrounds. The home languages of the students are as varied as their individual trajectories and include Belvie (Swahili French), Karen, Spanish, Gujarati, Arabic, Russian, Telugu, Tamil, and Bosnian.

Although her school doesn't provide any additional materials aside from the science-related textbooks, Maria is excited about this unit, because she will be able to use the city aquarium as a teaching tool. Together with her grade-level peers, Maria decides on the essential knowledge and skills that students need for this ecology unit. They select scientific knowledge as the basis of the unit with literary elements as a subtheme. After selecting a science content target and a language arts content target, Maria creates an overall language target for the unit in its entirety, as depicted in the box below.

> **Consider this . . .**
>
> The NGSS set high expectations in science for all students, and teachers of ELLs must employ effective strategies to deepen their students' understanding of science while the students are learning English. Case Study 4 in Appendix D of the NGSS lists five areas where teachers can support science and language for ELLs: (1) literacy strategies for all students, (2) language support strategies with ELLs, (3) discourse strategies with ELLs, (4) home language support, and (5) home culture connections. (NGSS, 2013)

Science Content Target:	Students will describe and explain how various organisms contribute to an ocean ecosystem.
Language Arts Content Target:	Students will summarize plot and examine character development in a novel.
Language Target:	Students will use present tense verbs to report on how a marine ecosystem nurtures and impacts the surrounding animals and humans who are dependent upon it; students will use past tense verbs and adverbials of time to map and report on chronological events in a novel.

For this unit, Maria uses two main science-related texts: an informational text and a work of historical fiction. Since she has a large number of ELLs at different levels of English language proficiency, and since many of her students had never seen the ocean, Maria carefully plans this unit with support from her grade-level colleagues. One important aspect of her planning involves examining the language demands of the two main texts for the unit. Figure 4.8 presents an abbreviated analysis of these texts in terms of the range of academic language.

Maria begins her unit with a picture walk and carousel brainstorming activity that raises students' interest in the organisms found in marine ecologies. She feeds that interest by mentioning that many exotic fish species live in tropical environments. As students look at the maps around the classroom, they see the names of the students who have lived in or visited some of those regions. This is one regular practice in Maria's classroom—making connections to her students and their families, homes, languages, and cultures. Another example includes asking families for their favorite seafood; for this activity students catalogue pictures of "Food Fish From

Figure 4.8 Brief Comparison of the Academic Language in Two Science Texts

Text Type	Discourse Level	Sentence Level	Word/Phrase Level
Our Wet World	Informational text	• Simple present tense • Prepositional phrases • Signal words • Comparative and descriptive adjectives in noun phrases	• Scientific vocabulary: consumer, producer, predator, prey, ecosystem • Live, grow, hunt for, survive, compete
Island of the Blue Dolphin	Historical fiction	• Past tense verbs • Prepositional phrases • Signal words of chronology and cause/effect • Dependent clauses (adjectival and adverbial) • Conditionals	• Crept • Not long after dawn, for many suns, before night • During, while, as, so, because • Like the, not unlike the • Vocabulary specific to novel: names of organisms in the island ecosystem

Source: Adapted from McCloskey & New Levine, 2014

Many Cultures," use cognates, and have many parents volunteer in their classroom.

This unit is packed with enticing activities and readings. For example, during the second week of this unit, selected activities include the following:

- Engaging in daily scaffolded reading of texts
- Intensive reading of a section of *Island of the Blue Dolphin* (O'Dell, 1988) with study guides
- Identifying types of organisms in an ecosystem: organism card game
- Using the words and phrases *predators and prey; producers, consumers, and decomposers; mutually beneficial*
- Discussing food web and examples after introduction of food web
- Watching *Shape of Life* starfish video; making connections to text and book video
- Creating model food chains from organisms in *Island of the Blue Dolphin*
- Preparing for the aquarium trip; learning about groups' focus ecosystems via WebQuests and aquarium study guides

With all these interesting activities, students are hooked! Clearly, Maria is a strong supporter of activities that encourage oral participation in class. She constantly interacts with students individually, in small groups, or in a whole class setting and provides structured opportunities for students to speak in class.

To encourage and support students' oral language development, Maria uses a variety of scaffolds to facilitate their access to content. A few of the strategies she uses include these:

Consider this . . .

Accompanying the NGSS is a document that identifies essential science and engineering practices for student learning. These practices are the following:

1. Asking questions (for science) and defining problems (for engineering)

2. Developing and using models

3. Planning and carrying out investigations

4. Analyzing and interpreting data

5. Using mathematical and computational thinking

6. Constructing explanations (for science) and designing solutions (for engineering)

7. Engaging in argument from evidence

8. Obtaining, evaluating, and communicating information (NGSS, 2013)

What role does language play in these essential practices? How can ELLs engage in these essential practices when they are in the early stages of language learning?

Wait time—The teacher waits from five to seven seconds after asking a question.

Repetition—The teacher repeats and may expand on a student's utterance.

Recasting—The teacher provides needed academic vocabulary.

Reformulation—The teacher models the necessary academic language.

Prompting—To address a need for a student reformulation, the teacher provides opportunities for the students to restate using academic language. (Levine & McCloskey, 2013, p. 104)

The discussion above paints with broad strokes a few aspects of this unit. In the next section we explore selected aspects of the language of science textbooks. While science textbooks should not be the only source of information for students in the science classroom, unfortunately in many classrooms, this is the case. It is important that both teachers and students be aware of the language demands posed by the language of science in textbooks.

The Language of Science Textbooks

Using the language of science (Lemke, 1990) is essential to the process of doing science. Students cannot conduct experiments, write their lab reports, or understand a film on genetics if they cannot use the appropriate terminology and grammatical structures that characterize the language of science. Much of the language in science classrooms and labs is used to describe natural phenomena, formulate hypotheses, propose alternate solutions, infer processes, gather and interpret data, and generalize, summarize, and report findings (Egbert & Ernst-Slavit, 2010).

Science textbooks are important sources of information for students. However, and as discussed earlier (see, for example, Chapter 2), scientific texts often present challenges to inexperienced and struggling readers. Science textbooks tend to include a variety of diagrams, illustrations, charts, tables, maps, headings, figures, photographs, and numbers. This variety of texts and illustrations requires that students not only know how to decode words but also be versed in additional literacies, such as the visual and mathematical. In Figure 4.9, we summarize work by de Oliveira (2010) regarding the language demands that science textbooks can pose for all students, but particularly for ELLs.

In general, the language of science is characterized by abstraction of reasoning, precision of expression, conciseness achieved by avoiding redundancy, and avoidance of personal opinions and relations. This kind

Figure 4.9   Linguistic Challenges Found in Science Textbooks

Technical terms and their definitions	Technical terms appear throughout science textbooks and are often set in bold or are highlighted. Definitions are sometimes difficult to find or may use complex language difficult for students to understand.
Conjunctions with specific roles	Conjunctions, such as *or,* may have multiple, specific meanings in science and all may occur within a few paragraphs. For example, *or* can introduce an explanation or paraphrase (e.g., "the moon lies on a straight line from Earth to or through the Sun") or a more abstract term (e.g., "the Moon's orbit is inclined or tilted at more than 5 degrees to Earth's orbit around the Sun").
Everyday questions and terms with specialized meanings	In many science texts, paragraphs begin with colloquial, informal questions but continue to provide the answers with highly technical language. Everyday words that have specialized meanings may appear repeatedly and confuse students who may know only the everyday meaning.
Zigzag patterning	Words are introduced, and then they are either repeated or are referred to within the passage. However pronouns are used in reference to some of those nouns, creating confusion for readers.

Source: Adapted from de Oliveira, 2010, and de Oliveira & Dodds, 2010

of abstraction and conciseness is clearly evident in one important scientific task: the creation of categories and taxonomies that represent conceptual relationships, often represented with one or few words. Lev Vygotsky (e.g., 1978) posited that the classification systems of the sciences represent abstract ways of thinking not captured with everyday language. Many terms used in scientific texts represent a construct packed with information. For example, let's explore the taxonomic hierarchy of the domestic cat.

Kingdom	Animalia
Phylum	Chordata
Class	Mammalia
Order	Carnivora
Family	Felidae
Genus	*Felis*
Species	*Felis catus Linnaeus*

Drawing of cat by Arthur Slavit

While many of these terms have Latin origins and may not be too difficult to memorize, each of these levels of the taxonomy and terms represents a very distinct category involving many years of research and classification. This form of taxonomic reasoning is pervasive in the sciences and requires abstract reasoning. When students encounter one of the terms from the list above, they need to infer the multiple and nested relationships from the term (Lee & Spratley, 2010).

In the next section we explore the features of academic language in social studies, a content area that includes a variety of disciplinary content.

EXPLORING ACADEMIC LANGUAGE IN A SOCIAL STUDIES CLASS

The content area of social studies is multidisciplinary and draws from history, anthropology, sociology, political science, economics, psychology, geography, religious studies, and civics. Because of the heavy emphasis on US history and geography in the early grades, social studies content can be particularly demanding for ELLs. Joy Egbert and Gisela Ernst-Slavit (2010) discuss selected challenges posed by conceptual and linguistic aspects of social studies content for these students; these are listed in Figure 4.10.

The Specialized Language of Social Studies Texts

A cursory look at the current social studies standards framework, the CCSS for English language arts (Grades 6-12 Literacy in history/social studies), current curricula, and recently published social studies textbooks reveals a clear emphasis on academic language use. If we couple this focus on academic language with the challenges posed by social studies content, we can surmise that academic language also involves cultural knowledge, "ways of being in the world" (Egbert & Ernst-Slavit, 2010, p. 11). This cultural knowledge is manifested in terms of disciplinary content as well as the manner in which the language of the materials and activities is constructed and organized. Additionally, the sociocultural contexts and historical perspectives of social studies are quite different from those of other content areas.

Discourse Level

During social studies, students are exposed to a variety of texts, each with a different set of discourse features. For example, when accessing primary sources such as historical documents, diaries, political cartoons, photographs, and letters, students encounter a variety of distinct organizational

Figure 4.10 Potential Challenges for ELLs in Social Studies Classrooms

Potential Issue	Explanation
Content may be new.	Concepts such as *democracy, taxation, freedom,* and *liberty,* among many others, may be new for students coming from nations with different types of governments (e.g., dictatorships) and political stances (e.g., communism).
Content suggests different worldviews.	The perspectives and values presented in public school curricula and textbooks may be very different from those held by ELLs' families and nations.
Topics are abstract and language dependent.	Many concepts are abstract (e.g., *justice, civil rights, individual rights*), and cognitively complex (King George III is to monarchy as Andrew Jackson is to democracy), which require students to depend on reading and listening.
The field of social studies relies on extensive background knowledge.	The lack of prior exposure to the elementary or middle school curriculum makes it difficult for ELLs to keep up with current content while trying to catch up with several years of social studies curricula.
History is generally presented in a linear manner and from an Anglocentric perspective.	For students coming from educational systems where history is learned in a circular manner around selected dynasties or historical periods, the linear approach might be confusing and the nuances implicit in events in US history incomprehensible.
Cultural differences may impede full participation of students.	These differences may preclude ELLs from asking questions of the teacher, stating their opinion, or providing a critical perspective. Participating in cooperative groups may be seen as not useful, since students may be accustomed to listening to teacher lectures and learning content through rote memorization.
Maps indicate different political constructions.	Issues of nationalistic and cultural focus can emerge when studying maps (e.g., most countries have their territory at the center of the world map).

Source: Adapted from Egbert & Ernst-Slavit, 2010, pp. 159–160

and linguistic features, including text organization, cohesion, voice, and complex and dense text, among others. Clearly, this kind of text variety challenges all students as they engage with new and cognitively complex language and contexts. Figure 4.11 presents a variety of social studies text types or genres that students have to process and produce in the social studies classroom.

Figure 4.11 Text Types Typical of Social Studies Classrooms

biographies	charts and tables	diagrams
digital maps	editorials	essays
historical arguments	journals	media analyses
personal accounts	photo essays	scenarios
theses	timelines	travelogues

In social studies classrooms, discourse extends to the use of primary sources. The examination of primary sources in social studies is beneficial because it gives students opportunities not only to study history but also to become anthropologists and historians as they analyze, for example, artifacts, photos, recordings, authentic documents, and transcripts of interviews (Mason & Ernst-Slavit, 2010). In this regard, 20th century history can easily be studied via the use of smartphones, tablets, and personal computers. In terms of language development, exposure to and analysis of primary sources, such as oral history interviews, video memoirs, and face-to-face interviews, helps students correlate written and spoken language, see spelling and sentence construction, and listen to content language as it is used by different speakers in meaningful ways. The use of primary sources also helps students learn many aspects of oral interaction, such as how to ask meaningful questions, how to provide short or long answers, and how to draw conclusions based on individual or collective narratives.

Sentence and Word Levels

At the sentence level, features pervasive in social studies textbooks and materials include the passive voice, and abundant dependent clauses or multiple clauses that connect series of facts, ideas, and concepts in one long sentence. Learning to construct well-designed and meaningful sentences matched to a specific purpose can be difficult.

As discussed in Chapter 1, students need opportunities to construct sentences orally, even if only using everyday language. The following vignette shows how a teacher scaffolds students' language as they are learning to construct meaningful sentences using the word *migration* to describe personal trajectories. The teachers' deliberate and systematic efforts in this area prepare students to move along the mode continuum (Gibbons, 2009), where they can engage in oral conversations and produce academic text around the topic.

In their study of a social studies fourth grade unit on 19th century westward migration to the Pacific Northwest, Ernst-Slavit and New (2013) observed how Mrs. Piaf, the classroom teacher, consistently scaffolds students' oral construction of sentences as they are using their newly acquired concept of migration. In the following segment, we hear Mrs. Piaf having a lively conversation with her 26 students, including six ELLs, four students receiving learning support, and two homeless students. While students are sitting on the carpet, and after they have discussed with a partner the last time their families moved, they engage in the following dialog.

56 T	You're . . . you can talk about this. Talk about
57	when you did it last summer.
58 Sarah	Okay, so, I migrated cause I was in Old Town and we moved to
59	New Town.
60 T	Okay. So how can you use that in a sentence?
61 Sarah	Uh . . . let's see. I migrated to [from] Old Town to New Town over . . .
62	the summer.
63 T	Okay. Did you do it by yourself?
64 Sarah	With my family.
65 T	Okay, so put that in your sentence.
66 Sarah	I migrated with my family to New Town through the
67	summer.
68 T	From . . .
69 Sarah	Yeah, from Old Town.
70 T	From Old Town over the summer. Okay. Kevin . . .

The class had previously discussed that the use of the word *migration* required three key components: the act of relocating (lines 56–57), a location (line 60), and a group of people (line 63). On those instances, Mrs. Piaf, explicitly directs Sarah to use all three pieces of information in her sentence, helping her to produce a clear and precise statement showing the meaning of *migrate*. After her interaction with Sarah, Mrs. Piaf turns to Kevin and encourages him to produce his sentence and share it with a partner, and she asks the whole classroom to do the same.

This kind of interaction, fairly common in Mrs. Piaf's classroom, offers an interesting insight into the teaching and learning of academic language.

The propensity of many educators is to focus solely on vocabulary, or the word level of academic language. However, the dialog above exemplifies the importance of sentence level development within academic language (New, 2013). In addition, Mrs. Piaf is not only modeling how to put a sentence together in relation to the concept of migration, she is explicitly teaching students to be "hyperclear" (Zwiers, 2008, p. 30) in their production of the English language. Last, but of utmost importance, she is connecting the concept of migration with students' own experiences.

Effective Instruction in Content Classrooms Around a Unit of Learning

When we share examples like this one in our teaching or professional learning efforts, a question we are often asked is, "What does effective instruction look like in such diverse classrooms with students with so many different needs?" While there is not a bulletproof recipe for effective teaching, one common characteristic across classrooms where all students enjoy academic success is differentiated content and language instruction. However, a precursor to successful instruction includes identifying the needs and strengths of the students, reviewing both content and language proficiency/development standards, identifying the linguistic demands (that is, academic language) within the unit, and developing content and language targets for the unit. (For a more complete discussion of preparation for successful instruction, see Chapter 5.)

For example, consider how National Board Certified veteran teacher Marcy March plans for her social studies unit on civil rights, biographies, and the Southeast region in her fourth grade classroom in the Midwest (Silvers, Shorey, Eliopoulos, & Akiyoshi, 2014). After going through the above steps, she maintains her instructional focus on the intended outcomes of the unit. While she has one overall target for content and one for language, shown below, she also knows that later she will divide these targets into differentiated lesson objectives as the unit progresses.

Content Target for Students:	Students will understand the attributes of democracy and the significance of the people who were leaders in the civil rights movement.
Language Target for Students:	Students will discuss biographies and describe details of important people and connected events.

Taken together, the content and language targets complement each other to represent the focal points of the unit. While the content target relates to the "big idea," or "essential understanding" of the unit, the language target reflects the language function or communicative purpose that best fits the concept for all learners (Gottlieb & Ernst-Slavit, 2013).

In today's diverse classrooms, an important next step is to set realistic and differentiated expectations from lesson to lesson that will challenge and yet engage all students in learning. While differentiated content objectives provide different paths to acquiring the skills and concepts named or implied in grade-level content standards, differentiated language objectives provide ELLs, in particular, specific options for accessing and achieving grade-level content for their current levels of English language proficiency. Keeping this in mind, Ms. March outlines a set of differentiated oral language and literacy objectives for her students. Figure 4.12 provides a detailed account of those objectives by the students' English language proficiency levels.

With these sets of content and language targets and differentiated language and content objectives in hand, Ms. March and her students continue working on this rich unit about civil rights, biographies, and the Southeast

Figure 4.12 Differentiated Oral Language and Literacy Objectives

All students, including recently reclassified and soon to be reclassified ELLs (proficient in English)	• Use content vocabulary, expressions, sentences, and discourse to describe concepts, events, ideas, and famous people. • Use comparative and analytical language. • Use adjectives to describe events, people, and ideas. • Make personal connections to themes, issues, and concepts.
Intermediate ELLs with growing English language proficiency (ELP Levels 3–4)	• Recognize and use some content vocabulary, expressions, and sentences to describe important events. • Use comparative language. • Use descriptive language for people, events, and ideas. • Make personal connections to events, people, and concepts.
Beginning ELLs with minimal English language proficiency (ELP Levels 1–2)	• Recognize and use some content vocabulary and expressions, or draw some content information. • Identify names of people, places, and ideas (e.g., marching, bus). • Use visuals to compare people and events. • Show connections visually, through drama, or with a few words in English.

Source: Silvers, Shorey, Eliopoulos, & Akiyoshi, 2014, p. 104

region. Through inquiry and collaborative work, students learn to use language tools and process information from a variety of sources (i.e., visual, digital, and print). Ultimately, with scaffolding and support from teachers, materials, and tools, students in this classroom were able to adopt a critical but caring perspective about the world that surrounds them.

FOR FURTHER THINKING . . .

In spite of its ubiquitousness in schools, academic language can be invisible or misunderstood. Just as we forget that buildings and houses lie on top of a well-designed and solid foundation, we sometimes overlook the role that academic language plays in supporting students' content area learning. If we consider only vocabulary, we are only providing a shallow foundation that might not support the kind of academic tower that students will need to be successful throughout their schooling and beyond. Providing a deep and well-planned foundation of academic language that considers its multiple dimensions will allow students to reach disciplinary skyscraper-like success.

One important goal of this chapter was to make visible the role that academic language plays in student learning throughout the school day. Academic language is the foundation needed by all students to be successful in content area learning. This register, found throughout different classrooms and spaces in schools, includes typical disciplinary discourse (e.g., lab reports, essays, word problems, timelines), application of rhetorical conventions and devices at the sentence level (e.g., compare and contrast), and discipline-specific vocabulary, phrases, and expressions. While the extent of academic language used throughout the day by teachers and students, as seen in these brief vignettes, is diverse and ample, so are the different skills and prior knowledge that students may bring to the learning situation. Building upon what students bring and making connections to their home languages and cultures contribute to solidifying the structures for academic success.

As you reflect on this chapter, the following issues and questions might be helpful to consider:

1. In the social studies classroom, many of the topics and concepts are new to ELLs. As you plan a new unit or discuss a lesson for your content area, consider what topics and concepts might be unknown to students who did not grow up in the United States. What are some activities you can design or strategies you can use to make these topics more accessible?

2. Jeff Zwiers (2008) highlights the role of academic language in the talk, texts, tasks, and tests used in the content area classroom. One useful exercise is to analyze the language we use during content area instruction. For that purpose, divide a sheet of paper in four and label each fourth with one the four categories listed above. Then analyze all the materials you plan to use for a lesson along with instructional and assessment tasks. List all those instances in which academic language is used or needed in the pertinent quadrant. What can you deduce from this exercise?

3. As teachers or future teachers, how are you using academic language at school? What specific, deliberate efforts are you making to help students learn academic language beyond academic vocabulary?

4. In a given content area, what are some specific sentence level grammatical structures that students encounter as they read diverse texts or produce different writing pieces?

5. Have you ever shadowed an ELL? One useful exercise in teacher education classes is to have preservice teachers spend one day shadowing or following an ELL. While observers should try to be inconspicuous, the goal of this activity is to observe the kinds of linguistic demands encountered throughout the school day, including lunch and PE.

5

How Can Academic Language Be Integrated Into Instruction and Assessment?

Children must be taught how to think, not what to think.

—Margaret Mead

Language is the medium for thinking and doing; while in school, language is the medium of instruction and assessment. As academic language use crosses all disciplines, it only makes sense that utilizing this shared space between content and language encourages students to engage in higher order thinking and learning. Discourse, sentences, and word/phrases are the building blocks of academic language that vary according to the socio-cultural context and situation of language use, or in the case of schools, in each and every classroom.

In the previous chapter we saw how academic language use is ever present in school across all the content areas. This chapter focuses on becoming aware of academic language use in instruction and assessment in classrooms filled with linguistically and culturally diverse students.

MAINTAINING A FOCUS ON ACADEMIC LANGUAGE: A HISTORICAL PERSPECTIVE

It seems logical that academic language use has always been central to language education, but that has not always been the case. Language education has generally followed the trends from the fields of linguistics and psychology. Behaviorism of the late 1950s, marked by stimulus–response and memorization followed by recitation of rote dialogs, gave way to the view of language as a system of rule-governed structures that were hierarchically arranged and taught in isolation. Subsequently, structuralism of the 1960s had a strong grammatical base, where control over structures was primary, and forms were generally memorized. Noam Chomsky took this notion further by investigating the deep structure of language, while psychologists began to examine the affective and interpersonal nature of learning. With communicative competence theory of the 1970s and 1980s, the emphasis of language teaching and learning shifted to meaning as the center for interactive communication in authentic contexts (Brown, 2007).

Since the early 1990s, the literature in language education has been sensitive to content derived from language and from topics or tasks from subject matter classes. Largely known as content-based instruction, this methodology has applied to "foreign" language, bilingual immersion, and English as a second language education (Crandall & Tucker, 1990). Fred Genesee (1994) stated that content "can include any topic, theme or non-language issue of interest or importance to the learners," (p. 3) while Miriam Met (1999) proposed that "'content' in content-based instruction represents material that is cognitively engaging and demanding for the learner" (p. 150). The rationale behind this approach is that postponing content instruction until students reach a threshold of academic language (in English) is impractical and does not serve the complex needs of language learners (Grabe & Stoller, 1997). Consequently, the ultimate goal of content-based instruction is for students to simultaneously acquire subject matter concepts and proficiency in English when it is the medium of instruction.

The tenets of content-based instruction within language education circles have spurred several offshoots that have been applied to multiple contexts in the last 20 years. Within the K–12 educational setting, the principles behind content-based instruction still hold; however, the content is now directly related to content standards, while language is scaffolded according to levels of language proficiency as represented by language proficiency/development standards. Within this content-driven paradigm, another purpose for language use, with roots in social psychology, emphasizes language for social action, that is, use of language as a tool for problem solving and getting things done (Holtgraves, 2002).

Generally speaking there are two instructional pathways that interweave content and language teaching. The subtle distinctions between content-based instruction and language-based instruction reflect the changing roles of general education teachers and language teachers in relation to their language learners. Figure 5.1 outlines these nuances.

There are a variety of effective instructional practices that integrate content with academic language, just as there are eclectic views of language learning. However, there is general agreement that when it comes to instruction and assessment, students are to

1. Be exposed to and interact with academic language through stimulating content.

2. Use academic language that is embedded within discourse rather than language that is presented in isolated fragments.

3. Process and produce complex information through listening, speaking, reading, and writing applied to real-life situations.

4. Explore content of interest and cultural relevance while they engage in language-related activities.

And the units of learning that constitute curriculum should

5. Center on a theme or issue that is language rich.

6. Accentuate the linguistic and cultural resources of students, acknowledging and incorporating their unique perspectives and experiences.

7. Encourage students to build their metalinguistic and metacognitive awareness as a means to make greater connections with language and their prior knowledge.

Figure 5.1 Differences Between a Content-Based and a Language-Based Focus for Instruction

Content-Based Focus for Instruction	Language-Based Focus for Instruction
• Content is taught through language. • Content learning is primary. • Language is the medium for content learning. • Assessment centers on skills and conceptual understanding (academic achievement).	• Language is taught through content. • Language learning is primary. • Content provides the context for language learning. • Assessment centers on language use within sociocultural contexts (academic language proficiency).

With these tenets in mind, it's time to see how to plan and implement a unit of learning.

PLANNING A UNIT OF LEARNING AROUND ACADEMIC LANGUAGE USE

Planning a unit of learning takes time, thought, and energy; it is best accomplished when teachers can collaborate by partnering or participating in professional learning teams. The design of a unit of instruction using a Curricular Framework (see Chapter 6) should revolve around effective teaching practices. Above all, this means that curricular content be geared toward having students engage in higher order thinking (Gibbons, 2009). Consistent research findings identify key features of instruction likely to result in improved student learning; these include the following:

- Clear goals (targets) and objectives
- Appropriate and challenging material
- Well-designed instruction and instructional routines
- Clear input and modeling
- Active student engagement and participation
- Informative feedback to learners
- Application of new learning and transfer to new situations
- Practice and periodic review
- Structured, focused interactions with other students
- Frequent assessments, with re-teaching as needed
- Well-established classroom routines and behavior norms (Goldenberg, 2012, p. 40)

Effective research-based practices for English language learners (ELLs) are far reaching and are much more language centered. Over and above effective teaching for all students, ELLs benefit from having

1. additional instructional supports, such as visuals and graphics, to ensure comprehensibility of grade-level material,

2. ample opportunities for classroom interaction with English-proficient students and adult models to develop and enhance their English language proficiency, and

3. use of their home language to clarify and extend their conceptual understanding.

In summary, academic language is vital to content area instruction; however, ELLs must also have the necessary oral and written language to discuss, explain, and argue academic content (Coleman & Goldenberg, 2012).

In the series Academic Language in Diverse Classrooms, we witness these effective practices being enacted in classrooms around the United States, from California, Connecticut, Florida, Georgia, Illinois, Kentucky, Massachusetts, New Mexico, Oregon, Texas, Utah, Virginia, and Washington to American Samoa. In planning a unit of learning, we find synergy in teacher partnerships. There are many different configurations of teachers working together, such as language teachers cooperating with content teachers, researchers or instructional coaches guiding classroom teachers, teachers and media experts contributing to grade-level teams, and teachers with support of school leaders participating in professional learning communities.

> **Consider this . . .**
>
> Every school has its own culture and a unique combination of school leaders, coaches, teachers, and paraprofessionals. What are the defining structures of educators in your school, and who are the participants? How might you tap the expertise of educators in different ways to maximize educational opportunities for students?

Student and teacher diversity varies enormously from classroom to classroom and school to school. In a second-grade dual language setting, Karina and Irma team teach, sharing languages, cultures, and 40 students between their two classrooms. In fourth grade, a classroom teacher partners with a language specialist and the school librarian to provide the students with rich language and literacy experiences for their multidisciplinary units. In a newcomer academy, a fifth grade teacher is constantly thinking of ways for her multicultural students from 13 different countries to interact and share experiences in learning. When teachers have the opportunity to contribute to the design and implementation of curriculum, they become vested in the process and can also focus on the academic language needs of their students. Likewise, when the school culture is one of diversity, it reflects the students' and community's linguistic and cultural resources.

Capitalizing on Linguistic and Cultural Resources

Research on language use in homes and communities, such as that of Shirley Brice Heath (1983) and Gordon Wells (2009), points to the variability in the ways children and families use language. When coming to school and assuming their roles as students, these children must reconcile how to make sense of their experiences revolving around their cultures and communities, often using a new register. At the same time, teachers must be responsive to the fact that students have varied language repertoires. In addition, teachers, by embracing the rich linguistic and cultural resources of the communities in which the schools are located, help students feel that school is an extension of their homes. This fluidity between home and school perhaps can lead to more expansive academic language use in English and the home language. With teachers, students, and family members working together toward a unified goal of increased achievement inside and outside of school, together we can raise a new generation of culturally competent, distinguished, and academically astute individuals.

One set of strategies to promote academic language use in classrooms is to examine the home–school connection. A striking example of establishing home–school relations is one used by the kindergarten teacher who makes home visits to each and every family of her students. The practice of making home visits, which has been adopted by all teachers throughout the school, helps build grade-level teams and gives teachers a collective sense of shared personal and cultural knowledge to better meet the students' individual needs. It also provides teachers with vital background knowledge of the family histories and traditions that the students bring to school and the classroom. Equally important, the home visits foster a sense of trust between the teachers and the families (Cardenas, Jones, & Lozano, 2014).

Another way of highlighting the language of school is by having students extend their academic experiences through field trips. A first grade mathematics classroom, for example, takes their base-10 thinking to the local corn tortilla factory. As the entire school population is of Mexican descent, the surrounding community is a reservoir of Latino culture. Before the visit, the teacher poses the problem, "How many tortillas are necessary to make breakfast burritos for the kindergarten and first grade classes?" The students soon discover that tortillas come in packages of 10 or 100! Upon their return to the classroom, the students are better able to visualize base-10 thinking, apply it to solving problems, and explain their reasoning (Celedón-Pattichis & Musanti, 2013).

Yet one more strategy that utilizes the students' linguistic and cultural resources is seen in a fifth grade classroom studying ocean ecology. To involve the multicultural families of the students in the study of marine organisms and build background for the unit, the teacher prepares students to conduct an interview using sentence frames. The students then collect information from their family members in English or their home language on the types of seafood commonly eaten in their homes. The pride of the students is evident when they bring in their lists of seafood to school and share the cultural information. The teacher herself is surprised to discover that many of her ELLs, including students representing Indian, Burmese, Congolese, and Bosnian cultures, eat a wide range of seafood—a most personalized entrée into the unit (McCloskey & New Levine, 2014).

Deciding on a Theme for a Unit of Learning

Themes for instructional units might revolve around issues to examine, questions to explore, problems to resolve, or investigations to undertake. When students are involved in the selection of themes, their personalized interests are a motivator for them to learn. Inquiry and communication are activated for students in their desire to pursue the topic, and the classroom is ripe to become a community of learners. Teaching language through content around organized themes helps older ELLs develop the academic register of English in conjunction with academic content knowledge (Freeman & Freeman, 2002). A shared responsibility for teaching and learning emerges from the process of classrooms working within mutually agreed upon themes.

Themes may be multidisciplinary and comprehensive in scope, lasting an entire semester, such as elementary students studying "change" in every content area. At other times, themes may be interdisciplinary, spreading across language arts and science, for example, as in the pairing of literature and informational texts in the study of ecosystems. Themes may also be limited in scope, covering a specific topic within a single subject area, such as in an in-depth study of a work of Edgar Allen Poe.

Consider this . . .

Does your grade or department, if you work in teams, or do you personally have opportunities to select or modify themes for units of learning? Do students have a voice in the decision? Which type of themes is your preference—ones that are comprehensive, inclusive of multiple content areas, or those narrower in scope, confined to a single discipline?

Matching the Theme to Standards

In analyzing content standards, teachers need to identify the major concepts and skills to be taught, or, given a theme, teachers can then select the applicable standards. For each of the concepts, there are generally academic language functions that spell out how the students are to show what they understand and are able to do; for example, are they expected to be able to explain a process or argue a stance and support their claims?

Likewise, for the same theme, corresponding language development/ proficiency standards offer ways in which students can scaffold academic language to access grade-level content and participate in learning.

In a second grade classroom, the students and teacher brainstorm mathematical themes. Students have brought in coins from around the world, and the class now has a collection of pesos, reales, birrs, rupees, won, yuan, and dollars. Together the class thinks it might be a great idea to learn more about money from around the world and then to set up a classroom store to exchange goods. Building on the students' enthusiasm, the teacher searches the Common Core State Standards (CCSSI, 2010b) for mathematics and discovers, under Measurement and Data, that there is an apt second grade standard: "Solve word problems involving dollar bills, quarters, dimes, nickels, and pennies, using $ and ¢ symbols appropriately" (p. 20). She is also aware that with her growing number of linguistically and culturally diverse students, it is important to include the CCSS for English language arts for Speaking and Listening, Comprehension and Collaboration, where students "participate in collaborative conversations with diverse partners about grade 2 topics and texts with peers and adults in small and larger groups" (p. 23).

The next step in her unit planning is finding the corresponding language development/proficiency standards for the identified content standards so that integration of content and language can occur seamlessly during instruction. The teacher resides in a state that belongs to World-Class Instructional Design and Assessment (WIDA), and through professional learning, she has become familiar with WIDA's English language development (ELD) standards. Browsing through WIDA's standards document, she notices that the example topic for the Complementary Strand for Grade 1, the Language of Humanities, is multiculturalism—a natural fit for her multicultural group. In the standards matrix, the content Connection, taken from the Alaska Standards for Culturally Responsive Students (http://education.alaska.gov/ standards/pdf/cultural_standards.pdf), states that students will "acquire insights from other cultures without diminishing the integrity of their own" and "determine how ideas and concepts from one knowledge system relate to those derived from other knowledge systems." (p. 57). It would be easy (and fun) to ramp up the strand to fit into the second grade unit.

Furthermore, WIDA's Grade 2 English language development (ELD) Standard 3, the Language of Mathematics, has a perfect illustrative example that extends the theme of money across levels of English language proficiency. In fact, the identical Measurement and Data standard from the CCSS for mathematics is listed as the Connection! The reading matrix representing the ELD standard is shown in Figure 5.2. (Note how the Connection ties the concepts of the CCSS for mathematics standard to

Figure 5.2   A Representation of WIDA's ELD Standard 3, the Language of Mathematics, for the Example Topic Money

CONNECTION: Common Core Standards for Mathematics, Measurement and Data #8 (Grade 2): *Solve word problems involving dollar bills, quarters, dimes, nickels, and pennies, using $ and ¢ symbols appropriately.*

EXAMPLE CONTEXT FOR LANGUAGE USE: Students act out real-life mathematics scenarios related to money (e.g., to make purchases in a classroom store)

COGNITIVE FUNCTION: Students at all levels of English language proficiency will ANALYZE text of word problems.

	Level 1 Entering	Level 2 Emerging	Level 3 Developing	Level 4 Expanding	Level 5 Bridging	
READING	Match words and phrases (e.g., "more than," "less than," "take away") involving money and value to operations (e. g., +, –) using illustrated word cards and realia with a partner	Find words and phrases involving money and value from illustrated text using realia with a partner	Sequence sentences to decide how to solve word problems involving money and value using realia with a partner	Locate clues for solving problems involving money and value from simplified text (e. g., written in present tense with familiar contexts) using realia with a partner	Categorize word problems (e.g., by addition or subtraction) involving money and value using realia	**Level 6 - Reaching**

TOPIC-RELATED LANGUAGE: Students at all levels of English language proficiency interact with grade-level words and expressions, such as: total, enough, cost, change, left over, solve.

Source: WIDA, 2012, p. 60

possible ways of scaffolding the associated language across the five language proficiency levels.)

ACADEMIC LANGUAGE USE IN LEARNING TARGETS AND DIFFERENTIATED OBJECTIVES

The sociocultural context for learning built around the students' experiences, languages, and cultures needs to be part of the instructional planning process. Within a unit's multidisciplinary theme or subject-area topic, there should be a place for the students' interests and their prior experiences, with plenty of room for students to grow. At the same time, the theme should lend itself to both content and language standards.

In the design of curricular units of learning, as illustrated in the *Academic Language* series, the overall expectations for all students are expressed in content and language targets. Content and language targets serve as the "North Star," guiding the unit. For instruction, targets are broken down into differentiated content and language objectives that apply to a related set of lessons and particular groups of students. Figure 5.3 shows the hierarchical relationship among standards, learning targets, and differentiated objectives.

> **Consider this . . .**
>
> Why is the academic language present in standards important for all students? How might English language development/proficiency standards bolster or strengthen content standards, in particular the CCSS, for students in terms of their understanding and use of academic language?

Infusing Academic Language Into Unit Targets and Differentiated Lesson Objectives

We should remember that learning targets are intended for all students and extend across the entire unit, while objectives are differentiated for specific groups of students on a lesson-by-lesson basis. In formulating content and language targets, teachers have to delve into standards to identify

Figure 5.3 Connecting Curriculum and Instruction: From a Unit's Theme to a Lesson's Differentiated Objectives

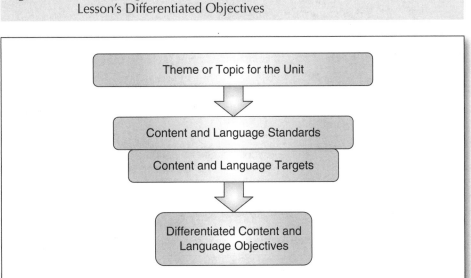

pertinent genres, sentence structures, phrases, and words for a given discourse. The targets, when broken down into differentiated objectives, provide concrete ways for informing instruction. Figure 5.4 shows how content and language standards might translate into corresponding targets, and subsequently, differentiated content and language objectives. This example is taken from a fourth grade mathematics unit on fractions where students are working with the discourses related to recipes and story problems.

The example targets and differentiated objectives that pertain to fractions give us an idea of the similarities and differences among the features

Figure 5.4 A Fourth Grade Example of Content and Language Targets Along With Differentiated Objectives for a Theme on Fractions

Content Target	Differentiated Content Objectives
All students will solve and explain mathematical problems involving fractional parts.	Students with conceptual understanding will • Represent fractions with creative examples. • Do mental math when multiplying fractions. • Determine equivalency of fractions using sports or other analogies. Students challenged by the concepts and skills will • Represent fractions relying on physical models. • Construct multiple fractions using realia or manipulatives. • Determine equivalency of fractions referencing the analogy (of the model).
Language Target	Differentiated Language Objectives
All students will describe and compare the use of fractions in a variety of situations.	Intermediate ELLs will • Use descriptive words, phrases, and modeled sentences to describe fractions. • Use comparative terms, such as *greater than 1* and *smallest common denominator,* to identify fractions. • Use sequential terms to describe steps of cooking recipes using a graphic organizer. Beginning ELLs will • Reproduce words and phrases from the math word/ phrase wall to describe fractions. • Distinguish between *bigger than* and *smaller than* to compare visually supported fractions. • Show basic steps of cooking recipes involving fractions using visuals.

Source: Ernst-Slavit, Gottlieb, & Slavit, 2013, pp. 92, 98, 99

of these two curricular components. Figure 5.5 compares and contrasts the uses of unit targets and differentiated objectives for related lessons in planning instruction and assessment.

INSTRUCTIONAL ACTIVITIES AND TASKS

A rich curriculum consists of real-life activities and tasks that offer multiple opportunities for students to actively participate, think, and express themselves in creative ways. Authentic tasks and activities should involve interaction among different configurations of

Consider this . . .

Learning targets and differentiated objectives provide distinct ways to organize curriculum and instruction. What is the contribution of each to curricular and instructional planning? In particular, how might you share or create content and language targets with grade-level teams of teachers?

Figure 5.5 Comparing and Contrasting Learning Targets and Differentiated Objectives

Both Learning Targets and Differentiated Objectives

- Help provide a sociocultural context for learning
- Offer ways to organize lessons and units for learning
- Provide a means for monitoring student progress
- Inform teachers of curricular scope and sequence
- Invite collaboration between content and language teachers

Content and Language Targets	*Differentiated Content and Language Objectives*
Relate to units of instruction	Relate to individual lessons or a series of related lessons
Represent content and language development standards	Represent conceptual understandings and skills along with communication of those understandings
Apply to all students	Differentiate students by academic performance and language proficiency levels
Match end-of-unit or summative assessment	Match formative assessment practices within lessons
Document student learning over time	Provide descriptive, criterion-referenced feedback to students on an ongoing basis

listening, speaking, reading, and writing that scaffold into a performance, product, or project. In participating in these tasks and activities, students should have opportunities to collaborate in collecting, organizing, analyzing, interpreting, and applying information to new or related situations.

Instructional tasks and activities should spur intellectual engagement of students. In fact, according to Pauline Gibbons (2009), there are seven intellectual practices that should characterize the curriculum:

1. Students engage with the key ideas and concepts of the discipline in ways that reflect how experts in the field think and reason.

2. Students transform what they have learned into a different form for use in a new context or for a different audience.

3. Students make links between concrete knowledge and abstract theoretical knowledge.

4. Students engage in substantive conversation.

5. Students make connections between the spoken and written language of the subject and other discipline-related ways of making meaning.

6. Students take a critical stance toward knowledge and information.

7. Students use metalanguage in the context of learning about other things. (pp. 21–29)

When students are able to see themselves within the sociocultural setting of the classroom, they become contributors to learning rather than recipients of teaching.

THE RELATIONSHIP BETWEEN ASSESSMENT AND INSTRUCTION

There is a close tie between assessment and instruction, so much so that at times it is difficult to distinguish between the two—hence the term *instructional assessment* (Gottlieb, 2006). Instructional assessment characterizes what happens in classrooms minute-by-minute, day-by-day. Sometimes assessment occurs spontaneously in a classroom between a single teacher and her group of students, such as the "teachable moment" based on students' understanding. At other times teachers pair up and engage in a thoughtful process of planning how to collect and interpret evidence of student performance within the instructional cycle and provide structured feedback to students. Instructional assessment can extend to common assessment when grade-level or professional learning teams agree upon the kind of documentation, such as a rubric, to interpret the end-of-unit product or project that they have planned together. These assessments, occurring at or building up to the culmination of a unit for learning, are embedded into and indistinguishable from real-world tasks in which students often partner or work in small groups to showcase their work. Many of these assessments tap relevant issues where students have time to think, defend their views, and later reflect on their learning. In doing so, students can demonstrate how they are acquiring and applying skills to succeed in school and in later life (Darling-Hammond, Ancess, & Falk, 1995).

The forms of assessment crafted by teachers are very much intertwined with instruction. In fact, when academic language use is the centerpiece of instruction, it naturally extends into assessment. Decisions based on instructional data rest with teachers who know their individual students best and are constantly making adjustments to their teaching based on individual student performance.

Two other forms of assessment are externally imposed upon teachers at either a district or a state level. They are not as closely connected to classrooms and everyday instruction, and they generally serve an accountability purpose rather than one for improving teaching and learning. Interim assessment generally is commercially developed and comes from the outside; it is administered at a school or district level three to four times a year. For the most part, these measures serve as practice tests or predictors of the annual standardized test. Standardized tests are either norm-referenced or criterion-referenced; they are the most secure, high-stakes state measures that are administered under strict, uniform conditions on an annual basis.

Each form of assessment is part of school life and provides insightful data into what students can do with content and language. With the current focus on grade-level rigor, sparked by both content and language standards, assessment is moving toward capturing students' processing and use of academic language. Figure 5.6 illustrates this assessment continuum.

Figure 5.6 The Placement of Forms of Assessment on a Continuum From Personalized Classroom Assessment to State Assessment

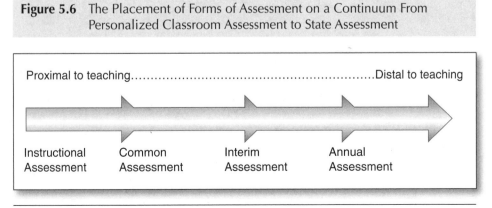

Source: Adapted with permission from Gottlieb, 2012b, p. 170

All assessment should provide information that is useful to students, the primary stakeholder, and teachers. In any assessment system, whether at a classroom, school, district, state, or consortium level, there should be a balance among data sources. Academic language use may be a unifying thread for student assessment, however, in reality, each form of assessment has a distinct purpose. Figure 5.7 identifies what is the primary purpose for each form, where it is implemented, and when it occurs. The first two rows of the figure encompass instructional assessment built into curricular frameworks; instructional assessment, including formative assessment practices, and common instructional assessment are most integral to the functioning of classrooms and teachers' understanding of student performance.

Placement of Assessment Within a Curricular Framework

Within a curricular framework instructional assessment prevails to focus on classrooms, their students, and their teachers. There are generally two

Figure 5.7 The Forms, Features, and Time Frames for Assessment

Form of Assessment	Primary Feature	Level of Implementation	Time Frame for Use
Instructional	Provides real-time descriptive feedback to students on their learning based on evidence that teachers collect and use to adjust instruction	Individual classrooms	Every day to weekly
Common Instructional	Provides teachers mutually agreed upon ways to collect, analyze, and use data to support content and language learning	Multiple classrooms	Monthly or the amount of time corresponding to the end of a unit
Interim	Provides teachers student-level data on student performance from an independent external source	Schools, programs, districts	Periodically, two to four times a year
Annual	Provides accountability data for student achievement and language proficiency	Districts, states, consortia	On a yearly basis

Source: Adapted with permission from Gottlieb, 2012b

schools of thought in regard to where and when assessment and instruction occur within curricular design. The first position is that assessment should precede instruction so that teachers are aware of an endpoint or goal for measurement; such is the case in Understanding by Design (Wiggins & McTighe, 2005). Assessment at the forefront of planning curriculum accentuates how student expectations are going to be measured. The second view is that instruction shapes assessment; thus instructional activities and tasks or even a final project determine how assessment should proceed. Figure 5.8 depicts the relationship between instruction and assessment acting independently, yet reliant on each other, or merged into a single construct.

Consider this . . .

What is the proportion of each form of assessment in your school or district? Using a pie chart, fill in the percent attributed to instructional, common instructional, interim, and annual assessment as it currently occurs in your setting. Now with a second pie chart, show how much each form of assessment contributes to your district's or state's accountability. Don't forget to include measures of both language proficiency and academic achievement in your estimation. Compare your pie charts, and explain the discrepancy in the proportion of each form of assessment.

Whichever perspective a state, district, or school takes, the end result is the same, that is, to measure and document the extent to which students are learning. To resolve this issue, we view the relationship between instruction and assessment as reciprocal.

Instructional assessment occurs within and across lessons within a unit of learning that has been designed by teachers. When measurement happens at the end of a unit, it is considered summative. It centers on ways in which students demonstrate their language learning and achievement that are directly in line with the unit's content and language targets, which

Figure 5.8 The Interaction Between Instruction and Assessment to Produce Instructional Assessment

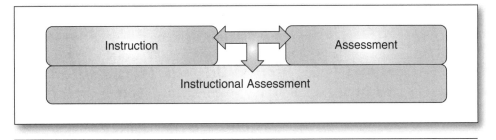

Source: Adapted from Gottlieb, 2012b, p. 170

in turn represent content and language development standards. Here are some ways in which teachers assess learning across related lessons.

Assessment Across Lessons of a Unit: Measuring Standards and Learning Targets

Instructional activities and tasks with multiple pathways for students to pursue go hand in hand with students having options to show what they understand and are able to do using their oral language and multiliteracies in a variety of formats and venues. These performances, accompanied by holistic or analytic rubrics and student self- or peer assessment, are usually given at the culmination of a series of lessons that fold into a unit's final project or product. Here are a couple of primary classrooms that show how young students can engage in scaffolded activities that lead to an end-of-unit task reflective of standards and learning targets.

In a first grade classroom, at the close of the unit of study on informational texts across content areas, students produce a written expository report on their individually selected animals. In addition the students create brochures that are displayed during their author celebration and shared with family members and reading buddies. The four-point analytic rubric that the teacher crafts to interpret the students' work is divided into a content and language side that matches the content and language targets; it is shown in a modified form in Figure 5.9.

As a culminating mathematics assessment, a second grade class goes on a treasure hunt around the school to integrate their content and language learning around odd and even numbers. On the content side, student pairs tally the number of designated objects and translate the findings onto an odd-even chart. Teams then add the results and cross check against another team. On the language side, students recount the route they took around the school and describe how they collected their data. After giving an oral summary, the students then explain how they arrive at their sums in writing (Silverstone & Zacarian, 2013).

Common Instructional Assessment

Common instructional assessment generally occurs at the end of a unit of learning and involves teachers as decision makers. Designed by teachers, whether in pairs, grade level teams, or professional learning communities, it is a performance, product, or project along with mutually agreed upon criteria for student success that is implemented uniformly across classrooms (Gottlieb, 2012a). With its close ties to curriculum and related standards, common instructional assessment lends authenticity, credibility, and validity to the inner workings of each grade or department. The systematic

Figure 5.9 An Example of a Grade 1 Project-Based Rubric for Language and Content Targets

Rubric Score	Language: Writing Development The student	Content: Knowledge and Skills The student
4	• Produced a paragraph of 3–5 cohesive sentences. • Used informational discourse to create extended written text.	• Identified vivid details about the animal. • Provided a description of the animal's habitat and why the animal survives there.
3	• Produced a paragraph of 2–3 sentences. • Used informational discourse to create written text.	• Identified key details about the animal. • Provided a description of the animal's habitat.
2	• Produced 1–2 related sentences. • Used limited informational language to create written text.	• Identified the animal with scant details. • Matched the animal to its habitat.
1	• Produced some phrases. • Used isolated words to relate informational discourse.	• Identified the animal. • Named an animal's habitat.

Source: Adapted from Mora-Flores, 2014, pp. 110–111

collection, analysis, and interpretation of relevant data help teachers who work together gain a collective sense of the achievement and the language proficiency of their students. Here are a couple of scenarios where common assessment has helped inform instruction.

In a dual immersion school, sixth grade partner teachers Claire and Eduardo, one using English as the medium of instruction and the other instructing in Spanish, joined forces in designing an oral language development rubric to be used in both classrooms and for both languages. The three-point scale provided criteria to interpret evidence of Early Advanced and Advanced students' oral language performance on various tasks. First, the rubric was used to assess pair work. It was also applied to the students' final oral report on explaining the challenges and processes in surface area calculation in the creation of their piñatas. In addition, the teachers used the same scale to compare the students' direct measurement and mathematical calculation of various lengths of geometric solids. It is reproduced as Figure 5.10.

In a middle school, an eighth grade English language arts team tried to capture the oral and written use of academic language for their heterogeneous group of students. They decided on having students collaborate in dyads or

Figure 5.10 A Sixth Grade Speaking Protocol for Early Advanced and Advanced Language Learners

Meeting Language Objectives (Include evidence from student's speech)	Consistently	More Often Than Not	Infrequently
Early Advanced: Explaining Use of regular and irregular verb forms in past tense, with declarative, complex, and compound sentences: *"We measured the sides of all the faces. As we measured, we wrote down the lengths."*			
Advanced: Explaining Use of regular and irregular verb forms, especially past tense, adverbs of manner: *"First, we measured the length around the middle of the sphere, in order to find the circumference."*			
Early Advanced: Comparing/ Contrasting Use of language involving comparative adjectives, varied sentence structures: *"Finding the length of each side of the pyramid was easy. But finding the area of each face was harder."*			
Advanced: Comparing/ Contrasting Use of language involving comparative adjectives with complex sentence structure and specific comparative language and contrasting words: *"For a sphere, using the tape measure to directly measure the radius was hard, because we couldn't cut the sphere in half. In contrast, using the formula to calculate the radius was a lot easier."*			

Source: Villagómez & Wenger, 2013, p. 59

triads in planning, drafting, revising, and editing a gothic short story based on their studying and dissecting of "The Cask of Amontillado," by Edgar Allan Poe. Some students elected a second choice, a multimedia presentation that summarized strategies that they had learned and applied throughout this five-week literature unit. Given the group's differing conceptual understandings and language proficiencies, the teacher team wanted the students to be able to select their preferred performance assessment to demonstrate their individual growth in oracy or literacy (Minaya-Rowe, 2014).

> **Consider this . . .**
>
> Does your grade, department, school, or district engage in common assessment? If so, does it measure content, language, or both? Have the unique characteristics of different groups of students, including ELLs, been considered in the design of the assessment and the interpretation of the results? What might you suggest to make common assessment more linguistically and culturally responsive?

There are benefits for teachers to collaborate in crafting and implementing curricular units, but what do individual teachers do from day to day to monitor student learning? The next section addresses how to interweave assessment within classroom instructional activities and tasks.

Assessment Within Lessons: Measuring Differentiated Objectives

As assessment within lessons is instructionally bound, it serves to support learning. Instructional assessment occurring on a daily basis is a continuous, ongoing cycle that occurs from the moment the students arrive until they slip an exit card of what they have learned on their way out the door. At times assessment within a lesson is a quick check, signaled by thumbs up, thumbs down by students, or a tale-telling expression on a student's face. Other times, instructional assessment is planned around the academic language contained in differentiated content and language objectives.

Clear descriptive feedback where students understand their performance in relation to criteria for success benefits learning by supporting student achievement and cognition (Moss & Brookhart, 2009). Figure 5.11 gives some suggestions for students to produce evidence for learning while learning and for teachers to provide constructive, not evaluative, feedback.

An umbrella term often used to describe a more intentional or planned assessment embedded in instruction with purposeful feedback to students and teachers within the confines of a classroom is *formative assessment practices*.

Figure 5.11 Ideas for Instructional Assessment Within Lessons

Students Produce Evidence Through	Teachers Elicit and Provide Feedback Through
• Learning logs • Interactive journals • Interactive learning walls • Exit cards or slips • Sticky notes or response cards • Academic conversations • Accountable talk • Visual displays of information • Graphic organizers • Partner feedback from peer assessment • Self-assessment checklists, rating scales, or other documentation of language and content learning	• Planned, open-ended questions asked of students • Criterion-related remarks in logs or journals • Observation checklists or rating scales • Anecdotal notes • Collaborative student structures • Interactive whiteboards • Observation with oral student feedback for language and content • Descriptive written feedback on learning logs or assignments • Student-led conferences on language and content learning

Formative Assessment Practices

Formative assessment is considered a subset of instructional assessment; it is a tricky term, as there are many interpretations and uses. Even among theorists and researchers there seems to be substantial divergence as to what constitutes its formative nature. Figure 5.12 points to the differing perspectives in regard to formative assessment.

What is undeniable about formative assessment strategies is that research confirms their value for improving teaching and learning, especially student learning outcomes for low achievers (Black & William, 1998). Overall, there are five robust principles for teachers to adhere to in implementing formative assessment practices:

1. Clarifying, sharing, and having learners understand learning intentions and success criteria

2. Eliciting evidence of learners' achievement

3. Providing specific feedback that moves learning forward

4. Activating students as instructional resources for one another

5. Acknowledging students as owners of their own learning. (William, 2011)

Formative assessment implies a partnership where there is trust between teachers and students within the confines of the classroom. Students receive

Figure 5.12 Varying Views of Formative Assessment

View of Formative Assessment	Researchers/Theorists in Support of The Stance
"Any assessment can be formative. . . . Assessment functions formatively when it improves the instructional decisions that are made by teachers, learners, or their peers."	William (2011, p. 45)
A planned, continuous **process** integrated into instruction that includes the criteria for success, collection of evidence of learning, interpretation of the evidence, and pointed descriptive feedback (never grades) to students on the status of their learning.	Heritage (2010); Moss & Brookhart (2009); Popham (2008)
A comprehensive **system** grounded in the classroom that consists of unobtrusive, obtrusive, and student-generated measures that yield scores that can be converted to grades.	Marzano (2010)
Assessment *for* learning: a collection of continuous (not frequent) **practices** where instructional decision making is predicated on teachers and students working as a team using standards-based curriculum maps with clear visions of the learning targets to inform students about themselves.	Stiggins (2005)

descriptive feedback about their learning in relation to criteria for success, motivated by standards but ideally set by teachers in collaboration with students. Teachers, in turn, use the assessment information to adjust and improve their teaching. Formative assessment strategies that are geared around students' academic language use allow teachers to pace and differentiate instruction to enable all students to successfully meet the objectives at hand.

CRAFTING INSTRUCTIONAL ACTIVITIES AND TASKS

The heart of academic language use lies in the intersection between instruction and assessment. When instruction is rich, it more readily yields strong evidence for student learning. Rich instruction means that within a unit of learning, the majority of the activities and tasks

- Reflect the characteristics of the students and are connected to their lives.
- Are engaging, hands on, and performance based, resulting in a creative product.

- Involve challenges, higher level thinking, and self-reflection.
- Reward innovative ideas that lead to original work.
- Have clear performance criteria that are mutually agreed upon by students and teachers.
- Exemplify content and language standards, learning targets, and differentiated objectives. (Gottlieb, 2012a)

Activities and tasks are the heart of instruction and assessment. When they are crafted with both language and content in mind, and ELLs are invited to use their home language to support, clarify, or summarize their learning, then instruction becomes comprehensible and meaningful to every student. In instructional activities and tasks, content does not have to be sacrificed, and language does not have to be diminished; notwithstanding, there have to be substantial supports for students to grasp the meaning as they are internalizing the concepts, processing the language, and providing evidence for learning.

REFLECTING ON TEACHING AND LEARNING

Reflection on teaching and learning invites thinking; it is a metacognitive process that leads to improved performance on the part of teachers and students. It takes into account who the students are, what the demands of the task are, and how the sociocultural context is framed. Teachers, or teachers and students together, should formulate and decide on criteria for success for the unit as a whole. Throughout the unit, teachers engage in instructional assessment practices to collect, analyze, and respond to evidence produced by students in a timely fashion. Students act on teacher (or peer) feedback, and teachers, in turn, adjust their instructional practices.

Teacher Reflection

When teachers are members of professional learning teams or professional learning communities, discussion and reflection are a natural course of action. In this environment, there is devoted time for teachers to debrief, share ideas, discuss issues, come to consensus, and decide on next steps. Teacher reflection, however, does not occur only with fellow professionals; it is equally important as part of the classroom culture.

When both teachers and students have opportunities to be reflective, then the classroom is transformed into a community of learners (Lave & Wenger, 1991). When teachers and students plan for and ask strategic questions of each other during instruction, classroom discourse is enriched. Equally important is for students to come to use questioning as a means of contributing to a classroom dialog and as a tool for thinking and learning rather than as a means for providing a right answer (Moss & Brookhart, 2009).

Student Reflection

When students engage in self- and peer reflection, they build metacognitive (knowledge of one's thinking) and metalinguistic (knowledge of the features and use of language) awareness. To be effective in self-assessment, it is important for students to hold a conception of quality similar to that of their teacher; in other words, they need to be thoroughly familiar with the criteria for success to be able to set mutually agreed upon goals (Heritage, 2010; Sadler, 1989).

Even young learners can engage in self-reflection. In a first grade classroom where the final products for the unit are both a written report and a brochure, the teacher methodically includes students in self-assessment along the way so that the students see their expertise as writers grow over time. Throughout the writing process the students complete criteria checklists as part of self-assessment—from Preparing for Writing to Drafting Writing to finally Preparing for Sharing (see Mora-Flores, 2014, p. 109).

Older students can and should be involved in formulating criteria for success and then using the criteria on some form of documentation for self- and peer assessment. Such is the case for sixth graders when a team of English language arts teachers facilitates the design of a four-point analytic scale for an argumentative writing project. What is unique in this instance is that the teachers use the life stages of a coconut in the students' home language, Samoan, as the descriptors for the rubric, making feedback more culturally relevant. The rubric is intended for use numerous times over the course of the unit; students will assess their group, their partner, and their own writing. In that way, the students come to internalize the criteria and are able to apply them with greater automaticity (Lam, Low, & Tauiliili-Mahuka, 2014).

FOR FURTHER THINKING . . .

As part of schooling, students need to develop academic uses of language. As academic language is inherent in standards, pedagogical action must revolve around translating clusters of standards into targets for learning, differentiated objectives, and related lessons along with embedded assessments that form instructional units with a final performance, project, or product. The organizing structure for this work is a Curricular Framework that is unveiled in the next chapter.

School leaders must support a learning culture for teachers and students where language and content are equal partners. Academic language use is critical to this discussion, as it is

- Integral to college and career readiness standards, built into the CCSS English language arts anchor standards, CCSS standards of mathematics practice, and NGSS cross-cutting concepts.
- The centerpiece of language development/proficiency standards.
- An inextricable part of every school discipline.
- Key to navigating complex text and using technology to further learning.
- The focal point for building multiple literacies.
- Central to developing 21st century cognitive, interpersonal, and intrapersonal competencies.

Quality instruction is quality assessment—they should be engaging, challenging, intentional, planned, and ideally matched to students' characteristics, experiences, languages, and cultures.

As you reflect on this chapter, personally or with colleagues, think about how you might respond to the following questions:

1. How can you ensure that academic language crosses instruction into assessment, or the converse, from assessment into instruction? What kinds of instructional supports and strategies might assist students, in particular ELLs, in both instructional and assessment contexts?

2. Why are content and language targets as well as content and language objectives necessary for a unit of learning, or are they? If not, how can you guarantee that curriculum, instruction, and assessment are aligned and referenced back to standards throughout a unit of learning?

3. How might you and your school or district infuse academic language into the different forms of assessment? What might be necessary to create a full complement of content and language assessments for diverse students?

4. Which examples of classrooms that are sprinkled throughout this chapter resonate with you? Which aspect or component of curriculum do you find useful that might apply to your setting?

6 How Is Academic Language Situated in Curricular Design and Infused Into Professional Learning?

At this point, we appear to have a 19th century curriculum, 20th century buildings and organizations, and 21st century students facing an undefined future.

—Bruce Wellman, 2010

In the context of school and this new age of rigor, academic language is essential for all students, as everyone is a language learner. But how can it be interwoven into the organization for teaching and learning? The answer lies in how we design and enact curriculum. First, curriculum planning has to be approached systematically, with utmost consideration for the characteristics of the students, the grade-level content, and the accompanying richness of language. Second, as standards are ripe in academic language, teachers and school leaders must have dedicated time to explore and experiment with their contents. Third, instructional materials filled with academic language have to be relevant, culturally responsive, and accessible to students. In sum, academic language situated within curricular design is central to building multiliteracies for students to be competitive in the 21st century.

Moving from examining student standards to formulating curriculum requires thoughtful interpretation. In this last chapter, we illustrate how a curricular framework can facilitate learning that highlights language used for academic purposes. A brief literature review that traces curriculum from the early 20th century to the present provides the rationale for a Curricular Framework used by all the contributors in the Academic Language in Diverse Classrooms series. Having a rationale for the Framework, we describe the usefulness and contribution of each component as it relates to academic language use within the mainstay of educational practice. Last, we discuss how professional learning opportunities for teachers and teacher leaders are requisite to integrating academic language use within the curriculum and promoting its use schoolwide.

A THEORETICAL BASIS FOR CURRICULAR FRAMEWORKS

The shaping of curriculum involves school leaders and teachers making judgments on what constitutes meaningful pedagogy. Curricular frameworks are conceptual structures that guide the building of units of learning. In essence a framework, such as the Curricular Framework used throughout the series (Gottlieb & Ernst-Slavit, 2013, 2014) and graphically represented in Resource C, provides a vision of the relationship among the major components of learning and teaching. The theoretical basis for current curricular frameworks can be traced from the last century to the present.

Early Thinking on Curriculum

At the onset of the 20th century, progressive education reformers promoted a pedagogy that emphasized critical thinking and looked to schools for the political and social regeneration of the nation. Increasingly, the progressive movement of that time became focused on a child-centered approach to education. Next to the educational philosopher John Dewey, William Kilpatrick was the most renowned of the progressive educators of this time. Kilpatrick's article "The Project Method: The Use of the Purposeful Act in the Educational Process," published in 1918, has had long-lasting impact (including a recent resurgence in project learning). According to the project method, curriculum centers around problem-solving issues relevant to students' lives. It was originally aimed at promoting student interaction with peers, family members, and the community in an effort to produce self-reliant individuals. The teachers' role was one as facilitator, encouraging students to initiate, cooperate, and enjoy the learning process (Beineke, 1998).

The origins of curriculum design of the 21st century classrooms can be traced back to Ralph Tyler and his seminal book *Basic Principles of Curriculum and Instruction* (1949). Continuing the thinking of his predecessors, Tyler described learning as an activity that takes place through the action or agency of the student. "It is what he does that he learns, not what the teacher does" (p. 63). In envisioning the process of curriculum design, Tyler formulated four questions that became the basis for planning, delivering, and evaluating instruction:

> **Consider this . . .**
>
> Why is it important to explore the historical roots of curriculum? What insights carry over into teacher education today? At the same time, how has curriculum evolved to be more reflective of classrooms filled with diverse students?

1. What educational purposes should the school seek to attain?

2. How can learning experiences be useful in attaining these purposes?

3. How can learning experiences be organized for effective instruction?

4. How can the effectiveness of learning experiences be evaluated?

Tyler's major contribution to educational practice is an objectives-based evaluation model. The four essential questions from Tyler's model still apply for use by grade-level professional learning teams or even school-level professional learning communities. They are easily converted to action steps for teachers to use in planning lessons or units of learning. The steps, stated below, are displayed as a cycle in Figure 6.1.

1. Define learning (targets and) objectives (intents). The purpose of (targets and) objectives is to indicate how students will change as a result of learning.

2. Introduce relevant learning experiences that are useful in attaining the purpose (through the integration of content and language).

3. Organize the learning experiences to maximize their effect (through instruction).

4. Evaluate the effectiveness of the process and make revisions as necessary (through assessment).

Figure 6.1 Tyler's Essential Steps in Curriculum Design

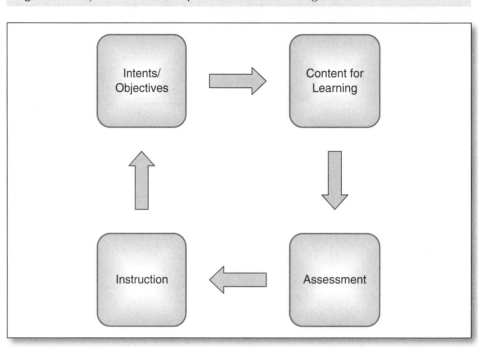

Consider this . . .

How relevant do you find the curricular framework from the mid 20th century? To what extent do teachers in your grade/department or school use its four components? What other components have been added to make the framework more up-to-date and responsive to a diverse student population?

In the 1960s, influences from curriculum designers such as Hilda Taba resulted in a curricular rationale being converted into a procedure (Taba, 1962). This theorizing of curriculum design provided a blueprint that prevailed throughout the rest of the 20th century. The curriculum development process that Taba proposed, still visible today, included having teachers

1. Diagnose student needs.

2. Formulate objectives.

3. Select and organize content.

4. Plan learning experiences.

5. Determine what to evaluate and the method for data collection.

In the 1970s and 1980s, during the era of mastery learning, Madeline Hunter was tremendously influential in shaping curriculum design. She was best known for codifying a lesson plan template that consisted of essential steps as part of a curriculum guide:

1. Anticipatory Set (activating prior knowledge and experiences of the students)

2. Objective/Purpose (determining what students will be able to know and do by the end of the lesson in relation to an overarching understanding)

3. Instructional Input (deciding how knowledge is to be communicated to students)

4. Modeling (demonstrating the skill or competence the student is expected to learn to perform)

5. Checking for Understanding (selecting strategies to determine the extent to which students have met the objective)

6. Guided Practice (engaging students in activities under teacher supervision)

7. Independent Practice (having students work on their own) (Hunter, 2004)

A curricular wave during the late 1980s and early 1990s saw the emergence of interdisciplinary approaches. Many configurations establishing connections around topics, themes, concepts, problems, or issues surfaced around the integration of different content areas to create multidisciplinary units (Drake, 2007). With the introduction of content standards for mathematics (NCTM, 1989), a national standards movement began to gain momentum, reshaping teaching. Still viable today, standards-referenced thematic instruction is a remnant from this era.

This brief historical overview of curricular trends in the United States of the last century paves the way for our current thinking on how to organize learning for students and how students can actively participate in the process within the context of school.

Recent Thinking on Curriculum

Starting with the new millennium and the 2002 reauthorization of the Elementary and Secondary School Act (aka No Child Left Behind), curriculum has evolved from a static state consisting of a prescriptive, lock-step procedure dictated by educators into a dynamic process where students have both voice and choice in learning. Put another way, there has been a general shift in orientation from curriculum that is largely transmissive, where students are the passive recipients of information and the teacher is viewed as the authority, to a more transactive one, where students have a more active role and are often purposely interacting with their peers. Some schools have gone one step farther and are engaged in a transformative curriculum, where students are genuinely empowered and take greater control over their learning, often making real-world choices from a social justice perspective. Figure 6.2 illustrates the continuum of curricular orientations.

Figure 6.2 A Continuum of Curricular Orientations from Teacher-Directed to Student-Centered

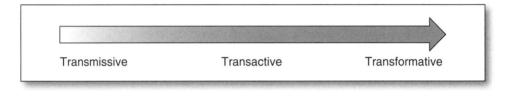

Transmissive   Transactive   Transformative

Consider this . . .

What is the curricular leaning of your district or school, or is it a combination of orientations? Do you agree with how your school is approaching curriculum, especially for its linguistically and culturally diverse students? If you could, what might you suggest to move your school's or district's view of curriculum in another direction?

Whichever the orientation, it remains that the structure of curriculum, in large part, shapes student learning in school and ultimately has come to be viewed as a pathway toward student achievement. In other words, each curricular framework provides for a distinct quality of experience and an opportunity to learn for students. With that in mind, let's return to the most recent history of the influences on curriculum design.

Increased accountability for schools and districts has been a force in revamping 21st century curriculum. State standards have become a nonnegotiable component of how educators have come to organize teaching—first the federal mandate for content standards in 1994 and then the subsequent reauthorization of the Elementary and Secondary School Act of 2002 requiring English language proficiency standards. Eight years later, a state-led initiative produced the Common Core State Standards for English language arts and mathematics in 2010; the Next Generation of Science Standards followed in 2013. Today, "a curriculum works with the [CCSS] standards to frame optimal learning experiences" (McTighe &

Wiggins, 2012, p. 3). In fact, the backward design curricular model launched by Jay McTighe and Grant Wiggins has helped thousands of educators set clear, standards-referenced learning goals for planning authentic assessment that serves as the anchor for instruction.

The current centrality of standards in educational life is cause for educators to center on 21st century college and career readiness understandings and skills as the end products of curriculum. The Partnership for 21st Century Skills concludes that curriculum should focus on the following (see www.p21.org/overview/skills-framework for a more complete discussion):

1. Deep understanding of 21st century skills across content areas

2. Standards that articulate essential concepts and skills

3. Educator and stakeholder involvement around the essential questions and enduring understandings of 21st century skills

4. Curriculum-embedded, performance-based assessments

5. Continuous reflection and revision in curriculum design processes that result in improved teaching and learning

6. Collaboration among key stakeholders

Since the early 2000s, Carol Ann Tomlinson's (2004) notion of differentiated teaching and learning has become part of curriculum design and an accepted practice in mainstream classrooms. This approach is a response to the maxim that one size does not fit all and recognizes that students come to school with varying background knowledge, preferences in learning, and interests. Differentiation involves tailoring instruction and assessment to meet individual student needs. Its intent is to provide different pathways for acquiring content so that all students can learn effectively, regardless of their ability, within a classroom environment.

Looking back at this broad synopsis of the history of curricular design in the United States, there has been little mention of the ever present role of language in schooling. Rather, the focus has been on the organization of content and its associated knowledge and skills. Most recently, with increased curricular attention to the ideas of globalization, social action, and multiliteracies comes recognition of the role of academic language use within sociocultural contexts. That said, there is a growing need to explore and identify the linguistic requirements of classroom discourse across all subject areas (Lee, Quinn, & Valdes, 2013).

CONCEPTUAL FRAMEWORKS THAT INTEGRATE LANGUAGE AND CONTENT

Since the mid to late 1980s, there has been a changing perspective on how to approach language teaching, from a curriculum that approaches language learning in isolation to one that accentuates meaningful and intentional communication in social and academic settings. Along with this shift has come the belief that when language instruction is purposely interwoven into content instruction, learning becomes stronger and more meaningful. As a result, content and language have come to have equal status in curriculum planning and implementation (Mohan, 1986). The co-occurrence of envisioning language teaching around authentic, meaningful communication and integrating language and content during instruction has given way to a new conceptualization of effective practices in language education.

A lesson learned from this period is that when curriculum is built around academic language, content and language tend to reinforce each other to deepen student learning. More aptly said, "When the learner's second language is both the object and medium of instruction, the content of each lesson must be taught simultaneously with the linguistic skills necessary for understanding it" (Cantoni-Harvey, 1987, p. 22). A framework for integrating language and content first mentioned in the literature revolved around the use of content-related objectives to relate linguistic purposes for learning (Snow, Met, & Genesee, 1989). In it, we see overtures for collaboration between content and second or "foreign" language teachers, representatives of the curriculum of their respective disciplines. Together the teachers engaged in ongoing evaluation of a learner's needs that became translated into content-obligatory language (necessary for students to develop and communicate specific content) and content-compatible language (complementary to the concepts or information being taught). Figure 6.3 is an adaptation of a framework that illustrates how language and content teachers determine the use of language in formulating content objectives from ongoing needs assessment of students.

Another way for helping older students build an integrated set of language, concepts, and skills is through a project framework (Beckett & Slater, 2005). In addition to simultaneously learning content and language, several goals are associated with this student-centered approach; these include (1) challenging students

Consider this . . .

Do you agree that it is important to consider both content and language in universal curriculum design? Why or why not? How might addressing both content and language improve the possibility for increased achievement of all students?

Figure 6.3 A Framework for Infusing Language Into Content in Curriculum Design

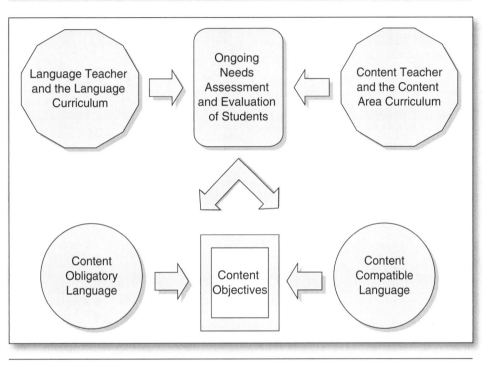

Source: Adapted from Snow, Met, & Genesee, 1989, p. 206

to think creatively, (2) fostering collaboration among students, and (3) encouraging socialization of students, with attention to English language learners (ELLs). In it, the curriculum is broken into projects that address the forms (grammatical structures) and functions (purposes) of language use, the conceptual load of the content, and the necessary skills in using language and content. Figure 6.4 shows how language can be intentionally incorporated into a project-based curriculum.

Around this time, Pauline Gibbons (2006) introduced an integrated curriculum framework for mainstream classrooms with considerations for teaching language within content. It was intended to stimulate discussion and systematic planning between language and content teachers around the language needs of ELLs. This language-centered process consisted of five steps:

1. Finding out about learners' language needs

2. Unpacking the topic for language

3. Selecting the language focus

Figure 6.4 A Curricular Framework Around Projects With Consideration for Content and Academic Language Use

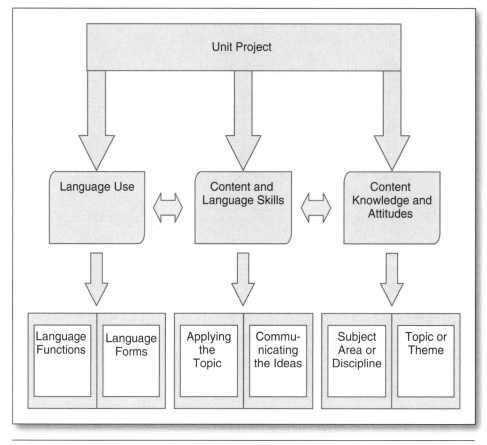

Source: Adapted from Beckett & Slater, 2005, p. 110

4. Crafting activities to develop the focus language

5. Evaluating the unit (Gibbons, 2006, p. 223)

Using Gibbons's framework as a starting place, Margo Gottlieb, Anne Katz, and Gisela Ernst-Slavit (2009) elaborated the steps necessary for folding English language proficiency standards into instructional planning. As a result, a three-phased framework for curriculum development emerged: (1) previewing—examining the context for language instruction, (2) planning—incorporating language considerations into lesson design, and (3) reflecting—assessing the extent that language learning has occurred. Using each phase as an overarching category, seven steps were interspersed into the process of designing a language-centered curriculum. They included the following:

Previewing

1. Determine ELLs' current language performance.

2. Analyze the language demands of the content topic.

3. Match English language proficiency standards to language demands, decide whether transformations (or changes in the representation of standards) are necessary, and, if so, which ones.

Planning

4. Develop language objectives.

5. Differentiate instructional activities according to (the students') levels of language proficiency.

6. Plan for instructional supports.

Reflecting

7. Review evidence of language learning and decide on next steps. (Gottlieb et al., 2009, p. 123)

Looking back at the historical treatment of curriculum, first from the perspective of content and later from the view of content in relation to language, we can now assemble the components of a comprehensive curriculum framework for districts and schools inclusive of all students.

Consider this . . .

Which of the frameworks that center on language and content presented in this chapter resonates with you? Why? Drawing on your own experience, if you were to create a curricular framework, what would be some of its key components?

The Value of an Integrated Curricular Framework for Diverse Schools and Districts

College and career readiness standards were ushered onto the US landscape in 2010. With the Common Core State Standards (CCSS) and the Next Generation Science Standards (NGSS), among others, adopted by states, standards-referenced curriculum has become a stronghold in districts and schools across the nation. Equally important have been the unearthing of the language and literacy of the new content standards, headed by the Understanding Language group (www.ell.stanford.edu) and identifying the features of academic language in language development

Consider this . . .

Does your school or district rely on an exclusive curricular framework or design? If so, have there been input or adjustments made for language learners who may be receiving content instruction in more than one language? Have any considerations been made for students with interrupted formal education or those who are considered long-term ELLs? Have any modifications been made for students with special needs? Explain how all student groups can access the curriculum and be successful learners.

standards, as noted by World-Class Instructional Design and Assessment (www.wida.us). Together, these entities have elevated the role of language in instructional practices, in particular in classrooms with ELLs.

With the adoption of uniform sets of standards, many schools and districts have moved toward the use of a common curricular framework. Consequently, teachers may not have had much latitude in implementing curriculum and often have had to resort to creativity to enhance its meaningfulness for diverse learners (McKay, 2006). The use of a single curricular framework for all students has both pros and cons. Figure 6.5 weighs the benefits and pitfalls of relying on a sole way of organizing instruction within districts with diverse students, including ELLs, ELLs with disabilities, and students who use diverse dialectical forms of English.

Figure 6.6 features the global components of curricular frameworks implemented in today's diverse classrooms. It is hierarchically nested, starting with academic language at its core. Content and language standards represent shared grade-level academic language use, which in turn

Figure 6.5 The Pros and Cons of Districts Adhering to a Single Curricular Framework

Benefits of Having a District Curricular Framework	Pitfalls of Having a District Curricular Framework
• It is reflective of a district's overall mission and vision to be inclusive of all students. • There is a uniform set of expectations for each grade level or department. • There is a shared language among school leaders and teachers.	• School-level variables, such as influence of specific languages and cultures, may not be taken into account. • Student-level variables, such as the number of students with learning disabilities, students' prior school experiences, or the range of English language proficiencies among ELLs, may not be considered. • The shared language may not extend to the integration of language and content instruction or the use of multiple sets of standards.

Figure 6.6 Proposed Components of Integrated Curricular Frameworks

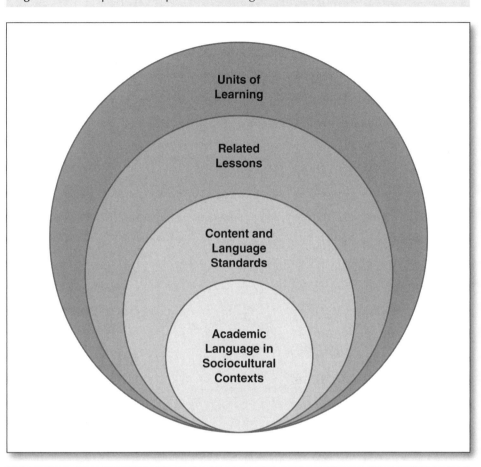

Source: Gottlieb & Ernst-Slavit, 2013

contributes to the formulation of a series of related lessons that scaffold to form units of instruction and assessment. These components can apply to all students in diverse settings where one or more languages are the media of instruction.

A CURRICULAR FRAMEWORK THAT FEATURES ACADEMIC LANGUAGE USE

This chapter has presented an historical overview of the work of major educational theorists who have contributed to our understanding of curricular frameworks. In addition, it has offered a strong theoretical and practical basis for frameworks that integrate content and language for students from diverse backgrounds. These two streams come together to provide the rationale for the development of a curricular framework that centers on academic language. Figure 6.7 identifies each of the major components of a framework that revolves around academic language use and provides a brief description along with evidence from the research literature. The Curricular Framework itself, reproduced in Resource C, serves as the foundation for the *Academic Language* series on mathematics and English language arts, kindergarten to grade 8 (Gottlieb & Ernst-Slavit, 2013, 2014).

Figure 6.7 The Evidence-Based Components of a Curricular Framework Highlighting Academic Language Use

Component of the Framework	Description	Evidence
Student Characteristics	Experiences inside and outside of school; languages and cultures; academic achievement, literacies, and language proficiencies (in home languages and English)	Collier & Thomas (2009); Peregoy & Boyle (2013)
Teacher Qualifications	Certificates and endorsements, experience in working with linguistic and culturally diverse students	Darling-Hammond (2000); Darling-Hammond & Richardson (2009); Rice (2003); Tellez & Waxman (2006); Wong Fillmore & Snow (2000)
Unit Topic or Theme	Use of thematic units as a mark of high-quality instruction	Drake (2007), Freeman & Freeman (2008); Stoddart, Pinal, Latzke, & Canaday (2002)
Student Content Standards, Including CCSS and NGSS	Grade-level conceptual understandings and content-related skills	Ainsworth (2013); Marzano, Yanoski, Hoegh, & Simms (2013)
Language Development Standards	Language expectations expressed as a series of language proficiency levels that scaffold with increased complexity across a continuum of language development	Council of Europe (2001); Gottlieb, Katz, & Ernst-Slavit (2009); Morrow (2004)
Academic Language Within the Unit (present in standards and instructional materials)	Presence and use of the language of school at the discourse, sentence, and word/phrase levels	Arias & Faltis (2013); Bunch (2006); Derewianka (1990); Egbert & Ernst-Slavit (2010); Gibbons (2006); Graves & Lopriore (2009); Scarcella (2003); Schleppegrell, 2004

Component of the Framework	Description	Evidence
Content and Language Targets for the Unit	Overall foci for a unit of learning for all students	Gottlieb (2012a); Lyster (2007)
Linguistic and Cultural Resources	Assets-based approach to curriculum design and schooling that capitalizes on linguistic and cultural capital and treats community as an extension of school	González, Moll, & Amanti (2005); Miramontes, Nadeau, & Commins (2011); Saifer, Edwards, Ellis, Ko, & Stuczynski (2011); Valdés, Capitelli, & Alvarez (2011)
Instructional Supports	Sensory, graphic, and interactive scaffolds for language (and content) learning	Egbert & Ernst-Slavit (2010); Gottlieb, Katz, & Ernst-Slavit (2009); WIDA (2007, 2012)
Differentiated Content and Language Objectives for Related Lessons	Instructional grouping of students by performance and by language proficiency levels	Bailey & Heritage (2008); Egbert & Ernst-Slavit (2010); Echevarria, Vogt, & Short (2008); Goldenberg & Coleman (2010); Gottlieb (2012a, 2006)
Assessment Within and Across Instructional Activities	Formative assessment strategies measuring individual lesson objectives, and summative assessment tasks measuring a unit's targets	Heritage (2010); Stevens, Butler, & Castellon-Wellington (2000); Tomlinson (2004)
Instructional Activities and Tasks	A series of related lessons within units of learning	New Levine & McCloskey (2012); Rothenberg & Fisher (2007)
Student and Teacher Reflection	Opportunities for building students' metalinguistic, metacultural, and metacognitive awareness; reflection on teaching and learning	Andrews (2007); Marzano (2012); Schön (1983); Zeichner (1999)

Mastery of academic language is arguably the single most important determinant of academic success for individual students. . . . It is not possible to overstate the role that language plays in determining students' success with academic content. Proficient use of—and control over—*academic language* is the key to content area learning. (Francis, Rivera, Lesaux, Kieffer, & Rivera, 2006, p. 7)

To maximize students' opportunities for academic success, not only is a linguistically and culturally responsive curricular framework necessary, but

Consider this . . .

A comprehensive Curricular Framework, such as the one presented in Resource C, considers the many components involved in the interaction among teachers, students, resources, and tasks. Why is an evidence-based justification necessary for each component? Which components do you feel are essential for all students? Which are particularly important for linguistically and culturally diverse students?

schools and districts must also ensure that all educators have multiple venues to engage in ongoing professional learning.

THE ROLE OF PROFESSIONAL LEARNING IN UNDERSTANDING AND PROMOTING ACADEMIC LANGUAGE USE

There is an all out effort by schools, districts, and states to implement rigorous content standards, including the CCSS, to prepare students for college and careers and, simultaneously, to ready students to perform well on the next generation of achievement tests. Ultimately, to make a difference in educational outcomes, this massive effort has to be supported and sustained through extensive professional learning and changes in teacher accreditation. Professional learning must contribute to expanding teachers' knowledge of content, increasing their understanding and use of academic language, and extending teachers' repertoire of pedagogical practices for both content and language.

As academic language is situated at the nexus of content and language standards, professional learning offers the ideal opportunity to promote collaboration between content teachers and language teachers. Working together, whether in grade-level teams or with colleagues across the hall, teacher partners or professional learning communities might explore and discuss the following:

- Academic language in content and language standards
- The language demands of instructional materials
- Connections between the languages and cultures of home and the language of school
- Data and decisions from content and language measures
- Content and language targets for units of learning
- Differentiated content and language objectives
- Common content and language assessments
- Assessment for formative purposes embedded within instruction
- Instructional strategies that highlight academic language use in content instruction

- Instructional strategies that highlight academic language use in language instruction
- Documentation of student growth in academic language use over time

Implementing Professional Learning: From Two Participants to District Level Participation

In response to the reauthorized version of the Elementary and Secondary School Act post 2002, Learning Forward, a professional learning association, states that *professional development* refers to a "comprehensive, sustained, and intensive approach to improving teachers' and principals' effectiveness in raising student achievement" (Learning Forward, n.d.a.) Furthermore, the vision of this national organization is "ensuring that every educator engages in effective professional learning every day so every student achieves" (Learning Forward, n.d.b.). (Refer to http://learningforward.org for more information).

Professional learning involves the facilitation and support of school (and district) leadership including principals, coaches, mentors, master teachers, or other teacher leaders who, along with teachers, paraprofessionals, and tutors, work toward a unified goal. Figure 6.8 shows some of the many ways in which professional learning for educators can be organized,

Consider this . . .

Examining the academic language embedded in content standards is a starting point for communication among teachers and school leaders. How might long-term professional learning help facilitate interaction and communication between content and language teachers? How might the cross-disciplinary integration of literacy and the content areas presented in the CCSS for English language arts as well as English language development standards be a focus of professional learning for content and language teachers?

Figure 6.8 Configurations for Professional Learning and Their Levels of Implementation

Structure for Professional Learning	Level of Implementation
1. Learning Networks	Across schools within a district
2. Professional Learning Communities	A school
3. Professional Learning Teams	A grade level or department
4. Communities of Practice	A classroom of learners
5. Coteaching or team teaching	A pair of teachers

from pairs of teachers to teachers throughout an entire district. Internal to the functioning of schools, principals need to create and maintain structures for teachers to freely exchange ideas around teaching and learning. One major theme for discussion should be how academic language can be embedded in curriculum design and day-to-day instruction.

A potentially far-reaching type of professional learning is through personal learning networks (Richardson & Mancabelli, 2011). Through networks, educators reach out into cyberspace and connect with others who share interest in the same topic. Webinars, wikis, blogs, and discussion boards form, in essence, an online community in pursuit of self-directed academic learning. At times teachers or school leaders collaborate across a district through virtual environments, where documents are shared and meaningful interactions occur. Virtual spaces are open 24/7; thus, education becomes a personal learning experience that extends to people making connections to one another, to relevant content outside the classroom, and to global contexts at any time, in any place.

> **Consider this . . .**
>
> There are many ways in which teachers and teacher leaders can engage in professional learning: protected time during a school day for joint planning, an afterschool workshop, an early release day to delve into an issue, a hybrid course, or virtually through other online opportunities. Which venues have you used? Which ones do you prefer and why?

Linda Darling-Hammond and Nikole Richardson (2009), in examining two decades of research on professional development that improves instruction and student achievement, state that the most successful framework for teachers' professional learning is one inclusive of professional learning communities. An extension of this finding is that in diverse schools or in districts with heterogeneous student populations, professional learning communities should include representatives with content and language expertise. Language experts, such as English as a second language, dual language, or bilingual teachers, mentors, or coaches, need to work side by side with their content colleagues. When every educator is an accepted member of a professional learning community, all participants benefit from collective (1) pedagogical knowledge of diverse student populations, (2) content/subject matter knowledge, (3) linguistic knowledge, (4) knowledge of the language development process, (5) cross-cultural understanding, and (6) interpersonal skills (Honigsfeld & Dove, 2010).

Similar to professional learning communities, communities of practice operate internal to individual classrooms, where the culture of learning stems from a shared set of expectations and anticipated outcomes between the teacher and students. The teacher, as a facilitator for learning, contributes to the students' development of strong identities as learners and as effective participants in the social practices of their learning community. Students participate in these community practices as part of their daily routine so that over time, the collective practices are codetermined (Lave & Wenger, 1991).

Communities of practice can readily be formed around students' academic language use. Acquiring and using linguistic resources to participate in a community of practice is of utmost importance. Teachers have to realize how language must scaffold incrementally so that students can practice the language of each discipline and eventually act independently (Walqui & Heritage, 2012). For example, a fourth grade classroom exemplifies a community of practice throughout a multidisciplinary unit when students center their attention on an interactive learning wall. While the teacher guides the process,

> the students add or rearrange items on the wall and work to complete assignments . . . using academic language while collaborating with peers, solving problems as they work on their projects, and developing an expanded expressive vocabulary as they discuss important information. The learning wall provides opportunities for shared expertise among all the students incorporating their diverse background knowledge, technological abilities, and authentic use of language to successfully engage in everyday classroom learning experiences. (Silvers, Shorey, Eliopoulis, & Akiyoshi, 2014, p. 109)

Grade-level professional learning teams are ideal for the collaborative crafting and implementation of standards-referenced units of learning with their related lessons and common assessment. When district or school leadership provides designated, protected time on a regular basis, professional learning teams can tackle important issues. Coteaching is another powerful professional learning structure between two teachers or two school leaders that requires joint planning and setting mutual goals. When its key elements are in place—coordinated work plans, a shared belief system and philosophy of education, equal distribution of leadership, parity of roles, and cooperation—it becomes obvious that both teachers assume responsibility for student achievement (Villa, Thousand, & Nevin, 2008).

In schools with linguistic and culturally diverse students, all forms of professional learning should revolve around forwarding an alliance between language and content teachers. In participating in professional learning opportunities, teachers working together can offer each other pedagogical expertise, content knowledge and strategies, second language development theories and strategies, cross-cultural understanding, and culturally appropriate, interpersonal skills (Honigsfeld & Dove, 2010). Figure 6.9 illustrates how the complementary roles of content and language teachers can lead to a strong partnership.

To summarize, content and language teachers, in identifying and examining academic language of standards and instructional materials, enrich each other's expertise through the following:

- Exchanging ideas and strategies related to academic language use
- Choosing themes and topics rich in academic language that represent multiple perspectives for classroom instruction and assessment
- Formulating individual student learning plans
- Examining student performance in their home language in relation to English
- Understanding students' academic achievement in relation to their language proficiency
- Enhancing interaction between proficient English students and ELLs through academic conversations
- Providing linguistically and culturally responsive practices relevant to diverse students
- Facilitating differentiated small group instruction and assessment
- Enabling students to represent what they can do with content and language

Figure 6.9 Contributions of Content and Language Teachers to Reciprocal Professional Learning

Content Teachers	Language Teachers
Rely on furthering students' content knowledge	Rely on furthering students' language development
Help students socialize to the classroom	Help accentuate and embed cross-cultural insights into classroom routines
Ease students into the norms of school	Promote understanding of the unique characteristics of students' languages and cultures
Select content standards for instructional planning	Select corresponding language proficiency/development standards for instructional planning
Design content targets	Design language targets
Craft differentiated content objectives	Craft differentiated language objectives

Above all, teachers must ensure that students are able to relate to and thrive in a place called school.

MAKING SCHOOL A MEANINGFUL EXPERIENCE FOR 21ST CENTURY STUDENTS

To further the conversation on teaching and learning, we reiterate: Every student is a language learner, and every educator is a language teacher. Furthermore, as Luciana de Oliveira states, "Academic language is a 'second' language for all students" (2013, p. 149). Put another way, in school each and every student is acquiring academic language as an additional language. Therefore, all teachers must have the academic language and linguistic knowledge of their discipline to identify and address the language demands required of instruction. Culturally and linguistically responsive teaching, by being sensitive to individual student characteristics, facilitates student attainment of academic language within and across disciplines.

Culturally and Linguistically Responsive Teaching and Learning

State standards cannot be implemented in isolation, especially for a diverse student population. Only when standards are couched within a motivating and personally meaningful classroom environment can they yield the benefits of academic success for students. When the academic understandings and skills defined in

> **Consider this . . .**
>
> What is your personal reaction to the statement, "Every student is a language learner and every educator is a language teacher"?

the standards can also be situated within the life experiences and frames of reference of the students, classroom instruction is better matched to the students' cultural and experiential bases. Ultimately, the cultural characteristics and perspectives of linguistically and culturally diverse students serve as conduits for more effective teaching practices (Gay, 2000).

Students become disenfranchised when what is culturally valued at home and in the community and what is educationally valued in school are incongruent. One approach for connecting with students is through culturally and linguistically responsive teaching. Teaching is considered culturally and linguistically responsive when it validates and affirms the home cultures and home languages for the purposes of building and bridging students to success in academia and mainstream society. It revolves around an instructional dynamic and an inclusion mindset that honors and accentuates language and cultural inputs as the basis for teaching and learning (Muhammad & Hollie, 2012; Nieto, 2004). Culturally responsive teachers and school leaders are critical to the education of today's youth.

Schools must be focused on having students develop high levels of language and literacy within academic contexts, school-to-work contexts, global contexts, and sociocultural contexts. As language is always situated within cultural contexts, teachers must commit to deeply understanding who their students are and how to build their capacities to navigate the world around them. When teachers connect with students' backgrounds and bring them to the foreground to foster learning, students begin to form new identities and see themselves in academic roles. It is grade-level language used for academic purposes that enables students to accomplish this goal. Figure 6.10 gives some ideas for embedding academic language use into culturally responsive teaching.

Figure 6.10 Ideas for Embedding Academic Language Use Into Culturally Responsive Instruction

Features of Culturally Responsive Instruction	Infusing Academic Language Into Culturally Responsive Instruction
• Communicate high expectations for learning • Support learning within a sociocultural context • Embed multiculturalism into the curriculum • Encourage participation of family members and the community	• Identify academic language within grade-level standards to share with students along with criteria for success • Make provisions for teaching academic language with a sociocultural backdrop • Create academic content and language targets for multicultural units of learning • Encourage academic language connections among school, home, and the community

The use of cognates to compare academic language in two languages is an effective instructional strategy reflective of culturally and linguistically responsive teaching, especially for students from Spanish-speaking backgrounds or proficient English students who are participating in Spanish dual language settings. Spanish–English cognates can be a means for students to make connections between their two languages and become more metalinguistically aware of the similarities and differences in linguistic patterns. (For examples, see Ernst-Slavit, Gottlieb, & Slavit, 2013, for cognates related to fractions and Minaya-Rowe, 2014, for cognates related to gothic literature.) These pairs of words often represent technical academic language, as both terms are derived from Latin or Greek roots, and provide a window into students' content knowledge. Another culturally and linguistically responsive teaching strategy is to extend the school experience into the community. For example, a first grade class of students of Mexican descent visits the local tortilla factory to discover how base-10 thinking operates in their local neighborhood and the real world (see Celedón-Pattichis & Musanti, 2013). By thinking of the students first and their potential contributions to their own learning in an ever changing world, we begin to see the transformation of schools.

> **Consider this . . .**
>
> Students in linguistically and culturally responsive classrooms are comfortable with their environment and, by being able to more readily relate to the material, are generally intrinsically motivated to learn. How might you make your classroom and school more culturally and linguistically responsive? How might you make stronger connections between the students' home cultures and the school or classroom culture?

Transformation of Schools

> Until the needs (of linguistically and culturally diverse students) are placed squarely in the mainstream of teaching, learning, planning, and educational reform, it is unlikely that these students will have access to equitable educational opportunities. In order for school-reform efforts to be successful, educators must understand how to include all students, weigh program choices, and anticipate and evaluate the decisions of particular decisions. (Miramontes, Nadeau, & Commins, 2011, p. 8)

This statement underscores the need for districts to formulate and enact missions and visions that view diversity as a strength and to design programs around the assets of their students. Bringing this notion of strengths-based education to the school level, Debbie Zacarian (2011) suggests several principles for transforming schools that include ELLs:

- Connect academic learning to socially relevant issues that are personal to students' lives.
- [Ensure that] thinking skills are explicitly taught and visually displayed.

- [Plan and] deliver lessons that are comprehensible [for all students].
- Use cooperative learning to practice, apply, and learn the language of content. (pp. 94, 96, 98, & 104)

As the changing student demographic comes up against the implementation of the next generation of standards and assessments, our educational system is at a crossroads. This new reality is cause for a shifting of the status quo. Research on school effectiveness has converged on several key characteristics that, used in combination, help raise student performance, namely,

- Strong leadership
- Effective teaching
- Data-driven decisions
- A culture of excellence
- More instructional time

The Council of Great City Schools reached similar conclusions based on their research on effective policies and practices that lead to improved student achievement for school districts with large numbers of ELLs. Specifically, the Council identified a series of contextual features—(1) a shared vision for reform, (2) supportive leadership and advocacy on behalf of ELLs, (3) empowerment of district ELL directors, and (4) external forces—along with promising practices—(a) comprehensive districtwide planning and adoption of language development strategies for ELLs, (b) extensive and continuous support for implementation of initiatives, (c) a culture of collaboration and shared accountability, (d) high-quality, relevant professional development, and (e) the use of student data as a cornerstone for decision making)—as the catalysts for reform (Horwitz et al., 2009).

We believe that in today's diverse classrooms, schools, and districts, academic language use must be added to the equation for increasing and sustaining student achievement. Ensuring that students reach high levels in their use of academic language must be a priority for every teacher and school leader. This agreed-upon goal, reachable through multimodal, multicultural pathways, holds promise for students as they engage in 21st century learning and life.

PROMOTING ACADEMIC LANGUAGE FOR ALL STUDENTS AND TEACHERS

All students must be held to high expectations where content standards, exemplified by the CCSS and the NGSS, set the bar. According to Aida Walqui & Margaret Heritage (2012),

> Every teacher will now need to be a teacher of the language and literacies that all their students, including ELLs, must possess to act in disciplinary valued ways in their classes. . . . This will require a different level of teacher expertise than currently exists among most teachers. (p. 1)

Students must be encouraged to think critically and creatively and to become their own agents. Students must be encouraged and motivated to become responsible for and be active participants in their own learning.

Seeking Advocacy Within the Educational Community

Teachers, school leaders, and administrators first and foremost must advocate on behalf of students and their families. Without their advocacy through leadership, guidance, support, and tireless work, the pathways to educational success can be blocked for a substantial number of students. Advocacy includes promoting equity and taking actions to ensure that all students are held to high expectations and have access to educational opportunities to be able to meet and exceed them.

Advocacy extends to stakeholders making use of linguistic and cultural resources of students and their communities and bringing them into the educational fold. It involves educators stepping in and providing a voice for students, in particular ELLs, and their families (Staehr Fenner, 2013). In fact, advocacy can take on many forms for teachers and school leaders of linguistically and culturally diverse students, including these:

> **Consider this . . .**
>
> Advocacy is a natural outgrowth of educational policy from a state level all the way down to an individual classroom. What steps might you take as an advocate for students and their families? What suggestions might you make to others in your school or district? What can you do to advocate on behalf of linguistically and culturally diverse students?

- Shaping the linguistic and cultural identities of students
- Understanding and valuing diversity inside and outside of school
- Using diversity in a positive way to organize classrooms and schools
- Providing multilingual, multicultural opportunities for all students
- Analyzing student data through a linguistically and culturally diverse lens
- Linking students' language, literacy, content knowledge, and sociocultural development to short-term and long-term outcomes
- Articulating a multilingual discourse that promotes policies and practices inclusive of all students and community members (de Jong, 2012)

Finally, advocacy implies that educators believe in students and know that they have the potential to succeed, despite the adversities they may face. It means that the use of academic language must become part of the school culture, modeled by coaches, mentors, teachers, and school leaders throughout the day, not just in specified lessons. When the community at large becomes the voice of the school community, when students and parents have shared goals with teachers, and when linguistically and culturally responsive practices become the norm in our schools, then advocacy can help replace the challenges facing the youth of the 21st century.

FOR FURTHER THINKING . . .

In this chapter we have examined the theoretical and historical underpinnings of a curricular framework that revolves around academic language. We provide ideas for professional learning to enable school leaders and teachers to deepen their understanding and uses of academic language along its application within and across content areas in linguistically and culturally responsive settings. The following questions help personalize the ideas presented in this chapter:

1. Do you feel that academic language use serves as the equalizer for all students and teachers? To what extent does academic language present in state standards promote collaboration among teachers and school leaders? Give some local examples.

2. What types of professional learning opportunities have you had that promote academic language learning for all students? Which type (face to face, hybrid, online) of professional learning do you believe is most effective for furthering your academic language development and why?

3. To what extent do you consider your school's or district's curriculum to be linguistically and culturally responsive? What suggestions might you make to increase the involvement of your students and utilize the linguistic and cultural resources of the community?

4. The field of language education has been moving toward having more integrated models of simultaneous instruction of language and content. How can integrated instructional models, along with curricular frameworks, be a source of advocacy at a school or district level?

At the End . . .

We can't solve problems by using the same kind of thinking we used when we created them.

—Albert Einstein

Our rapidly changing and increasingly complex world presents new challenges to and demands on our educational system. Many students live in diverse communities, where technology is becoming omnipresent and where access to knowledge is readily available in small handheld devices. Yet, these same students are often totally disengaged and disconnected from the material in their classrooms. Other students do not have access to 21st century technologies, are using dated materials, and have not had an experienced teacher during their school years. There are also students who are trying to learn how to "do school" in the United States while learning English as a second, third, or fourth language, and who are unable to catch up with their English-proficient peers. This heterogeneity of students is pushing schools and educators to develop new and creative ways of thinking about teaching and learning.

Within this context, academic language has become central to schooling and a strong factor influencing academic success. To participate in content area learning, students now need to simultaneously learn the language of the disciplines, including the unique linguistic features at the discourse, sentence, and word/phrase levels. Yet, as we have emphasized throughout this book and the series, learning academic language requires more than acquiring linguistic knowledge; it includes cultural knowledge about the ways, practices, actions, and interactions used in different academic communities.

Academic language is a tool to help students broaden their thinking and understanding of complex problems, scientific phenomena, and local and global issues. Ultimately, what we want is for students to be able to think, talk, act, and interact as members of a variety of academic, professional, scientific, and mathematical communities. The ability of students to use academic language for varying purposes and in a variety of situations is especially critical given that they will need to solve problems that do not yet exist and pursue careers that are not yet charted.

Fifteen tenets are exemplified in this book and throughout the series that afford educators promising ways of thinking about academic language use in school. While the success of several of these practices and principles has been documented in the literature, the uniqueness of this vision lies in their careful orchestration in a range of school contexts that leads to the academic success of diverse students, particularly English language learners (ELLs). The following is a brief explanation of each tenet.

1. Focus on the gifts that students bring to school.

    Students do not come to classrooms as *tabula rasa*—they are not blank slates to be written on. Each student comes into classrooms bringing many gifts, including languages, cultures, values, beliefs, and ways of learning and knowing. Since students are the consumers of and central focus for curricular planning and educational action, knowing students' individual backgrounds and trajectories is of the essence. Prior schooling experiences, individual interests, learning styles, personality traits, and motivation all play a role in how students connect to and learn from the experiences afforded by the school.

2. Plan and teach language and content simultaneously.

    We know that learning *aspects* of language alone does not facilitate language development. Many adults took a foreign language in high school, learned many vocabulary words, memorized conjugations, and rehearsed buying a ticket at the train station, yet when they had an opportunity to practice their new language to buy a bus ticket, they realized that they did not know how to "use" the language in meaningful ways in real-life situations. When teachers seamlessly integrate language and content within authentic instructional activities and tasks, students are able to simultaneously blend language learning within their content learning.

3. Examine content standards for academic language.

    The move toward standards-based education is a national effort to improve instruction and learning in public schools. It is based on the assumption that all students can reach higher levels of achievement if expectations for all students are raised, standards are clearly defined, instruction and classroom assessment are differentially planned, leadership supports learning, and students are held accountable for their performance. Within this context, the new generation of content standards, including the CCSS and NGSS, represent a step forward in updating educational expectations based on new understandings of how students learn, their personal needs, and the needs of our changing world. The academic language associated with these standards along with that of language proficiency/development standards helps raise the bar for student performance.

4. Identify corresponding language development or language proficiency standards.

Many states and consortia have developed, adapted, or adopted English language development/proficiency standards that correspond with current academic content standards so that ELLs, along with all students, can graduate from high school or college and be career ready. In conjunction with content standards, language proficiency/development standards contribute to our understanding of how academic language spirals vertically from grade to grade and horizontally from one proficiency level to the next. Together, language and content standards provide a powerful base for academic language use in a variety of contexts.

5. Remember, "It takes a village to raise a child."

In all societies, children learn how to be members of the world from their parents/guardians, siblings, family members, peers, neighbors, and friends, as well as teachers and other professionals. They also learn in different settings, such as the home, neighborhood, libraries, religious institutions, businesses, and community organizations and through the media in addition to school. With this in mind, it behooves educators to be aware of sociocultural configurations surrounding the lives of the students they teach. Old models of parent involvement are being replaced by more inclusive approaches of school–family–community partnerships that bring together not only parents and teachers but also grandparents, other family members, caregivers, community partners and business leaders—united by common goals linked to academic achievement and school success for all students.

6. Capitalize on the linguistic and cultural resources of students, homes, and communities.

Within the growing diversity in our communities, there is an abundance of rich resources. Community members, places, traditions, and events can offer educators invaluable perspectives on the students and the neighborhoods in which they reside. Having teachers learn about their students' lives and traditions help them better understand the rich cultural resources of the community and is an important first step in getting to know their students in deeper and more meaningful ways. Home visits and community events offer tremendous opportunities to become familiar with the students and their families outside the confines of school walls. From these rich resources can grow linguistically and culturally responsive curricula and instruction for the entire school.

7. Engage in academic, scientific, and mathematical practices.

In the last two decades, the notion of "practices" within a professional or scientific community has become prevalent in educational research and content standards. This notion emphasizes the importance of not only *knowing* scientific or academic concepts but also being able to *apply* those understandings to engage in disciplinary work, investigate issues, or solve problems. In essence, *practices* refers to disciplinary processes and competencies needed to engage in a variety of ways and contexts, including inquiry, scholarly examination of documents, empirical research, problem solving, and using evidence to support claims. Students and teachers alike should be active participants in these practices.

8. Involve multiple modes of communication in teaching and learning.

Education has shifted from an emphasis on the 3 Rs—Reading, wRiting, and aRithmetic—to preparing students for college and a multicultural global community. Traditional distinctions between oral and written language are being blurred in electronic communication. Texts, tweets, and instagrams are written (or multimodal) messages that resemble oral language. In fact, for the digital natives sitting in today's classrooms, both multiliteracies and electronic devices are used to construct meaning and communicate with others. Our repertoire of literacies is ever growing and has expanded to include digital literacy, visual literacy, financial literacy, and assessment literacy, to name a few. As we prepare students for tomorrow, an important skill they will need is to be able to communicate well and collaborate effectively with diverse people, in various settings, through a variety of modes.

9. Use instructional supports.

Visual, sensory, graphic, and interactional supports enhance instruction and carry over to classroom assessment. These kinds of supports give students an entrée to content and allow them to engage in higher order thinking regardless of their level of language proficiency and school experiences. Supports for instruction and assessment allow students to demonstrate what they know and are able to do without total dependence on print or oral language. With instructional supports, teachers are able to provide scaffolding for ongoing language development and content learning. Students, in turn, have more opportunities to access grade-level content and thrive in class.

10. Understand that one size doesn't fit all.

Curricular expectations are usually expressed in content and language targets for all students. Given the content and language targets, that is, the big ideas or essential understandings that guide instruction, educators need to break them down into differentiated content and language objectives. Differentiated content objectives apply to the specific academic needs and strengths of each student in relation to the activities of the lessons. For ELLs, differentiated language objectives, aimed at their levels of language proficiency, are key for them to participate in content learning.

11. Design integrated units of learning.

Integrated units, where different content areas are brought together around a common theme, have several characteristics: They cut across disciplines, are aligned with academic content and language standards, and allow students to experience learning in coherent ways. In addition, integrated units make learning more in tune with the real world; connect to students' interests, needs, and strengths in more meaningful ways; and result in authentic learning experiences.

12. Match learning targets to assessment practices.

In creating learning targets, teachers, whether as partners, in grade-level or departmental teams, or in professional learning communities, are encouraged to engage in conversations and reach consensus on the most critical aspects of content and language learning for each unit of instruction. Designed for all students, these targets enable teachers to concentrate on an essential understanding or big idea for the subject area topic and simultaneously pair it with an overall language focus that enables students to access and achieve that content. With these targets in hand, teachers can then generate ideas for an end-of-unit project, performance, or product along with rubrics or other documentation to interpret student work.

13. Create engaging instructional assessment activities.

Instructional activities, tasks, and projects, along with their embedded assessment, are the backbone for teaching and learning academic language and content in K–12 classrooms. Challenging or new content becomes comprehensible to students when educators integrate grade-level material and its related language into activities where students purposefully interact with each task and each other. In addition, when innovative engaging activities within lessons draw from the students' linguistic and cultural resources, students are able to move past understanding to integrate new concepts into their learning.

14. Form learning communities.

In today's educational settings, there is no room for the outdated model of one language teacher in charge of the education of ELLs for a single grade, multiple grades, a school, a language education program, or even a district! An important tenet apparent throughout the exemplar cases in the mathematics and language arts books is that there is strength in teacher collaboration. Students have greater opportunities for academic success when teachers cooperate in working together as a team or as members of learning communities inclusive of the students. Teacher teams can engage in dialogue, inquiry, and reflection to design curricula or plan instruction and assessment, to improve their professional practice.

15. Reflect on teaching and learning.

Given the complexities, ambiguities, and dilemmas that characterize the work of teachers in today's classrooms, educators have to take on the role of reflective researchers of their own practice. Beyond global statements such as "my students didn't understand" or "that lesson rocked," educators need to be deliberate, thoughtful, and systematic in collecting evidence of learning, often tied to standards, to inform their thinking and planning. Today's smartphones and other technology afford ways of recording moment-by-moment classroom interactions or taking pictures of students' work for assessment or further analysis. Of course, diaries, peer observation, and student feedback are always useful ways of exploring our practices and underlying beliefs. Teaching is a profession; its backbone is reflective practice.

Today's classrooms have unique configurations of students who represent many different languages, cultures, and life experiences. In recognition of this individuality, the thematic units of learning cited in this book are not step-by-step, foolproof teaching formulas. What we have tried to accomplish is to offer a smorgasbord of options and ideas for academic language use that are bound by a Curricular Framework (see Resource C). What is most valued are the thoughtful, intentional, and evidence-informed practices of dedicated educators who see strength in diversity, possibilities amidst challenging times, and academic success on the faces of all their students.

Resources

State content standards, in particular the Common Core State Standards (CCSS), have influenced mathematics education greatly. What has not been taken into account until recently is that embedded in each mathematical concept and skill is accompanying academic language. That is, for every domain and cluster of standards, there are also grade-level language expectations requisite for accessing and achieving those skills. In essence, language is the communicative tool used to negotiate mathematically.

The figures in this resource are but a slice of the grades K–8 mathematics curriculum. The in-depth presentation of mathematical thinking and doing offers much insight into typically diverse classrooms across the country. However, to provide greater coverage of the scope of each grade level and a sense of its academic language, we have created a set of individual figures with examples of the language of key concepts within each mathematical domain, according to the CCSS. In this way, teachers might anticipate how language might be used to relay mathematical content throughout the year.

The selected examples of the language of mathematics, shown on the right-hand side of each grade-level figure, may be challenging to students. They are just a sampling of the many ways in which the academic language of particular mathematical domains can be expressed, and are intended to illustrate an array of patterns that represent the dimensions of academic language. The words shown in italics are examples of academic language, including words and expressions with multiple meanings, technical vocabulary, complex grammatical constructions, and forms idiosyncratic to English as well as sequential and comparative language.

The figures in the following pages may be useful in (1) prompting collaboration between content and language teachers, (2) serving as points of departure in discussions within professional learning communities and grade-level teams, or (3) giving teachers some ideas for formulating language targets for their units of instruction or differentiating language objectives for their individual lessons. When educational stakeholders, especially teachers and school leaders, become aware of the reciprocal roles of language and content in subject-area instruction, all students benefit. Thus, ultimately, the integration or interweaving of content and language allows students to engage in meaning making during learning.

Content and Language Learning in Mathematics, Kindergarten

Key Concepts From the Common Core State Standards for Mathematics	Examples of Related Academic Language
Number Names and Count Sequence	Put the numbers *in a row*.
Counting	*Time to put our things away, 1, 2, 3!*
Comparison of Numbers	Which group has *more?* Which one is *greater?*
Concepts of Addition and Subtraction	How many do you need to *make* 10? Let's *put Jane's and Sam's M&Ms together.*
Foundations of Place Value	Let's trade these 10 sticks for *one bundle of 10* sticks. Twelve is *one ten and two ones.*
Measurable Attributes	The table is *longer than* the desk. The crayon is *shorter than* the pencil.
Classification of Objects	A triangle has *3 sides and 3 corners.* A circle has *no sides and no corners!*
Shapes: Identification and Description	There is a circle on the wall *in the front of* the room; what is it? There is a rectangle on the wall *in the back of* the room; what is it?
Shapes: Analysis, Comparison, and Creation	This side is *the same as* that side.

Content and Language Learning in Mathematics, Grade 1

Key Concepts From the Common Core State Standards for Mathematics	Examples of Related Academic Language
Addition and Subtraction	There are 9 pieces of fruit on a table. Two are apples and *the rest* are bananas. How many bananas are there?
Relationship Between Addition and Subtraction	*In a fact family, all the numbers are related! If* 15 − 9 = 6, *then* 6 + 9 = 15.
Fluency of Addition and Subtraction Within 20	*What is . . . ? How many are . . . ?*
Addition and Subtraction Equations	What is the *missing* number? Which number is *unknown?*
Counting	Let's *count down from* 20 and then *count back up!*
Place Value	Thirty means 3 *bundles of ten.*
Using Place Value for Addition and Subtraction	*When finding* 71 − 26, *why don't you count up by 10s from 26 first?*
Measurement of Length	Put the 3 crayons *in order.* First is the *short* one, then a *shorter* one, and last, the *shortest* one.
Time	Recess is in *a half hour.* Lunch is in *an hour and a half.*
Representation and Interpretation of Data	*Bar graphs, picture graphs, tally charts, tables, hundreds chart*
Reasoning With Shapes and Their Attributes	*Put shapes together* to make a new shape. *Combine different shapes* to make a new one.

Content and Language Learning in Mathematics, Grade 2

Key Concepts From the Common Core State Standards for Mathematics	Examples of Related Academic Language
Problem Solving With Addition and Subtraction	*How many more* do you need? How many are *left?*
Fluency of Addition and Subtraction Within 20	Think of a number from 2 to 10. *Add* 6. What is *2 less?* What is *4 more? Take away 3. Subtract 2* more. How many *remain?*
Groups of Objects	I know *there are an odd number of objects because.* . . .
Place Value	Use your base-10 *blocks* to show me 247. Remember, use *flats* for the hundreds place, *sticks* for the tens place, and *bits* for the ones place.
Using Place Value for Addition and Subtraction	Here is my *place value strategy* for 55 + 12. *First,* I *broke* 55 and 12 *into* tens and ones. Five tens plus one ten equals 6 tens. *Then* I added the ones, 5 plus 2. *Finally,* I *combined* the tens and the ones.
Lengths in Standard Units	*Estimate* the length of each object. Is each one *about a yard* in length? Or is it *around a foot* in length?
Addition and Subtraction of Length	Mimi's backpack is *15 inches long.* Hana's backpack is *18 inches long.* Who has the *shorter* backpack?
Time and Money	*If* you have 4 dimes and 5 pennies, how many *cents* do you have?
Representation and Interpretation of Data	Make a graph to show 9 insects, 4 spiders, 13 fish, and 2 frogs. Answer the question, "How many more spiders *would there have to be* in order for the number of spiders to equal the number of fish?"
Reasoning With Shapes and Their Attributes	If I put these two *triangles* next to each other, what new shape do I get? How many *sides* and *corner points* does it have?

Content and Language Learning in Mathematics, Grade 3

Key Concepts From the Common Core State Standards for Mathematics	Examples of Related Academic Language
Multiplication and Division: Representation and Problem Solving	Use *arrays* to find the *product* of 11 and 8. Show me 5 groups of 8 M&Ms. Now take the M&Ms and put them into equal groups of 10. What is the difference in these two *representations?*
Multiplication and Division: Properties of Multiplication and the Relationship Between Multiplication and Division	Can you *show me* why the *commutative property* always works? *Tell me how to read the equation two different ways:* $14 \times ? = 98$; ___ $\div 14 = 7$.
Multiplication and Division Within 100	Use the *times table* to recite the 3s *family.*
Basic Operations: Problem Solving and Patterns in Arithmetic	Describe the pattern using the phrase *each and every.*
Place Value in Multidigit Arithmetic	*Round* the number to the nearest hundred. Then tell me the rule of when to *round up* and when to *round down.* When comparing the numbers 436 and 612, why do we only need to worry about the *hundreds place?*
Fractions as Numbers	*Shade* in 3 of the 5 squares; what is the fraction amount? What does the *shaded area* show? How can we take *1/5 of the amount of* candy in the bowl? Only *6 out of the 23* children in the classroom are boys.
Measurement and Estimation of Intervals of Time, Liquid Volumes, and Masses of Objects	It takes 15 minutes for water to boil on a low flame. *If* you put a pot on the stove at 3:10, *when* will the water boil? Approximately *how much* water will the tub hold? How can we find its *volume?*
Data Representation and Interpretation	*Construct a table* that shows the number of students from various countries who attend your school.
Geometric Measurement: Area	Show that finding the area *is the same as* multiplying the lengths of the sides of a figure.
Geometric Measurement: Perimeter	You add *up* the length of the sides to *find* the perimeter.
Reasoning with Shapes and Attributes	How is a rhombus *like a* rectangle? How is a square *like a* rectangle?

Content and Language Learning in Mathematics, Grade 4

Key Concepts From the Common Core State Standards for Mathematics	Examples of Related Academic Language
Four Operations With Whole Numbers	How many *altogether?* How many are *left?* What is the *product?* How many times does ____ *go into* ____?
Factors and Multiples	A whole number is a multiple *of each of its factors.*
Patterns	1. Determine if the *order of numbers* is ascending (getting larger in value) or descending (becoming smaller in value). 2. Find the difference between numbers that are *next to each other.* 3. Use the difference between numbers to find the missing number.
Place Value with Multidigit Whole Numbers	A digit *in one place* is ten times what it represents *in the place to its right.*
Fraction Equivalence and Ordering	One half *is the same as* three sixths.
Fraction Building	Three and two thirds *means.* . . . *Another way of saying* four and two fifths *is* _____.
Decimal Notation for Fractions	*Convert* .55 to a fraction; *rewrite* .55 as a fraction; *express* .55 as a fraction.
Measurement and Conversion of Measurements	What *do you do* to double the amount? How do you *change* ____ *into* ____?
Data Representation and Interpretation	From a line plot, find and interpret the difference in height *between the tallest and shortest* zoo animals.
Angle and Angle Measurement	Which angle is between 20 and 40 *degrees?*
Shapes With Lines and Angles	Name the *types of angles* that *make up* each shape.

Content and Language Learning in Mathematics, Grade 5

Key Concepts From the Common Core State Standards for Mathematics	Examples of Related Academic Language
Numerical Expressions	Express the calculation, "Subtract 5 *from* 10; then multiply *by* 3."
Patterns and Relationships	Show the *sequence* for the *rule* "add 5" with the *starting number* 0. Then show the *sequence* for the *rule* "add 10" with the *starting number* 0. What is the *pattern between* the two *sequences?*
Place Value System	How do you *round* the decimal to the next *place?*
Multidigit Whole Number Operations With Decimals	*Explain how* to add, subtract, multiply, and divide decimals.
Equivalent Fractions: Addition and Subtraction	What are the steps in converting an *unlike denominator* into a *common denominator?*
Multiplication and Division of Fractions	6/8 means 6 *is divided by* 8. When 6/8 *is multiplied by* 8, the answer is 6.
Conversion of Measurement Units	To convert centimeters to millimeters, the decimal point moves *to the right;* to convert millimeters to centimeters, the decimal point moves *to the left.*
Data Representation and Interpretation	Look at the line plot. *How many players scored no runs last season?*
Geometric Measurement: Volume	What are the differences among a *cube,* a *unit cube,* and *one cubic unit?*
Graphing	In 2005, our school *had* 200 students. Every year, it *has grown* by 15 students. How many students *will it have* in the year 2015? Make a graph to show the growth.
Two-Dimensional Figures	All rectangles have 4 right angles. Squares are rectangles. *Therefore,* all squares have 4 right angles.

Content and Language Learning in Mathematics, Grade 6

Key Concepts From the Common Core State Standards for Mathematics	Examples of Related Academic Language
Ratios	A is X times *more than* B. The ratio *of* boys *to* girls is 3 *to* 2 (3:2).
Proportion	A *is to* B *as* C *is to* D. A is *directly/inversely proportional* to B.
Division of Fractions	To divide fractions, *flip* the second fraction to its *reciprocal; then multiply across.*
Common Factor of A and B	A number that *divides evenly into* both A and B is a common factor.
Multiple of A	Any number that can be *evenly divided* by A is a multiple of A as is any number of the form *A x k, where k is an integer.*
Rational Numbers	Every whole number is a rational number, *because it can be written as* a fraction. Rational numbers are written as the *numerator over (divided by) the denominator.*
Algebraic Equations	An equation is a number sentence *with an equal sign.*
Two-Variable Equations and Inequalities	The number of cats is twice *the number of dogs in a kennel.* What is *the greatest number of cats* if there are at most a total of 48 animals in the kennel?
Dependent and Independent Variables	Scores on tests help determine your final grade. The *independent variable* is a test, and the *dependent variable* is your grade.

Key Concepts From the Common Core State Standards for Mathematics	Examples of Related Academic Language
Area, Surface Area, and Volume	Area is *a two-dimensional measure; surface is a three-dimensional measure.* The volume of a sphere *is found* by the formula *"four-thirds pi r cubed"* ($4/3 \ \pi r^3$). The surface area can be found by *adding all of the areas of each face of the figure.*
Statistical Average and Variability	*Average* is a common term for a *measure of central tendency.* The *standard deviation* gives you an idea of how *close or far apart the data points are.*
Distributions	To draw a box *plot, first* sort the data from least to greatest. *Then* find the median of the entire set of data. *Now* find the median of the upper and lower halves of the data or its quartiles. *Next,* draw a number line starting with the minimum and ending with the maximum. *After that,* plot the median, upper quartile, and the lower quartile on the number line. *Finally,* draw a box around the upper and lower quartile points and divide the box in two parts at the median.

Content and Language Learning in Mathematics, Grade 7

Key Concepts From the Common Core State Standards for Mathematics	Examples of Related Academic Language
Proportional Relationships	How do *simple interest, tax, markups, markdowns, tips,* and *commissions* show proportional relationships? Each 2 inches on a scale drawing equal 5 feet. What are the *actual dimensions* of the room?
Number Operations With Fractions and Rational Numbers	*Adding fractions* requires a common denominator. *Multiplying denominators* will enable you to find the common denominator between fractions.
Equivalent Expressions	The expression a + 0.05a = 1.05a means that *increase by* 5% is the same as *multiply by* 1.05.
Numerical and Algebraic Expressions and Equations	*If* a teacher who is making $25 an hour gets a 10% raise, she will *then* make an additional 1/10 of her salary an hour. *If* you add the raise of $2.50 an hour to the base salary, she *then* will make $27.50 per hour.
Geometric Figures	*Parallelograms* and *pyramids* represent two- and three-dimensional figures.
Angle Measure, Area, Surface Area, and Volume	The seventh graders are building a *minigolf game.* The *end* of the *putting green* is a circle. If the circle is 10 feet in diameter, how many square feet of *grass carpet* are needed to *cover* the circle?
Inferences From Random Sampling	Data are collected from two random samples of 100 students regarding their *school lunch preference.* Make *at least* two inferences based on the results.
Comparative Inferences About Two Populations	The *mean height* of players on the basketball team is 10 centimeters greater than the *mean height* of players on the soccer team, which makes the separation between the two *distributions of mean heights* noticeable.
Probability Models	If a student is selected at random from a class of 20, find the probability that a girl *will be chosen.*

Content and Language Learning in Mathematics, Grade 8

Key Concepts From the Common Core State Standards for Mathematics	*Examples of Related Academic Language*
Rational and Irrational Numbers	It is irrational because it cannot be written as a ratio (or a fraction), *not because it is crazy!*
Radicals and Integer Exponents	Use square root and cube root symbols to represent solutions to equations of the form $x_2=p$ and $x_3=p$, *where p is a positive rational number.*
Proportional Relationships, Lines, and Linear Equations	A tree replanted as a sapling grows 3 inches every 2 months, which is 3/2—or 1.5—inches each month; *therefore,* the rate of change is constant. *Consequently,* how is the tree's height computed when it was replanted? (Answer: Take its height at month X and subtract Y months of growth.)
Pairs of Simultaneous Linear Equations	For example, *3x + 2y = 5* and *3x + 2y = 6* have no solution, because *3x + 2y* cannot *simultaneously* be 5 and 6.
Functions	A *function table* is also called an *input/output table,* where you write the equation that the *table is expressing.*
Relationships Between Quantities Using Functions	Sally created a table for a function she knows to be linear. She thinks something must be wrong with her table, because she can't find the original function from the table. Find the error and the original function. *Explain your strategy for finding the error.*
Congruence	Two triangles are congruent *when* their corresponding sides and angles are the same.
Pythagorean Theorem	The *legs of a right triangle* are 6 and 7 inches long, *respectively. Explain how to* find the hypotenuse.
Volume of Three-Dimensional Figures	Volume is the number of cubic units needed to *fill* a three-dimensional figure, *while* the surface area is the number of square units needed to *cover* all its surfaces.
Bivariate Data	*Bivariate* data are data from *two variables,* usually related, such as the amount of ice cream sales *in relation to* the average temperature on a given day.

RESOURCE B
EXAMPLES FROM THE CCSS FOR ENGLISH LANGUAGE ARTS OF RELATED ACADEMIC LANGUAGE

Current content standards, led by the Common Core State Standards Initiative, center on college and career readiness as a universal goal for schooling. According to George Bunch, Amanda Kibler, and Susan Pimentel (2012), the four areas of concentration for English language arts— (1) engaging in complex text, (2) using evidence in writing, (3) collaborating in speaking and listening, and (4) developing language to carry out communication effectively—should be the primary foci for educators of English language learners (ELLs). To accomplish this demanding agenda for 21st century schools, teachers have to partner across instructional settings and content areas. The question at hand is how do we begin to decipher the use of academic language required for academic success?

The Framework for English Language Proficiency Development Standards corresponding to the Common Core State Standards and Next Generation Science Standards states that the language competencies spelled out in the CCSS and NGSS "implicitly demand [that] students acquire ever-increasing command of language in order to acquire and perform the knowledge and skills articulated in the standards" (Council of Chief State School Officers [CCSSO], 2012, p. ii). In the following figures, we begin to chip away at the underlying academic language, bringing it to the surface for teacher use. Specifically, we identify example text types, text features, and text structures associated with the CCSS for each grade level, K through 8, and modality within English language arts—reading, speaking and listening, and writing.

In our case studies of English language arts classrooms, teachers and teacher teams pair the content standards with language proficiency/ development standards, making them come to life in their design of instructional units (see the Academic Language in Diverse Classrooms series for English language arts, 2013).

Reading: Example Text Types/Genres, Example Text Features, Example Text Structures, and Example Language Structures by Grade (Derived From the CCSS)

Grade	Text Types/ Genre-Based Discourse	Text Features	Text Structures	Language Structures
K	Storybooks, poems, informational texts	Front cover, back cover, title page, author & illustrator	Comparison and contrast of attributes, concepts of print	Where is the *large* monkey? Where is the *small* monkey?
1	Storybooks, poems, opinion pieces, informational texts	Headings, tables of content, glossaries, electronic menus, icons	Explanation of differences between narrative and informational text	This book *tells a story.* This book *gives information.*
2	Stories, fables, folktales, opinion pieces, content-area texts (history/ social studies, science, technical subjects)	Rhymes, captions, bold print, subheadings, indexes	Description of the overall structure of a story	*A fable is a story* about animals. *A fable has a moral.*

Reading: Example Text Types/Genres, Example Text Features, Example Text Structures, and Example Language Structures by Grade (Derived From the CCSS)

Grade	Text Types/ Genre-Based Discourse	Text Features	Text Structures	Language Structures
3	Stories, dramas, poems, myths, opinion pieces, content-area texts (history/ social studies, science, technical subjects)	Chapters, scenes, stanzas, sidebars, hyperlinks, key words	Explanation of actions and their contributions to sequence of events	*Tell me how* Mrs. O'Leary's cow led to the great Chicago fire.
4	Stories, myths, traditional literature from different cultures, dramas, poems, charts, graphs, diagrams, timelines, animations, web pages, opinion pieces, content-area texts (history/social studies, science, technical subjects)	Poems: verse, rhythm, meter Dramas: cast of characters, setting, dialogue, stage directions Stories: first- and third-person narration	Description of characters, settings, or events	This story *takes place* a long time ago in a country *far far away.* It's about a girl named Sadako who lived in the *island nation of* Japan. She made a thousand paper cranes *in hope of* curing her disease.
5	Stories, dramas, poems, graphic novels, multimedia presentations, mysteries, adventure stories, digital sources, opinion pieces, content-area texts (history/social studies, science, technical subjects)	Quotations, figurative language (metaphors and similes)	Comparison and contrast of two or more characters, settings, or events	In the book *Lost,* Donald doesn't have any friends. *However,* he is kind and considerate. *In contrast,* Drew is very popular and confident.

Reading: Example Text Types/Genres, Example Text Features, Example Text Structures, and Example Language Structures by Grade (Derived From the CCSS)

Grade	Text Types/ Genre-Based Discourse	Text Features	Text Structures	Language Structures
6	Stories, dramas, poems, memoirs, biographies, historical novels, fantasies, multimedia texts, literary nonfiction	Citation of textual evidence	Analysis of text structure in relation to the theme, setting, or plot	Biographies are often written in the historical present. *As a result,* it seems *as if* Lincoln is living today *instead of* over 150 years ago.
7	Audio text, digital text, video, multimedia, literary nonfiction, sonnets, soliloquies	Citation of pieces of textual evidence	Comparison of text to a multimedia version	The audio text helped me understand the plot. *On the other hand,* the digital text helped me see the action.
8	Digital text, video, multimedia, literary nonfiction, film, scripts, live productions	Allusions, analogies	Evaluation of the use of different mediums	Which form of technology is *most effective* for your learning style? Describe and compare the different forms from most beneficial to least useful for you.

Speaking and Listening: Example Functions, Text Structures, and Language Structures by Grade (Derived From the CCSS)

Grade	Example Language Functions	Example Text Structures	Example Language Structures
K	Ask and answer questions	Interrogatives	*Who* is the author? *It's* Alma Flor Ada.
1	Describe people, places, things, and events	Descriptive language	The election *is in* November. The inauguration *is on* January 20th.
2	Recount key ideas	Descriptive language	The grocery store *was at the corner.* The bank *was across the street.*
3	Discuss with others	Dialogue	*"How do you think we should* make stone soup?" *"I think we should* use water, vegetables, and stones!" *"What do you think* we should use?"
4	Paraphrase from diverse media	Prepositional phrases	Twitter makes you say things *in 140 characters* or less. Facebook allows you to have pictures *of your friends.*
5	Summarize others' points	Connectives	*Basically,* you are opposed to a longer school day. *In other words,* you don't think we need extra time to learn.
6	Interpret information	Technical vocabulary	Read the problems and decide whether to use a *circle graph, bar graph,* or a *stem and leaf plot.*
7	Evaluate reasoning of a speaker's argument	Linking words and phrases	The pros of having school guards outweigh the cons. *Therefore,* I favor police officers in school.
8	Analyze the purpose of information	Multiple meanings	This article *argues* for the use of qualitative data.

Writing: Example Text Types, Text Structures, and Language Structures by Grade (Derived From the CCSS)

Grade	Example Text Type	Example Text Structures	Example Language Structures
K	Preferences	First person	*I like* ice cream.
1	Opinions	Relative clauses	*I think* it's going to rain.
2	Recounts of events	Sequential language	First, I washed the dishes. *Then* I did my homework. *Finally,* I played outside.
3	Information pieces	Linking words and phrases	The weather is changing. *For example,* it has not rained very much. *Also,* the days are warmer than last year.
4	Explanations	Relational language related to cause and effect	Juan picked out a new blue backpack because he lost his old one. If he *would have chosen* the red one, he *would have gotten* a ten-dollar coupon.
5	Narratives of experiences or events	Past tense	Late one night, a loud bang *woke me up*. I *searched* and *searched* all around but *saw* nothing strange.
6	Arguments focused on discipline-specific content	Persuasive language	You *definitely* need to read this article. The author is *confident* that global warming is a reality. Scientists are *certain* that greenhouse gas emissions are rising more rapidly than predicted.
7	Narration of historical events, scientific procedures/ experiments, or technical processes	Descriptive language	*During the final hours of the battle,* it was evident that the Allies would win.
8	Action research	Propositional language	*I propose that* if I study longer each day, I will get better grades.

REFERENCES

Bunch, G. C., Kibler, A., & Pimentel, S. (2012, January 13). *Realizing opportunities for English learners in the common core English language arts standards and disciplinary literacy standards.* Paper presented at the Understanding Language Conference, Stanford University, Palo Alto, CA.

Council of Chief State School Officers (CCSSO). (2012). *Framework for English language proficiency development standards corresponding to the Common Core State Standards and Next Generation Science Standards.* Washington, DC: Author.

RESOURCE C
A CURRICULAR FRAMEWORK HIGHLIGHTING
ACADEMIC LANGUAGE

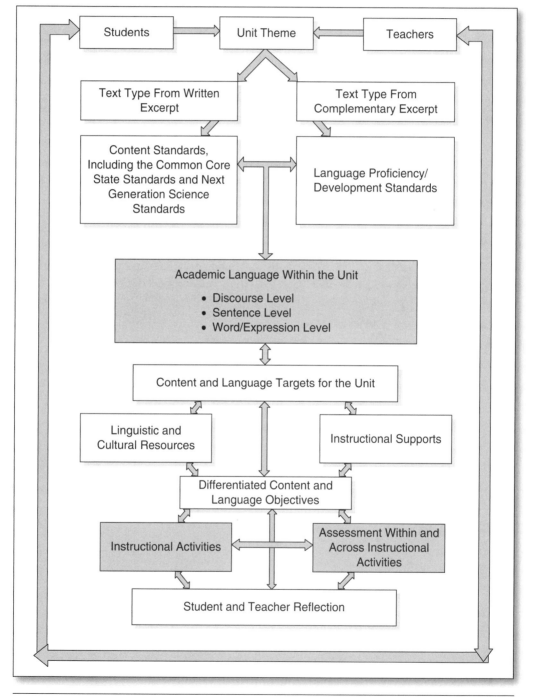

Source: Gottlieb & Ernst-Slavit, 2013

Glossary

Academic achievement: demonstration of the concepts, skills, and knowledge base associated with content area curricula.

Academic language: the language of school related to acquiring new and deeper understandings of content related to curriculum, communicating those understandings to others, and participating in the classroom environment. These understandings revolve around specific dimensions of language use including discourse, sentence, and word or expression levels within sociocultural contexts.

Accountable talk: teachers modeling different ways of discussion and leading the interchange of ideas in classroom activities as a means of expanding students' thinking as they engage in academic conversations.

Assessment: the planning and gathering of information from multiple sources over time that, when analyzed, interpreted, and reported, provide evidence of student performance in relation to standards, targets, or objectives.

Backward design: front-loading standards, learning targets, and assessment in the instructional cycle to guide the implementation of activities and tasks for student learning.

Cognates: words in one language that correspond in both meaning and form to words in another language (e.g., *park* in English and el *parque* in Spanish).

Common assessment: a multistep process by which measures have been crafted based on mutually agreed upon decisions by educators for use in multiple classrooms, or a uniform set of procedures for collecting, interpreting, reporting, and using data across multiple classrooms.

Communities of practice: groups that share information and experiences and whose members learn from each other, such as a classroom of students.

Content-based instruction: an approach in which discipline-specific content is integrated with language teaching; the concurrent teaching of academic subject matter along with language skills.

Content-compatible language: the language that complements content-obligatory language of the specific concepts or information being taught.

Content objectives: a component of a curricular framework or design that identifies observable student behavior or performance expected at the end of a lesson related to specific concepts or skills of a discipline.

Content-obligatory language: the vocabulary, grammatical structures, and expressions necessary for language learners to develop and communicate content knowledge and to participate in classroom tasks.

Content standards, including the Common Core State Standards and Next Generation Science Standards: the skills and understandings descriptive of student grade-level expectations, minimally in English language arts, mathematics, and literacy in history/social studies, science, and technical subjects, along with their accompanying practices.

Content target: a component of a curricular framework or design that identifies the overall concepts, ideas, or knowledge of a topic or theme expected of all students for a unit of study.

Coteaching: two or more educators who work together and share the responsibility for instructing some or all of the students in a classroom.

Criteria for success: specific, measurable outcomes for learning, often tied to standards and related targets or objectives that are shared by teachers and students.

Cultural resources: the traditions, values, experiences, and artifacts that are part of students' lives that bridge home and community to school.

Curricular designs: ways of organizing learning experiences that are relevant and meaningful for students; the process of developing academic plans for teaching.

Curricular framework: an organized plan that defines the processes and products of a unit of learning that includes academic language associated with both grade-level content and language.

Differentiated instruction: an approach based on the philosophy that all students can learn; it provides groups of students with different avenues to acquire content (and language) based on challenging teaching materials.

Differentiated language objectives: language expectations defined so that teachers gear lessons according to English language learners' levels of English language proficiency.

Digital literacy: the ability to make meaning by critically navigating, collecting, and evaluating information using a range of digital technologies including computers, the Internet, educational software, and cell phones.

Discourse: broadly, the ways in which oral and written language are connected and organized.

Descriptive feedback: a formative assessment strategy important for student achievement where students gain understanding of their performance in relation to objectives, learning targets, or standards.

English language learners (ELLs): linguistically and culturally diverse students who are in the process of developing English language competencies as they access grade-level content.

English language proficiency levels: designations that are descriptive of where English language learners are positioned on the language development continuum.

Formative assessment practices: strategies that provide timely, descriptive, and relevant feedback to students related to their progress toward meeting learning targets or objectives; a process in which information is gathered during the instructional cycle for teachers to ascertain the effectiveness of their instruction.

General academic vocabulary: words and expressions applicable to a wide range of contexts and content areas.

Genres: ways to organize and define various types of oral and spoken language (e.g., blogs, oral book reports).

Home language: students' primary language spoken at home and generally one of their first languages acquired.

Informational texts: factual material whose purpose is to inform about the natural or social world.

Instructional activities: a component of curricular frameworks that describes the opportunities students have to interact with each other, with media, or independently to acquire or reinforce concepts, understanding, skills, or language.

Instructional assessment: varied measures of learning embedded in teaching, such as performance tasks, that use various forms of documentation to interpret student performance.

Instructional supports: sensory (e.g., photographs), graphic (e.g., T-charts), and interactive resources (e.g., paired collaborative learning) integrated into instruction and assessment and used to assist students at various levels of language proficiency in constructing meaning from language and content.

Language forms: the grammatical structures, syntax, and mechanics associated with sentence-level meaning.

Language functions: the purposes for which language is used to communicate (e.g., sequence, compare/contrast, justify).

Language objectives: specified, observable language outcomes designed for individual lessons and often differentiated by students' levels of language proficiency.

Language proficiency: demonstration of a person's competencies in processing (through listening and reading) and using (through speaking and writing) language at a point in time.

Language proficiency/development standards: language expectations for students marked by performance definitions and descriptors/performance indicators of language proficiency levels across the language development continuum.

Language targets: overall literacy and/or oral language outcomes designed for all students for a unit of learning.

Learning logs: an instructional assessment tool where students make entries on a regular basis that shows student growth in language or knowledge of content over time.

Levels of language proficiency: stages along the pathway of language development, generally expressed as descriptors of performance along the language continuum.

Linguistic complexity: the amount or density of information in oral or written discourse as determined by the compactness of words along with morphological and syntactic structures.

Linguistically and culturally responsive education: instruction and assessment that support students' learning by using resources and experiences from their homes and communities to relate to and build on what they already know about a topic.

Linguistically diverse students: students who are exposed to languages in addition to English in their home backgrounds.

Linguistic resources: language-related capital that can be brought into the classroom to enhance instruction, such as the reference to or use of the students' home languages.

Long-term ELLs: linguistically and culturally diverse students who have not reached linguistic parity with their English-proficient peers, although they have generally participated in language support programs for seven or more years.

Metacognitive awareness: the understanding and expression of the mental processes involved in learning.

Metalinguistic awareness: the understanding and expression of the nuances and uses of language, including the process of reflecting upon its features and forms.

Multimodal tools: visual, digital, and print materials that give students opportunities to creatively show their learning.

Multiliteracies: a 21st century approach to making meaning that relies on multimodal ways for people to make sense of the world and subsequently communicate and connect with each other to learn.

Multiple meanings: words or expressions that carry more than one interpretation in social situations or within or across content areas (e.g., *base* or *ring*).

Newcomer ELLs: students who are recent arrivals to the United States (generally within the last two years) whose conceptual understanding and communicative skills are most likely in a language other than English.

Peer assessment: descriptive feedback on student work given by fellow students, generally based on standards-referenced criteria.

Performance assessment: the planning, collection, and analysis of original student work, such as curriculum-related tasks and projects, that is interpreted based on specified criteria, such as a rubric.

Professional learning community (PLC): a group of educators, including teachers and school leaders, that meets, communicates, and collaborates on a regular basis to reach common educational goals.

Personal learning networks (PLN): a type of professional learning where educators reach out into cyberspace to create an online community in pursuit of self-directed academic learning and connect with others who share interest in the same topic.

Professional learning team: a group of educators, such as grade-level teachers, who collaborate on a regular basis to work toward a mutually agreed upon goal related to teaching and learning.

Register: a variety of language used according to the setting or purpose of the communication.

Rubric: a criterion-referenced tool that enables teachers and students to interpret student work using the same set of descriptors.

Scaffold: the use of instructional supports or strategies to allow students to work within their zones of proximal development to facilitate learning.

Self-assessment: students' application of performance criteria or descriptors to monitor and interpret their own work as a means of reflecting on their language or content learning.

Sheltered instruction: a set of strategies whereby teachers deliver grade-level subject matter in ways that are accessible and comprehensible to language learners.

Social media: a highly interactive means of communication in which people create, share, and exchange information and ideas in virtual communities and networks using mobile and web-based technologies.

Sociocultural awareness: familiarity with the nuances, norms, traditions, and histories of different cultural groups and their impact on learning.

Sociocultural context: the social and physical settings in which people interact.

Specialized academic vocabulary: words or expressions representative of a content area or discipline.

Summative assessment: the "sum" of evidence for learning gathered over time, such as at the culmination of a unit of study, that is generally used for grading or accountability purposes.

Syntax: the rules that govern the ways words are arranged to form phrases, clauses, and sentences.

Task: two or more related instructional activities that generally involve multiple modalities or language domains (e.g., research report requires reading and writing, often with the use of technology).

Technical academic vocabulary: words or expressions tied to a specific topic within a content area (e.g., *phylum, polar vortex*).

Text types: different forms or genres, mainly of writing, with distinct purposes and features (e.g., a "state of the union" speech).

Transactive curriculum: a curriculum taught in rich learning environments that motivate students to take social action in response to their learning.

Transformative curriculum: organization of learning in a way that involves critical thinking and the application of learning to real-world problems; it includes student voices in decision making.

Transmissive curriculum: organization of learning that is totally directed by teachers around the acquisition of student skills.

Translanguaging: the use by bilingual speakers of a linguistic repertoire that includes more than one language; in school, for example, students often interact in two or more languages in naturally occurring situations.

Visual literacy: ability to express complex concepts and ideas without heavy reliance on print, such as through photographs, images, and film among other media.

Vocabulary: the specific words, phrases, or expressions used in a given context.

References

Abbe, M. (2013, September 13). Claes Oldenburg's 1960s work at Walker Art Center [Art exhibit review]. *Minneapolis Star Tribune.* Retrieved from http://www.startribune.com/entertainment/stageandarts/224450811.html

Achugar, M., Schleppegrell, M., & Oteíza, T. (2007). Engaging teachers in language analysis: A functional linguistics approach to reflective literacy. *Teaching English: Practice and Critique, 6*(2), 8–24.

Ainsworth, L. (2013). *Prioritizing the Common Core: Identifying specific standards to emphasize the most.* Englewood, CO: The Leadership and Learning Center.

Allen, J. (1999). *Words, words, words: Teaching vocabulary in grades 4–12.* Portland, ME: Stenhouse.

Anderson, L., Krathwohl, R., Airasian, P., Cruikshank, K., Mayer, R., Pintrich, P., . . . & Wittrock, M. (Eds.). (2001). *Taxonomy for learning, teaching, and assessing: A revision of Bloom's taxonomy.* New York, NY: Longman.

Andrews, S. (2007). *Teacher language awareness.* Cambridge, UK: Cambridge University Press.

Anstrom, K., DiCerbo, P., Butler, F., Katz, A., Millet, J., & Rivera, C. (2010). *A review of the literature on Academic English: Implications for K–12 English language learners.* Arlington, VA: The George Washington University Center for Equity and Excellence in Education.

Arias, M. B., & Faltis, C. J. (2013). *Academic language in second language learning.* Charlotte, NC: Information Age.

Aristophanes. (405 BCE). *The frogs.* Retrieved from http://www.notable-quotes.com/l/language_quotes.html

Au, K. H. (1998). Social constructivism and the school literacy learning of students of diverse backgrounds. *Journal of Literacy Research, 30*(2), 297–319.

August, D., & Shanahan, T. (Eds.). (2006). *Developing reading and writing in second language learners: Report of the National Literacy Panel on Language-Minority Children and Youth.* Mahwah, NJ: Erlbaum.

Bailey, A. L. (2007). *The language demands of school: Putting academic English to the test.* New Haven, CT: Yale University Press.

Bailey, A. L., & Heritage, M. (2008). *Formative assessment for literacy grades K–6: Building reading and academic language skills across the curriculum.* Thousand Oaks, CA: Corwin.

Bartolomé, L. I. (1998). *The misteaching of academic discourses.* Boulder, CO: Westview Press.

Bay-Williams, J., Glasser, R. M., & Bronger, T. A. (2013). Algebra describes the world! In M. Gottlieb & G. Ernst-Slavit (Series Eds.), *Academic language in diverse classrooms: Mathematics, grades 3–5* (pp. 123–164). Thousand Oaks, CA: Corwin.

Beck, I. L., McKeown, M. G., & Kucan, L. (2008). *Creating robust vocabulary: Frequently asked questions and extended examples.* New York, NY: Guilford.

Beckett, G. H., & Slater, T. (2005). The project framework: A tool for language, content, and skills integration. *ELT Journal 59*(2), 108–116.

Beeman, K., & Urow, C. (2013). *Teaching for biliteracy: Strengthening bridges between languages.* Philadelphia, PA: Caslon.

Beineke, J. (1998). *And there were giants in the land: The life of William Heard Kilpatrick.* New York, NY: Peter Lang.

Bhatia, V. K. (2005). *Worlds of written discourse: A genre-based view.* London, UK: Continuum.

Blachowicz, C. L. Z., Fisher, P., Ogle, D., & Watts-Taffe, S. (2006). Vocabulary: Questions from the classroom. *Reading Research Quarterly, 41,* 524–539.

Black, P., & William, D. (1998). Assessment and classroom learning. *Assessment in Education, 5*(1), 7–71.

Boals, T. (2013, July 19). *Making the invisible, visible: Language & literacy development across the school for ELLs & everyone else!* Keynote address delivered at the Pacific Educational Conference, Saipan, Commonwealth of the Northern Mariana Islands.

Board of Education, Commonwealth of Virginia. (2010). *English standards of learning curriculum framework, grade 6–grade 8.* Retrieved from http://www.doe.virginia .gov/testing/sol/frameworks/english_framewks/complete/framewk_ english_k-12.pdf

Bravo, M. A., & Cervetti, G. N. (2008). Teaching vocabulary through text and experience in content areas. In A. E. Farstrup & S. J. Samuels (Eds.), *What research has to say about vocabulary instruction* (pp. 130–149). Newark, DE: International Reading Association.

Brown, H. D. (2007). *Principles of language learning and teaching* (5th ed.). Boston, MA: Pearson Longman.

Bunch, G. C. (2006). "Academic English" in the 7th grade: Broadening the lens, expanding access. *Journal of English for Academic Purposes, 5,* 284–301.

Cannon, J. (1993). *Stellaluna.* San Diego, CA: Harcourt.

Cantoni-Harvey, G. (1987). *Content-area language instruction: Approaches and strategies.* Boston, MA: Addison-Wesley Longman.

Cardenas, G., Jones, B., & Lozano, O. (2014). A window into my family and community. In M. Gottlieb & G. Ernst-Slavit (Series Eds.), *Academic language in diverse classrooms: English language arts, grades K–2* (pp. 45–77). Thousand Oaks, CA: Corwin.

Carrison, C., & Muir, E. (2013). Making sense of number sense. In M. Gottlieb & G. Ernst-Slavit (Series Eds.), *Academic language in diverse classrooms: Promoting content and language learning, mathematics, grades K–2* (pp. 39–86). Thousand Oaks, CA: Corwin.

Celedón-Pattichis, S., & Musanti, S. (2013). "Let's suppose that. . . . ": Developing base-10 thinking. In M. Gottlieb & G. Ernst-Slavit (Series Eds.), *Academic language in diverse classrooms: Mathematics, grades K–2* (pp. 87–128). Thousand Oaks, CA: Corwin.

Christie, F. (2005). *Language education in the primary years.* Sydney, Australia: UNSW Press.

Coleman, R., & Goldenberg, C. (2012, February). The Common Core challenge for English language learners. *Principal Leadership,* 46–51.

Collier, V. P., & Thomas, W. P. (2009). *Educating English learners for a transformed world.* Albuquerque, NM: Fuente Press.

Coltrane, B. (2003). *Working with young English language learners: Some considerations.* Retrieved from http://www.cal.org/resources/digest/0301coltrane.html

Common Core State Standards Initiative (CCSSI). (2010a). *Common Core State Standards for English language arts & literacy in history/social studies, science, and technical subjects.* Retrieved from http://www.corestandards.org/ELA-Literacy

Common Core State Standards Initiative (CCSSI). (2010b). *Common Core State Standards for mathematical practice.* Retrieved from http://www.corestandards.org/math

Council of Chief State School Officers. (2012). *Framework for English language proficiency development standards corresponding to the Common Core State Standards and the Next Generation Science Standards.* Washington, DC: Author.

Council of Europe. (2001). *Common European framework of reference for languages: Learning, teaching, assessment.* Cambridge, UK: Cambridge University Press.

Coxhead, A. (2000). A new academic world list. *TESOL Quarterly, 34*(2), 213–238.

Crandall, J. A., & Tucker, G. R. (1990). Content-based language instruction in second and foreign languages. In S. Anivan, (Ed.), *Language teaching methodology for the nineties* (pp. 83–96). Singapore: SEAMEO Regional Language Centre.

Cummins, J. (1981). The cross-lingual dimensions of language proficiency: Implications for bilingual education and the optimal age issue. *TESOL Quarterly, 14,* 175–185.

Cummins, J. (1986). Empowering minority students: A framework for intervention. *Harvard Educational Review, 56,* 18–36.

Darling-Hammond, L. (2000). Teacher quality and student achievement: A review of state policy evidence. *Education Policy Analysis Archives, 8*(1), 1–44.

Darling-Hammond, L., Ancess, J., & Falk, B. (1995). *Authentic assessment in action.* New York, NY: Teachers College Press.

Darling-Hammond, L., & Richardson, N. (2009). Teacher learning: What matters? *Educational Leadership, 66*(5), 46–53.

de Araujo, Z. (2013). Ratios and proportions in everyday life. In M. Gottlieb & G. Ernst-Slavit (Series Eds.), *Academic language in diverse classrooms: Mathematics, grades 6–8* (pp. 77–112). Thousand Oaks, CA: Corwin.

de Jong, E. J. (2012). What are some concrete strategies that administrators and teachers can use to guide advocacy of English language learners on the local level? In E. Hamayan & R. Freeman Field (Eds.), *English language learners at school: A guide for administrators* (2nd ed.), (pp. 232–233). Philadelphia, PA: Caslon.

de Oliveira, L. C. (2010). Enhancing content instruction for English language learners: Learning about language in science. In D. Sunal, C. Sunal, M. Mantero, & E. Wright (Eds.), *Teaching science with Hispanic ELLs in K–16 classrooms* (pp. 135–150). Charlotte, NC: Information Age.

de Oliveira, L. C. (2013). Academic language in the social studies for English learners. In M. B. Arias & C. Faltis (Eds.), *Academic language and second language acquisition* (pp. 149–170). Charlotte, NC: Information Age.

de Oliveira, L. C., & Dodds, K. N. (2010). Beyond general strategies for English language learners: Language dissection in science. *Electronic Journal of Literacy Through Science, 9*(1), 1–14. Retrieved from http://ejlts.ucdavis.edu

Derewianka, B. (1990). *Exploring how texts work.* Newtown, Australia: Primary English Teaching Association.

Drake, S. M. (2007). *Creating standards-based integrated curriculum: Aligning curriculum, content, assessment, and instruction* (2nd ed.). Thousand Oaks, CA: Corwin.

Echevarria, J., Vogt, M. E., & Short, D. J. (2008). *Making content comprehensible for English learners: The SIOP model* (4th ed.). Boston, MA: Allyn & Bacon.

Edelsky, C. (2006). *With literacy and justice for all: Rethinking the social in language and education.* Mahwah, NJ: Erlbaum.

Edelsky, C., Hudelson, S., Altwerger, B., Flores, B., Barkin, F., & Jilbert, K. (1983). Semilingualism and language deficit. *Applied Linguistics, 4*(1), 1–22.

Egbert, J. L., & Ernst-Slavit, G. (2010). *Access to academics: Planning instruction for K–12 classrooms with ELLs.* Boston, MA: Pearson Education.

Ernst-Slavit, G., Gottlieb, M., &. Slavit, D. (2013). Who needs fractions? In M. Gottlieb & G. Ernst-Slavit (Series Eds.), *Academic language in diverse classrooms: Mathematics, grades 3–5* (pp. 81–121). Thousand Oaks, CA: Corwin.

Ernst-Slavit, G., & Mason, M. R. (2011). "Words that hold us up": Teacher talk and academic language in five upper elementary classrooms. *Linguistics and Education, 22,* 430–440.

Ernst-Slavit, G. & New, J. (2013, April). *Teacher talk, academic language, and language awareness: A focus on English learners.* Paper presented at the annual meeting of the American Educational Research Association, San Francisco, CA.

Ernst-Slavit, G., & Slavit, D. (2013, March 18). Mathematically speaking. *Language Magazine,* 32–36.

Faltis, C. J. (2013). Demystifying and questioning the power of academic language. In M. B. Arias & C. J. Faltis (Eds.), *Academic language in second language learning* (pp. 3–26). Charlotte, NC: Information Age.

Fang, Z., & Schleppegrell, M. J. (2008). *Reading in secondary content areas: A language-based pedagogy.* Ann Arbor: University of Michigan Press.

Fisher, D., Frey, N., & Rothenberg, C. (2008). *Content area conversations: How to plan discussion-based lessons for diverse language learners.* Alexandria, VA: ASCD.

Fisher, D., Rothenberg, C., & Frey, N. (2007). *Language learners in the English classroom.* Urbana, IL: National Council of Teachers of English.

Francis, D. J., Rivera, M., Lesaux, N., Kieffer, M., & Rivera, H. (2006). *Research-based recommendations for instruction and academic interventions.* Portsmouth, NH: Center on Instruction. Retrieved from http://www.centeroninstruction.org/files/ELL1-Interventions.pdf

Freeman, Y. S., & Freeman, D. E. (2002). *Closing the achievement gap: How to reach limited formal schooling and long-term English learners.* Portsmouth, NH: Heinemann.

Freeman, Y. S., & Freeman, D. E. (2008). *Academic language for English language learners and struggling readers: How to help students succeed across the content areas.* Portsmouth, NH: Heinemann.

Garcia, G. E. (1991). Factors influencing the English reading test performance of Spanish-speaking Hispanic students. *Reading Research Quarterly 26*, 371–392.

García, O., & Leiva, C. (2013). Theorizing and enacting translanguaging for social justice. In A. Blackledge & A. Creese (Eds.), *Heteroglossia as practice and pedagogy* (pp. 199–216). New York, NY: Springer.

García, O., & Sylvan, C. E. (2011). Pedagogies and practices in multilingual classrooms. *The Modern Language Journal, 95*(3), 385–400.

Gay, G. (2000). *Culturally responsive teaching: Theory, research, and practice.* New York, NY: Teachers College Press.

Gee, J. P. (1990). *Social linguistics and literacies: Ideology in discourses.* London, UK: Falmer Press.

Gee, J. P. (1992). What is reading? Literacies, discourses, and domination. *Journal of Urban and Cultural Studies, 2,* 65–77.

Gee, J. P. (2004). Learning language as a matter of learning social languages within discourses. In M. R. Hawkins (Ed.), *Language learning and teacher education: A sociocultural approach* (pp. 13–31). Clevedon, UK: Multilingual Matters.

Gee, J. P. (2005). Language in the science classroom: Academic social languages as the heart of school-based literacy. In R. Yerrick & W. Roth (Eds.), *Establishing scientific classroom discourse communities: Multiple voices of teaching and learning research* (pp. 19–37). Mahwah, NJ: Erlbaum.

Gee, J. P. (2011). *An introduction to discourse analysis: Theory and method.* New York, NY: Routledge.

Genesee, F. (1994). *Integrating language and content: Lessons from immersion.* Santa Cruz, CA: National Center for Research on Cultural Diversity and Second Language Learning.

Genesee, F., Lindholm Leary, K., Saunders, W. M., & Christian, D. (Eds.). (2006). *Educating English language learners: A synthesis of research evidence.* Cambridge, UK: Cambridge University Press.

Gibbons, P. (1998). Classroom talk and the learning of new registers in a second language. *Language and Education, 12,* 99–118.

Gibbons, P. (2002). *Scaffolding language, scaffolding learning: Teaching second language learners in the mainstream classroom.* Portsmouth, NH: Heinemann.

Gibbons, P. (2003). Mediating language learning: Teacher interactions with ESL students in a content-based classroom. *TESOL Quarterly, 37*(2), 257–273.

Gibbons, P. (2006). Steps for planning an integrated program for ESL learners in mainstream classrooms. In P. McKay (Ed.), *Planning and teaching creatively within a required curriculum for school-age learners* (pp. 215–233). Alexandria, VA: Teachers of English to Speakers of Other Languages.

Gibbons, P. (2009). *English learners, academic literacy, and thinking: Learning in the challenge zone.* Portsmouth, NH: Heinemann.

Goldenberg, C. (2012). Research on English learner instruction. In M. Calderón (Ed.), *Breaking through: Effective instruction & assessment for reaching English learners* (pp. 39–61). Bloomington, IN: Solution Tree.

Goldenberg, C., & Coleman, R. (2010). *Promoting academic achievement among English learners: A guide to the research.* Thousand Oaks, CA: Corwin.

González, N., Moll, L. C., & Amanti, C. (Eds.). (2005). *Funds of knowledge: Theorizing practices in households, communities, and classrooms.* Mahwah, NJ: Erlbaum.

Gottlieb, M. (2006). *Assessment of English language learners: Bridges from language proficiency to academic achievement.* Thousand Oaks, CA: Corwin.

Gottlieb, M. (2012a). Common instructional assessment for English learners: A whole school effort. In M. Calderón (Ed.), *Breaking through: Effective instruction & assessment for reaching English learners* (pp. 167–182). Bloomington, IN: Solution Tree.

Gottlieb, M. (2012b). *Common language assessment for English learners.* Bloomington, IN: Solution Tree.

Gottlieb, M., & Ernst-Slavit, G. (2013). Academic language: A foundation for academic success in mathematics. In M. Gottlieb & G. Ernst-Slavit (Series Eds.), *Academic language in diverse classrooms* (pp. 1–38). Thousand Oaks, CA: Corwin.

Gottlieb, M., & Ernst-Slavit, G. (2014). Academic language: A centerpiece for academic success in English language arts. In M. Gottlieb & G. Ernst-Slavit (Series Eds.), *Academic language in diverse classrooms* (pp. 1–44). Thousand Oaks, CA: Corwin.

Gottlieb, M., Katz, A., & Ernst-Slavit, G. (2009). *Paper to practice: Implementing TESOL's preK–12 English language proficiency standards.* Alexandria, VA: Teachers of English to Speakers of Other Languages.

Grabe, W., & Stoller, F. L. (1997). Content-based instruction: Research foundations. In M. A. Snow & D. M. Brinton (Eds.), *The content-based classroom: Perspectives on integrating language and content* (pp. 5–21). White Plains, NY: Longman.

Graves, M. F. (2006). *The vocabulary book.* New York, NY: Teachers College Press.

Graves, M. F. (2007). Conceptual and empirical bases for providing struggling readers with multifaceted and long-term vocabulary instruction. In B. M. Taylor & Y. Ysseldyke (Eds.), *Effective instruction for struggling readers, K–6* (pp. 55–83). New York, NY: Teachers College Press.

Graves, M. F. (2009). *Teaching individual words: One size does not fit all.* New York, NY: Teachers College Press, & Newark, DE: International Reading Association.

Graves, M. F., August, D., & Mancilla-Martinez, J. (2013). *Teaching vocabulary to English language learners.* New York, NY: Teachers College Press.

Graves, K., & Lopriore, L. (Eds.). (2009). *Developing a curriculum for school age learners.* Alexandria, VA: Teachers of English to Speakers of Other Languages.

Halliday, M. A. K. (1978). *Language as semiotic: The social interpretation of language and meaning.* Baltimore, MD: University Park Press.

Halliday, M. A. K. (1993). Towards a language-based theory of learning. *Linguistics and Education, 5,* 93–116.

Halliday, M. A. K., & Martin, J. R. (1993). *Writing science: Literacy and discursive power.* Pittsburgh, PA: University of Pittsburgh Press.

Heath, S. B. (1983). *Ways with words: Language, life and work in communities and classrooms.* Cambridge, UK: Cambridge University Press.

Heritage, M. (2010). *Formative assessment: Making it happen in the classroom.* Thousand Oaks, CA: Corwin.

Hiebert, E. H. (2005). In pursuit of an effective, efficient vocabulary program. In E. H. Hiebert & M. Kamil (Eds.), *Teaching and learning vocabulary: Bringing research to practice* (pp. 243–263). Mahwah, NJ: Erlbaum.

Holtgraves, T. M. (2002). *Language as social action: Social psychology and language use.* Mahwah, NJ: Erlbaum.

Homza, A. (2011, April). *Disentangling the threads of linguistic difference from the tapestry of diversity: One program's documentary account.* Paper presented in the symposium Preparing Linguistically Responsive Educators: Challenges and Opportunities in One Teacher Education Program's Multifaceted Approach at the Annual Meeting of the American Educational Research Association, New Orleans, LA.

Honigsfeld, A., & Dove, M. G. (2010). *Collaboration and co-teaching: Strategies for English learners.* Thousand Oaks, CA: Corwin.

Horwitz, A. R., Uro, G., Price-Baugh, R., Simon, C., Uzzell, R., Lewis, S., & Casserly, M. (2009). *Succeeding with English language learners: Lessons learned from the Great City Schools.* Washington, DC: Council for the Great City Schools.

Hunter, R. (2004). *Madeline Hunter's mastery teaching: Increasing instructional effectiveness in elementary and secondary schools* (Updated ed.). Thousand Oaks, CA: Corwin.

Iorio, N. (2005). *Bats!* New York, NY: Harper Collins.

Kersaint, G. (2013). Are they similar or congruent? In M. Gottlieb & G. Ernst-Slavit (Series Eds.), *Academic language in diverse classrooms: Mathematics, grades 6–8* (pp. 113–147). Thousand Oaks, CA: Corwin.

Klingner, J. K., Hoover, J. J., & Baca, L. M. (2008). *Why do English language learners struggle with reading? Distinguishing language acquisition from learning disabilities.* Thousand Oaks, CA: Corwin.

Kuhn, T. S. (1962). *The structure of scientific revolutions.* Chicago, IL: The University of Chicago Press.

Ladson-Billings, G. (1995). But that's just good teaching! The case for culturally relevant pedagogy. *Theory into Practice, 34*(3), 159–165.

Lam, E. Y., Low, M., & Tauiliili-Mahuka, R. (2014). Legends and life. In M. Gottlieb & G. Ernst-Slavit (Series Eds.), *Academic language in diverse classrooms: English language arts, grades K–3* (pp. 79–116). Thousand Oaks, CA: Corwin.

Lave, J., & Wenger, E. (1991). *Situated learning: Legitimate peripheral participation.* Cambridge, UK: Cambridge University Press.

Learning Forward. (n.d.a.). *Definition of professional development.* Retrieved February 24, 2014, from http://learningforward.org/who-we-are/professional-learning -definition-test#.UwZjpf2e60s

Learning Forward. (n.d.b.) *Who we are.* Retrieved February 24, 2014, from http:// learningforward.org/who-we-are#.Uwj-xv2qU6I

Lee, C. D., & Spratley, A. (2010). *Reading in the disciplines: The challenges of adolescent literacy.* New York, NY: Carnegie Corporation of New York.

Lee, N. (2011, April). *District understandings of academic language and language standards in 20 states.* Paper presented in the symposium Perspectives on Academic Language and Its Role in Content and Language Standards at the Annual Meeting of the American Educational Research Association, New Orleans, LA.

Lee, O., Quinn, H., & Valdes, G. (2013). Science and language for English language learners in relation to Next Generation Science Standards and with implications for Common Core State Standards for English language arts and mathematics. *Educational Researcher, 42*(4), 223–233.

Lemke, J. (1990). *Talking science: Language, learning, and values.* Norwood, NJ: Ablex.

Levine, L. N., & McCloskey, M. L. (2013). *Teaching English language and content in mainstream classes: One class, many paths* (2nd ed.). Boston, MA: Pearson.

Lillie, K. E. (2013). Afterword. In M. B. Arias & D. J. Faltis (Eds.), *Academic language in second language learning* (pp. 225–234). Charlotte, NC: Information Age.

Lyster, R. (2007). *Learning and teaching languages through content: A counterbalanced approach.* Philadelphia, PA: John Benjamins.

Macedo, D. (1994). *Literacies of power.* Boulder, CO: Westview Press.

MacSwan, J., & Rolstad, K. (2003). Linguistic diversity, schooling, and social class: Rethinking our conception of language proficiency in language minority education. In C. B. Paulston & G. R. Tucker (Eds.), *Sociolinguistics: The essential readings* (pp. 329–340). Malden, MA: Blackwell.

Makkai, A., Boatner, M. T., & Gates, J. E. (2004). *A dictionary of American idioms* (4th ed.). New York, NY: Barron's Educational Series.

Marzano, R. J. (2010). *Formative assessment and standards-based grading: Classroom strategies that work.* Indianapolis, IN: Marzano Research Laboratory.

Marzano, R. J. (2012). *Becoming a reflective teacher.* Centennial, CO: Marzano Research Laboratory.

Marzano, R. J., Yanoski, D. C., Hoegh, J. K., & Simms, J. A. (2013). *Using Common Core Standards to enhance classroom instruction & assessment.* Centennial, CO: Marzano Research Laboratory.

Mason, M., & Ernst-Slavit, G. (2010). Representations of Native Americans in elementary school social studies: A critical look at instructional language. *Multicultural Education, 18*(1), 10–17.

McCloskey, M. L., & New Levine, L. (2014). No water, no life; No blue, no green. In M. Gottlieb & G. Ernst-Slavit (Series Eds.), *Academic language in diverse classrooms: English language arts, grades 3–5* (pp. 131–178). Thousand Oaks, CA: Corwin.

McKay, P. (Ed.). (2006). *Planning and teaching creatively within a required curriculum for school-age learners.* Alexandria, VA: Teachers of English to Speakers of Other Languages.

McTighe, J., & Wiggins, G. (2012). *From Common Core standards to curriculum: Five big ideas.* Retrieved from grantwiggins.files.wordpress.com/2012/09/mctighe_wiggins_final_common_core_standards.pdf

Mercuri, S., & Rodríguez, A. D. (2014). Developing academic language through ecosystems. In M. Gottlieb & G. Ernst-Slavit (Series Eds.), *Academic language in diverse classrooms: English language arts, grades K–2* (pp. 117–156). Thousand Oaks, CA: Corwin.

Met, M. (1999, January). *Content-based instruction: Defining terms, making decisions.* NFLC reports. Washington, DC: The National Foreign Language Center.

Minaya-Rowe, L. (2014). A gothic story: "The Cask of Amontillado." In M. Gottlieb & G. Ernst-Slavit (Series Eds.), *Academic language in diverse classrooms: English language arts, grades 6–8* (pp. 137–182). Thousand Oaks, CA: Corwin.

Miramontes, O. B., Nadeau, A., & Commins, N. L. (2011). *Restructuring schools for linguistic diversity: Linking decision making to effective programs* (2nd ed). New York, NY: Teachers College Press.

Mohan, B. (1986). *Language and content.* Reading, MA: Addison-Wesley.

Moll, L. C., Armanti, C., Neff, D., & Gonzalez, N. (1992). Funds of knowledge for teaching: Using a qualitative approach to connect homes and classrooms. *Theory into Practice, 31*(2), 132–141.

Mora-Flores, E. (2014). Bombarding students with informational texts: Writing across the curriculum. In M. Gottlieb & G. Ernst-Slavit (Series Eds.), *Academic language in diverse classrooms: English language arts, grades K–2,* (pp. 79–116). Thousand Oaks, CA: Corwin.

Morrow, K. (2004). *Insights from the Common European Framework.* Oxford, UK: Oxford University Press.

Moschkovich, J. N. (2002). A situated and sociocultural perspective on bilingual mathematics learners. *Mathematical Thinking and Learning, 4*(2), 189–212.

Moschkovich, J. N. (2013). Preface. In M. Gottlieb & G. Ernst-Slavit (Series Eds.), *Academic language in diverse classrooms: Mathematics* series (pp. vii–xi). Thousand Oaks, CA: Corwin.

Moss, C. M., & Brookhart, S. M. (2009). *Advancing formative assessment in every classroom a guide for instructional leaders.* Alexandria, VA: ASCD.

Muhammad, A., & Hollie, S. (2012). *The will to lead, the skill to teach: Transforming schools at every level.* Bloomington, IN: Solution Tree.

Nagy, W. E., & Anderson, R. C. (1984). How many words are there in printed English? *Reading Research Quarterly, 19,* 304–330.

Nagy, W. E., & Scott, J. A. (2000). Vocabulary processes. In M. L. Kamil, P. B. Mosenthal, P. D. Pearson, & R. Barr (Eds.), *Handbook of reading research* (vol. III, pp. 269–284). Mahwah, NJ: Erlbaum.

Nagy, W. E., & Scott, J. A. (2004). Developing word consciousness. In J. F. Baumann & E. J. Kame'enui (Eds.), *Vocabulary instruction: Research to practice* (pp. 201–217). New York, NY: Guilford Press.

Nagy, W. E., & Townsend, D. (2012). Words as tools: Learning academic vocabulary as language acquisition. *Reading Research Quarterly, 47*(1), 91–108.

Nation, I. S. P. (2001). *Learning vocabulary in another language.* Cambridge, UK: Cambridge University Press.

National Assessment Governing Board. (2008). *Reading framework for the 2009 National Assessment of Educational Progress.* Washington, DC: Author.

National Council of Teachers of Mathematics. (1989). *Curriculum and evaluation standards for school mathematics.* Retrieved from http://www.mathcurriculumcenter.org/PDFS/CCM/summaries/standards_summary.pdf

National Education Goals Panel. (1993). *Summary guide. The national education goals report: Building the best.* Washington, DC: Author.

New, J. (2013). *Academic language, teacher talk, and language awareness: A focus on science education and ELLs.* Master's thesis, Washington State University Vancouver.

New Levine, L., & McCloskey, M. L. (2012). *Teaching English language and content in mainstream classes: One class, many paths* (2nd ed.). Boston, MA: Pearson.

New London Group. (1996). A pedagogy of multiliteracies: Designing social futures. *Harvard Educational Review, 66*(1), 60–92.

Next Generation Science Standards (NGSS). (2013). Retrieved from http://www.nextgenscience.org/next-generation-science-standards

Nieto, S. (2004). *Affirming diversity: The sociopolitical context of multicultural education* (4th ed.). Boston, MA: Pearson.

O'Dell, S. (1988). *Island of the blue dolphins.* Boston, MA: Houghton, Mifflin, Harcourt (Original work published 1960).

O'Loughlin, J. (2013). What time is it? In M. Gottlieb & G. Ernst-Slavit (Series Eds.), *Academic language in diverse classrooms: Mathematics, grades K–2* (pp. 39–80). Thousand Oaks, CA: Corwin.

Osher, D., & Fleischman, S. (2005). Creating culturally responsive schools. *Educational Leadership, 63*(1), 83–84.

Partnership for 21st Century Skills. *Curriculum and Instruction: A 21st Century Skills Implementation Guide.* Retrieved from http://p21.org/storage/documents/p21-stateimp_curriculuminstruction.pdf

Payan, R. M., & Nettles, M. T. (2007). *Current state of English-language learners in the U.S. K–12 student population.* Retrieved from http://www.ets.org/Media/Conferences_and_Events/pdf/ELLsympsium/ELL_factsheet.pdf

Peregoy, S. F., & Boyle, O. F. (2013). *Reading, writing, and learning in ESL* (6th ed.). Boston, MA: Pearson Education.

Popham, W. J. (2008). *Transformative assessment.* Alexandria, VA: Association for Supervision and Curriculum Development.

Rice, J. K. (2003). *Teacher quality: Understanding the effectiveness of teacher attributes.* Washington, DC: Economic Policy Institute.

Richardson, W., & Mancabelli, R. (2011). *Personal learning networks: Using the power of connections to transform education.* Indianapolis, IN: Solution Tree.

Rieger, A., & McGrail, E. (2006). Understanding English language learners' needs and the language acquisition process: Two teacher educators' perspectives. *On Points.* National Institute for Urban School Improvement. Retrieved from http://www.urbanschools.org/pdf/understanding_ell.pdf

Romaine, S. (1994). *Language and society: An introduction to sociolinguistics.* Oxford, UK: Oxford University Press.

Rothenberg, C., & Fisher, D. (2007). *Teaching English language learners: A differentiated approach.* Upper Saddle River, NJ: Pearson Education.

Sadler, D. R. (1989). Formative assessment and the design of instructional systems. *Instructional Science, 18,* 119–144.

Saifer, S., Edwards, K., Ellis, D., Ko, L., & Stuczynski, A. (2011). *Culturally responsive standards-based teaching: Classroom to community and back.* Thousand Oaks, CA: Corwin.

Sanders, B. (2013). Common Core poses big challenge for students, big opportunity for teachers. *Ed Source.* Retrieved from http://www.edsource.org/today/2013/common-core-poses-big-challenge-for-students-big-opportunity-for-teachers/37065#.UhI4sxaXs9V

Saunders, B., & Goldenberg, C. (2010). Research to guide English language instruction. In *Improving education for English learners: Research-based approaches* (pp. 26–71). Sacramento: California Department of Education.

Scarcella, R. (2003). *Academic English: A conceptual framework* (Technical Report No. 1). Irvine: The University of California Linguistic Minority Research Institute.

Scarcella, R. (2008). Academic language: Clarifying terms. *AccELLerate!* The Quarterly Newsletter of the National Clearinghouse for English Language Acquisition (NCELA), *1*(1), 5–6.

Schleppegrell, M. (2001). Linguistic features of the language of schooling. *Linguistics and Education, 12,* 431–459.

Schleppegrell, M. J. (2004). *The language of schooling: A functional linguistics perspective.* Mahwah, NJ: Erlbaum.

Schleppegrell, M. (2007). The meaning in grammar. *Research in the Teaching of English, 42*(1), 121–128.

Schön, D. A., (1983). *The reflective practitioner: How professionals think in action.* New York, NY: Basic Books.

Schwartz, D. A. (2004). *How much is a million?* New York, NY: Harper Collins.

Scott, J., Jamieson-Noel, D., & Asselin, M. (2003). Vocabulary instruction throughout the school day in 23 Canadian upper-elementary classrooms. *The Elementary School Journal, 103*(3), 269–286.

Short, D., & Fitzsimmons, S. (2007). *Double the work: Challenges and solutions for acquiring language and academic literacy for adolescent English language learners: A report to the Carnegie Corporation of New York.* Washington, DC: Alliance for Excellent Education.

Short, K. (2013). The Common Core State Standards: Misconceptions about informational and literary texts. *Worlds of Words.* University of Arizona. Retrieved from http://wowlit.org/blog/2013/01/21/the-common-core-state-standards-misconceptions-about-informational-and-literary-texts/

Shuy, R. W. (1981). The rediscovery of language in education [Guest editorial]. *Educational Leadership, 38*(6), 435.

Silvers, P., Shorey, M., Eliopoulis, P., & Akiyoshi, H. (2014). Making a difference in the world: Civil rights, biographies, and the southeast region. In M. Gottlieb & G. Ernst-Slavit (Series Eds.), *Academic language in diverse classrooms: English language arts, grades 3–5* (pp. 87–129). Thousand Oaks, CA: Corwin.

Silverstone, M., & Zacarian, D. (2013). Evens and odds: How many in all? In M. Gottlieb & G. Ernst-Slavit (Series Eds.), *Academic language in diverse classrooms: Mathematics, grades K–2* (pp. 87–128). Thousand Oaks, CA: Corwin.

Skloot, R. (2010). *The immortal life of Henrietta Lacks.* New York, NY: Broadway Paperbacks.

Snow, C. E. (2010). Academic language and the challenge of reading for learning about science. *Science, 328*, 450–452.

Snow, C. E., & Uccelli, P. (2009). The challenge of academic language. In D. R. Olson & N. Torrance (Eds.), *The Cambridge handbook of literacy* (p. 112). Cambridge, UK, and New York, NY: Cambridge University Press.

Snow, C. E., Uccelli, P., & White, C. (2013). *The conditions for and significance of children's acquisition of academic language.* Strategic Education Research Partnership. Retrieved from http://www.serpinstitute.org/downloads/Snow,%20uccelli,%20white_final.pdf

Snow, M., Met, M., & Genesee, F. (1989). A conceptual framework for the integration of language and content in second/foreign language instruction. *TESOL Quarterly, 23*(2), 201–217. Retrieved from http://static.aston.ac.uk/lis/tesol/quarterly-1967–2003/Vol_23_2.pdf#page=10

Staehr Fenner, D. (2013). *Advocating for English learners.* Thousand Oaks, CA: Corwin.

Stahl, S. A., & Nagy, W. E. (2006). *Teaching word meanings.* Mahwah, NJ: Erlbaum.

Stevens, R. A., Butler, F. A., & Castellon-Wellington, M. (2000). *Academic language and content assessment: Measuring the progress of ELLs* (CSE Tech. Rep. No. 552). Los Angeles: University of California National Center for Research on Evaluation, Standards, and Student Testing (CRESST).

Stiggins, R. J. (2005). From Formative assessment to assessment for learning: A path to success in standards-based schools. *Phi Delta Kappan, 87*(4), 324–328.

Stoddart, T., Pinal, A., Latzke, M., & Canaday, D. (2002). Integrating inquiry science and language development for English language learners. *Journal of Research in Science Teaching, 39*(8), 664–687.

Svalberg, A. (2007). Language awareness and language learning. *Language Teaching, 40*, 287–308.

Taba, H. (1962). *Curriculum development: Theory and practice.* New York, NY: Harcourt, Brace & World.

Teachers of English to Speakers of Other Languages (TESOL). (2006). *PreK–12 English language proficiency standards.* Alexandria, VA: Author.

Tellez, K., & Waxman, H. C. (2006). Preparing quality educators for English language learners: An overview of the critical issues. In K. Tellez & H. C. Waxman (Eds.), *Preparing quality educators for English language learners: Research, policy, and practice* (pp. 1–22). Mahwah, NJ: Erlbaum.

Tomlinson, C. A. (2004). *How to differentiate instruction in mixed ability classrooms* (2nd Ed.). Alexandria, VA: Association for Supervision and Curriculum Development.

Turner, E., Celedón-Pattichis, S., Marshall, M., & Tennison, A. (2009). "Fíjense amorcitos, les voy a contar una historia": The power of story to support solving and discussing mathematical problems with Latino/a kindergarten students. In D. Y. White & J. S. Spitzer (Eds.), *Mathematics for every student: Responding to diversity, grades Pre-K–5* (pp. 23–41). Reston, VA: National Council of Teachers of Mathematics.

Tyler, R. W. (1949). *Basic principles of curriculum and instruction.* Chicago, IL: University of Chicago Press.

Unsworth, L. (2001). *Teaching multiliteracies across the curriculum: Changing contexts of text and image in classroom practice.* Buckingham, UK: Open University Press.

Valdés, G., Capitelli, S., & Alvarez, L. (2011). *Latino children learning English: Steps in the journey.* New York, NY: Teachers College Press.

van Lier, L. (1996). *Interaction in the language curriculum: Awareness, autonomy and authenticity.* London, UK: Longman.

van Lier, L. (2007). Action-based teaching, autonomy and identity. *Innovation in Language Learning and Teaching, 1*(1), 46–65.

van Lier, L. (2012). Language learning: An ecological-semiotic approach. In E. Hinkel (Ed.), *Handbook of research in second language teaching and learning* (vol. 2, pp. 383–394). New York, NY: Routledge.

van Lier, L., & Walqui, A. (2012). *Language and the Common Core State Standards.* Stanford, CA: Understanding Language. Retrieved from http://ell.stanford.edu/publication/language-and-common-core-state-standards

Vásquez, A., Hansen, A. L., & Smith, P. C. (2010). *Teaching language arts to English language learners.* New York, NY: Routledge.

Villa, R. A., Thousand, J. S., & Nevin, A. I. (2008). *A guide to co-teaching: Practical tips for facilitating student learning* (2nd ed.). Thousand Oaks, CA: Corwin.

Villagómez, A., & Wenger, K. J. (2013). Exploring possibilities with geometric solids. In M. Gottlieb & G. Ernst-Slavit (Series Eds.), *Academic language in diverse classrooms: Mathematics, grades 6–8* (pp. 39–76). Thousand Oaks, CA: Corwin.

Vygotsky, L. S. (1978). *Mind in society: The development of higher psychological processes.* Cambridge, MA: Harvard University Press.

Vygotsky, L. S. (1987). Thinking and speech (N. Minick, Trans.). In R. Rieber & A. Carton (Eds.), *The collected works of L. S. Vygotsky, Volume 1: Problems of general psychology* (pp. 39–285). New York, NY: Plenum Press.

Wagner, S., & King, T. (2012). *Implementing effective instruction for English language learners: 12 key practices for administrators, teachers, and leadership teams.* Philadelphia, PA: Caslon.

Walqui, A., & Heritage, M. (2012). *Instruction for diverse groups of English Language Learners.* Retrieved from http://ell.stanford.edu/sites/default/files/pdf/academic-papers/09- Walqui%20Heritage%20Instruction%20for%20Diverse%20Groups%20FINAL_0.pdf

Walsh, D., & Staehr Fenner, D. (2014). Diving into the depths of research. In M. Gottlieb & G. Ernst-Slavit (Series Eds.), *Academic language in diverse classrooms: English language arts, grades 6–8* (pp. 101–135). Thousand Oaks, CA: Corwin.

Wellman, B. (2010, December 21). Web log comment on "On being an agent of change," by David Truss. Retrieved from http://pairadimes.davidtruss.com/on-being-an-agent-of-change/comment-page-1/#comment-6947

Wells, G. (2009). *The meaning makers: Learning to talk and talking to learn* (2nd ed.). Bristol, UK: Multilingual Matters.

Wiggins, G., & McTighe, J. (2005). *Understanding by design* (2nd ed.). Alexandria, VA: ASCD.

William, D. (2011). *Embedded formative assessment.* Indianapolis, IN: Solution Tree.

Wong Fillmore, L. (2004). The role of language in academic development. In *Aiming High, Aspirando a lo Mejor* (pp. 3–7). Santa Rosa, CA: Sonoma County Office of Education. Retrieved from http://www.scoe.org/docs/ah/AH_language.pdf

Wong Fillmore, L. (2011, May). *English learners and the Common Core standards.* Presentation to the Council of the Great City Schools Bilingual, Immigrant, and Refugee Education Directors' Meeting, Las Vegas, NV.

Wong Fillmore, L., & Snow, C. (2000). *What teachers need to know about language.* Washington, DC: U.S. Department of Education, Office of Educational Research and Improvement.

World-Class Instructional Design and Assessment (WIDA). (2007). *WIDA consortium English language proficiency standards and resource guide: Prekindergarten through grade 12. (2007).* Madison, WI: Board of Regents of the University of Wisconsin System, on behalf of the WIDA Consortium—www.wida.us.

World-Class Instructional Design and Assessment (WIDA). (2012). *Amplification of the English language development standards, kindergarten–grade 12.* Madison, WI: Board of Regents of the University of Wisconsin System, on behalf of the WIDA Consortium—www.wida.us.

Young, T. A., & Hadaway, N. L. (2014). Taking a closer look at our changing environment. In M. Gottlieb & G. Ernst-Slavit (Series Eds.), *Academic language in diverse classrooms: English language arts, grades 3–5* (pp. 45–86). Thousand Oaks, CA: Corwin.

Zacarian, D. (2011). *Transforming schools for English learners: A comprehensive framework for school leaders.* Thousand Oaks, CA: Corwin.

Zeichner, K. M. (1999). The new scholarship in teacher education. *Educational Researcher, 28*(9) 4–15.

Zwiers, J. (2008). *Building academic language: Essential practices for content classrooms, grades 5–12.* San Francisco, CA: Jossey-Bass.

Zwiers, J., & Crawford, M. (2011). *Academic conversations: Classroom talk that fosters critical thinking and content understandings.* Portland, ME: Stenhouse.

Index

CORWIN
A SAGE Company

The Corwin logo—a raven striding across an open book—represents the union of courage and learning. Corwin is committed to improving education for all learners by publishing books and other professional development resources for those serving the field of PreK–12 education. By providing practical, hands-on materials, Corwin continues to carry out the promise of its motto: **"Helping Educators Do Their Work Better."**